Legal Reform in English Renaissance Literature

Edinburgh Critical Studies in Renaissance Culture

Series Editor: Lorna Hutson

Titles available in the series:

Visit the Edinburgh Critical Studies in Renaissance Culture website at
edinburghuniversitypress.com/series/ecsrc

Legal Reform in English Renaissance Literature

Virginia Lee Strain

EDINBURGH
University Press

Edinburgh University Press is one of the leading university presses in the UK. We publish academic books and journals in our selected subject areas across the humanities and social sciences, combining cutting-edge scholarship with high editorial and production values to produce academic works of lasting importance. For more information visit our website: edinburghuniversitypress.com

Edinburgh University Press Ltd
The Tun – Holyrood Road
12(2f) Jackson's Entry
Edinburgh EH8 8PJ

Typeset in 10.5/13 Adobe Sabon by
Servis Filmsetting Ltd, Stockport, Cheshire
and printed and bound in Great Britain.

A CIP record for this book is available from the British Library

ISBN 978 1 4744 1629 0 (hardback)
ISBN 978 1 4744 1630 6 (webready PDF)
ISBN 978 1 4744 1631 3 (epub)

Contents

Acknowledgements

Professional debts: Thanks to the anonymous press readers; to Lorna Hutson, Lynne Magnusson, Holger Syme, Elizabeth Harvey, David Galbraith, Bradin Cormack, Jessica Winston, Ian Williams, Simon Stern, Judith Owens, Glenn Clark, James Knapp, Suzanne Gossett, Richard Strier, Megan Heffernan, Andrew Cutrofello, Edward Wheatley, Jeff Glover and Joyce Wexler; and to the research librarians at the Folger Shakespeare Library, the Huntington Library and the Cudahy and Law Libraries at Loyola University Chicago.

Personal debts: Thanks to Sharon Lee Strain, JR and Kelly Struffin, Barb and Ron Evich, Erin Ellerbeck, Katherine Cox Knapp, Ryan Copi and Steven Kris, and Mary Mackay.

A portion of Chapter 2 is reprinted from 'The "Snared Subject" and the General Pardon Statute in Late Elizabethan Coterie Literature', in Donald Beecher, Travis DeCook, Andrew Wallace and Grant Williams (eds), *Taking Exception to the Law: Materializing Injustice in Early Modern English Literature* (Toronto: University of Toronto Press, 2015), pp. 100–19.

Chapter 5 was published as '*The Winter's Tale* and the Oracle of the Law', in *English Literary History* 78.3 (2011), pp. 557–84.

Note on Citations

In my citations of early modern print sources, I have retained the original spelling; contractions have been silently expanded except when they appear in verse; and i/j, long-s/s, u/v and vv/w have been modernised.

Series Editor's Preface

Edinburgh Critical Studies in Renaissance Culture may, as a series title, provoke some surprise. On the one hand, the choice of the word 'culture' (rather than, say, 'literature') suggests that writers in this series subscribe to the now widespread assumption that the 'literary' is not isolable, as a mode of signifying, from other signifying practices that make up what we call 'culture'. On the other hand, most of the critical work in English literary studies of the period 1500–1700 which endorses this idea has rejected the older identification of the period as 'the Renaissance', with its implicit homage to the myth of essential and universal Man coming to stand (in all his sovereign individuality) at the centre of a new world picture. In other words, the term 'culture' in the place of 'literature' leads us to expect the words 'early modern' in the place of 'Renaissance'. Why, then, 'Edinburgh Critical Studies in *Renaissance Culture*'?

The answer to that question lies at the heart of what distinguishes this critical series and defines its parameters. As Terence Cave has argued, the term 'early modern', though admirably egalitarian in conception, has had the unfortunate effect of essentialising the modern, that is of positing 'the advent of a once-and-for-all modernity' which is the deictic 'here and now' from which we look back.[1] The phrase 'early modern', that is to say, forecloses the possibility of other modernities, other futures that might have arisen, narrowing the scope of what we may learn from the past by construing it as a narrative leading inevitably to Western modernity, to 'us'. Edinburgh Critical Studies in Renaissance Culture aims rather to shift the emphasis from a story of progress – early modern to modern – to series of critical encounters and conversations with the past, which may reveal to us some surprising alternatives buried within texts familiarly construed as episodes on the way to certain

[1] Terence Cave, 'Locating the Early Modern', *Paragraph* 29.1 (2006), pp. 12–26, at p. 14.

identifying features of our endlessly fascinating modernity. In keeping with one aspect of the etymology of 'Renaissance' or 'Rinascimento' as 'rebirth', moreover, this series features books that explore and interpret anew elements of the critical encounter between writers of the period 1500–1700 and texts of Greco-Roman literature, rhetoric, politics, law, oeconomics, *eros* and friendship.

The term 'culture', then, indicates a licence to study and scrutinise objects other than literary ones, and to be more inclusive about both the forms and the material and political stakes of making meaning both in the past and in the present. 'Culture' permits a realisation of the benefits to be reaped after two decades of interdisciplinary enrichment in the arts. No longer are historians naive about textual criticism, about rhetoric, literary theory or about readerships; likewise, literary critics trained in close reading now also turn easily to court archives, to legal texts and to the historians' debates about the languages of political and religious thought. Social historians look at printed pamphlets with an eye for narrative structure; literary critics look at court records with awareness of the problems of authority, mediation and institutional procedure. Within these developments, modes of research that became unfashionable and discredited in the 1980s – for example, studies in classical or vernacular 'source texts', or studies of literary 'influence' across linguistic, confessional and geographical boundaries – have acquired a new critical edge and relevance as the convergence of the disciplines enables the unfolding of new cultural histories (that is to say, what was once studied merely as 'literary influence' may now be studied as a fraught cultural encounter). The term 'Renaissance' thus retains the relevance of the idea of consciousness and critique within these textual engagements of past and present, and, while it foregrounds the Western European experience, is intended to provoke comparativist study of wider global perspectives rather than to promote the 'universality' of a local, if far-reaching, historical phenomenon. Finally, as traditional pedagogic boundaries between 'Medieval' and 'Renaissance' are being called into question by cross disciplinary work emphasising the 'reformation' of social and cultural forms, so this series, while foregrounding the encounter with the classical past, is self-conscious about the ways in which that past is assimilated to the projects of Reformation and Counter-Reformation, spiritual, political and domestic, that finally transformed Christendom into Europe.

Individual books in this series vary in methodology and approach, sometimes blending the sensitivity of close literary analysis with incisive, informed and urgent theoretical argument, at other times offering critiques of grand narratives of the period by their work in manuscript transmission, or in the archives of legal, social and architectural history, or by social histories of gender and childhood. What all these books have in common, however, is the capacity to offer compelling, well-documented and lucidly written critical accounts of how writers and thinkers in the period 1500–1700 reshaped, transformed and critiqued the texts and practices of their world, prompting new perspectives on what we think we have learned from them.

Lorna Hutson

For Dad and Sidney, who should still be here; for Mom, who isn't going anywhere anytime soon; for Sawyer and Abigail, who will go everywhere; and for baby Ross, who will arrive here any day now . . .

Introduction

This book investigates rhetorical and representational practices that were used to monitor English law at the turn of the seventeenth century. While the majority of Law and Literature studies characterise the law as a force of coercion and subjugation, this book instead treats in greater depth the law's own vulnerability, both to corruption and to correction. Numerous writings from across early modern English culture represent disorder as the product not of 'an ungovernable people', but of the legal system itself and its magistrates.[1] The broad participatory structure of the justice system helped produce a population that was especially sensitive to the contribution of legal language, institutions, practices, and officers to the regulation of the commonwealth. The dominance of the law in everyday life made its failings and improvements of widespread concern: it was a regular and popular focus of criticism. I argue that the terms and techniques of legal reform provided modes of analysis through which legal authorities and literary writers alike evaluated form and character. Legal reform, together with the conflicts and anxieties that inspired and sprang from it, were represented by courtly, coterie, and professional writers. Close readings in subsequent chapters reveal that Spenser's *Faerie Queene*, the Gray's Inn Christmas revels of 1594–5, Donne's 'Satyre V', and Shakespeare's *Measure for Measure* and *The Winter's Tale* all examine the potential, as well as the ethical and practical limitations, of legal reform's contribution to local and national governance. The selection of literary texts is drawn from a variety of major writers who established individualistic styles and contributions, but who were all drawn to legal reform as a subject and as a method of analysing contemporary thought and experience. The selection of texts is also heavily weighted on the side of satire and comedy, capacious genres that are simultaneously critical and conservative, just like the principles and practices of legal reform that I discuss below.

These literary texts place us in a compact era, stretching only from the 1590s to the 1600s, that has nevertheless attracted extensive scrutiny from every kind of historian. The period was beleaguered by crises on all fronts – social, economic, religious, political, local, national and international. The demands on governmental and legal institutions, processes, officers, and doctrines increased as a result, making their shortcomings both more visible and more consequential. To the long list of tensions already associated with the turn of the seventeenth century, I recover a number related to the operation of the law that have been preserved in the language and structure of literary texts. Legal reform's role within Tudor governance was established earlier in the sixteenth century and, as Barbara Shapiro writes, '[w]ith the reign of Elizabeth we settle into roughly the agenda of reform that will persist throughout the seventeenth century'.[2] But efforts were re-examined and re-energised by a number of legal-political authorities in late Elizabethan and early Jacobean England.[3] The period witnessed the advancement of Thomas Egerton, Edward Coke, and Francis Bacon, major figures in the historical development of the English law and state whose writings helped shape an ethos of legal reform at the end of the century and, in the long run, contributed to the so-called 'rise of the common law': its historical ascendancy through the escalation of litigation, the maturation of its educational societies and profession, and the expansion of its jurisdiction. The energy of the era sprang not only from the convergence of remarkable events, individuals and texts, but from the contribution of these to traditions that instrumentalised receptions of the past and projections of the future. Each chapter below centres on a literary text in which synchronic affinities intersect with diachronic projects.[4] These works attend to contemporary legal culture and practices as well as to the perennial or inherent deficiencies within a human-made justice system. The questions and the insights that emerge from my close readings are pragmatic rather than utopian, ethical more often than ideological.

The general abundance of legal language, characters, plots and relationships within early modern English literature is a clear refraction of the law's cultural ubiquity. Apart from professionals like judges, lawyers, and law clerks, an extraordinary number of subjects participated in the English justice system – as plaintiffs and defendants, as witnesses and jury members, and as the legion of unsalaried and unsupervised volunteer officers selected from nearly every social level. Property and marriage laws mediated family relations, and secular and ecclesiastical courts and officers arbitrated among neighbours. Commerce and emergent contract law inter-animated one another. The rhetorical education provided by sixteenth- and seventeenth-century grammar schools incorporated the treatises of Cicero and Quintilian, who originally wrote for an audience of legal practitioners. Forensic rhetoric and ideas were thereby broadly disseminated in Elizabethan and Jacobean culture.[5] Nearly all relationships, all forms of exchange, were inflected by legal definitions, processes, officers, institutions, and traditions.

This study considers the law's central role in governance, or its function as the interface between the subject and the state. As Julian Martin explains:

> 'Law' was not simply a structure of rules and institutions for coercion and punishment; the term encompassed not only the ways by which disputes were settled, but the institutional structure of governance in the realm . . . To become 'learned in the law' was simultaneously to become learned in the practical minutiae of governance in England.[6]

The first English translation of Francis Bacon's *De augmentis scientiarum* presents at greater length a picture of the law as the enabling condition for a common weal in which individual and public prosperity were intertwined:

> the end of Publique Law is not only to be a Guardian to Private Right . . . or to represse Injuries: but it is extended also unto Religion, & Armes and Discipline, and Ornaments, & Wealth . . . finally to all things which any way conduce unto the prosperous estate of a Common-wealth . . . For the End and Ayme at which Lawes should level, and whereto they should direct their Decrees and Sanctions, is no other then this, That the People may live happily: this will be brought to passe, if they be rightly trained up in Piety and Religion; if they be Honest for Morall conversation, secured by Armes against forraine enimies; Munited [protected] by Lawes, against seditions, and private wrongs; Obedient to Government and Magistrates; Rich and Florishing in Forces and wealth: but the instruments and sinewes of all Blessings are Lawes.[7]

At the turn of the seventeenth century, the state was administered through legal institutions, officers, processes, instruments, concepts, and language. Despite Bacon's reference to the happiness of the people and the blessings derived from the law, however, the connection between law and governance was most apparent when it was under stress. Legal reform gave expression to pervasive anxieties over the weaknesses of the legal system that could foment disorder in the commonwealth. Its principles and practices developed in response to ongoing, periodic and emergent tensions between the law, the needs of governance and the principles of justice.

As a primary instrument of the state's self-regulation, legal reform entailed, in Nicholas Bacon's words, the 'perfection' and 'execution' of the law. The law was 'perfected' through improvisations on existing laws, legal instruments, and legal processes that contributed to 'the experimental nature of early modern governance'.[8] However counter-intuitively, these officially sponsored, institutionalised improvisations accommodated evolving social, economic and political conditions within a system that was ideologically and pragmatically committed to tradition and continuity. These reforms were calculated to prevent more radical innovations that would in turn generate 'inconveniences', a term used technically and less precisely to signify systemic contradictions, absurdities or uncertainties that threatened the law's ability to produce just results.[9] The perfection of the law, however, was wasted effort unless the law was effectively executed or administered. A widely circulated, repetitive discourse on duty and character targeted the largely unsupervised legal-political officers entrusted with the justice and governance of the realm. This tradition of character criticism, delivered directly from the Lord Keeper's mouth or circulated through other legal-political, literary, theatrical, didactic, or religious writings, encouraged self-surveillance in officers and a more conscientious execution of their responsibilities. At the same time, it educated the English public in the signs of abuses of authority; it provided a rubric for evaluating the job performance of members of parliament, magistrates, judges, justices, constables, and others. These two dimensions or stages of legal reform generated a distinct critical orientation toward legal and governing activities that was reproduced throughout the justice system and, consequently, throughout the socio-political hierarchy. These techniques of formal improvisation and character criticism were thus accessible to early modern writers and inspired literary representations and analyses of law and order.

The rest of this Introduction enlarges this initial account of legal reform and literature by unpacking the connotations of 'reform' in the later sixteenth century and by situating my argument in the context of recent early modern legal, literary and political studies. I then examine in detail the discourse on legal reform within Nicholas Bacon's opening and closing parliamentary speeches. As Elizabeth's Lord Keeper for two decades, Bacon repeatedly emphasised the importance of the law's perfection through the reform of its form and content and the surveillance and correction of the officers in charge of the law's execution. While Bacon's speeches illuminate the proper targets of reform, establishing priorities and speech patterns for his successors, the literary works that I subsequently examine develop the problematics of legal reform in practice, as the concluding descriptions of individual chapters make clear.

Legal Reform in History and Criticism

A 'spirit of reform' has long been attributed to the sixteenth century. Julian Martin cautions, however, that the senses of the verb 'to reform' did not convey 'the idea of sweeping changes for the better which we now automatically associate with the verb'.[10] Nor did it import a religious connotation.[11] Instead, the senses 'to renew', 'to restore', 'to rebuild, repair', 'to amend or improve by alteration of form, arrangement, or composition', 'to revise, edit', and 'to correct errors or remove defects' resonated with Tudor populations.[12] Martin Ingram explains that these connotations were in play when 'reform' was used to describe the routine repair work of early modern governance:

> These meanings of the word were a commonplace of parliamentary bills and debates, of proclamations, of petitions to the courts of equity, and of the work of county and borough magistrates. Likewise they were part of the stock-in-trade of constables and presentment juries in quarter sessions and in manorial courts, and of churchwardens and other local officers when they were called upon to make their regular reports . . .

At the same time, Ingram maintains, a 'sense of urgency' attached to the mundane, quotidian work of reform when it was intended to address pressing social concerns.[13] Moral and social anxieties that focused on the 'reformation of manners' increased dramatically by the end of the sixteenth century, and they were expressed in numerous acts of parliament that attempted to redress dangers to the commonwealth by seeking social and economic reform. While Tudor humanist and religious writings may have 'sensitised a gentleman to the worldly ills and evils that surrounded him', writes Martin, 'the instrumen[t] by which he might achieve the restoration of an earthly goodness or even the elimination of a specific ill . . . was legislation.'[14] The effectiveness of the law and its execution was thus the precondition for the Elizabethan reformation of manners which, as Steve Hindle writes, was 'pursued as part of a larger project of good governance'.[15] More shades of the verb's meaning come into effect when 'reform' is used to refer to the law's own housekeeping: 'to revise and amend (a judgement)'; 'to correct (an instrument) according to the original intention when an error has been introduced; to construe (a legal document, etc.) in this way'; 'to put a stop to or remedy (an abuse, malpractice, etc.) by enforcing a better procedure or course of conduct'. The distinction and the relationship between these two types of reform – the reformation of the law and the reformation of manners – can be detected in the progress of Spenser's *Faerie Queene*, in which the Book 'Of Courtesie' follows from the Book 'Of Justice'. 'The political message of the poem,' writes Andrew Hadfield, is 'that the difficult problem of justice needs to be solved before culture can flourish'; 'without the foundations of social order, the establishment of courtesy is not just difficult, but is a meaningless enterprise.'[16]

Historians of all stripes are well aware of the late Elizabethan and early Jacobean 'burst of regulatory activity' that resulted from the legislation and local enforcement of 'the reformation of manners', though its causes are still debated.[17] What has gone virtually unnoticed until recently is the degree to which the law was not only the means of social reform, but the object itself of numerous reform efforts and writings. 'The mounting criticisms of the legal profession and of certain courts such as Chancery have been the subject of some scholarly attention', writes Barbara Shapiro, yet '[h]istorians have been somewhat less aware of more general and diffuse demands for improvements in the common law courts, local justice and legal procedure'.[18] Wilfrid Prest explains that the influential work of G. R. Elton derailed the scholarly investigation into legal reform of the second half of the sixteenth century by averring that 'there was only idle talk and failed bills'.[19] In contrast with the earlier reform measures carried out under Thomas Cromwell's direction, Elton writes, 'Elizabeth's chief purpose throughout her reign was to make time stand still'. The 1580 moratorium on aging portraits of the Queen is simply one extreme expression of a wide-ranging policy of political consolidation that inhibited change and progress.[20] Indeed, legal reform, understood historically as the revision, refinement or restoration of the correct form and execution of the law, was certainly not intended to precipitate vast cultural and historical shifts. Instead, it contributed to a governing mentality and activities that shaped the structure and experience of local and national order.

Contrary to the implications of Elton's vision of the Elizabethan status quo, an enormous amount of effort was expended in attempts to protect the legal-political system from radical innovation or deterioration. This is readily apparent in Nancy Matthews' description of the wide range of early modern legal reform practices that moves far beyond Henry Maine's classic account of 'legal fictions, equity and legislation' as 'the ways the law adjusted to the needs of society'.[21] Matthews writes that legal reform

> could be broadly defined as an effort to achieve a greater degree of justice, an exercise that might be accomplished through procedural reform or by altering the laws themselves. It could also mean the endeavor to gain a better understanding of legal principles or to publicize what was known of the settled law. More practically, it could involve an effort to facilitate a greater efficiency in the administration of justice . . . [C]orruption and ignorance [were] problems which had long been recognized to be endemic in both law enforcement and in the administration of the courts. Proposals to exert effective controls over officials entrusted with responsibilities had been formulated by government administrators and members of parliament from Elizabeth's reign up to the time of the civil war . . . From the 1590s through the 1630s privy councillors,

judges and parliamentary committees all were raising questions about the state of the law and law enforcement . . .[22]

On Matthews' account, the topic of legal reform has been hiding from us in plain sight. Rather than standing out as a special measure or response, it regularly motivated the activities of legal-political officers at every level.

While Matthews enumerates the kinds of historical activities that inform my literary analyses, Francis Bacon provides a contemporary account of the extensive intellectual or analytical labour that those activities demanded from legislators, legal authorities and magistrates. In his treatment of the deficiency of law, in the section on 'Civil Knowledge' in Book Two of the 1605 edition of *The Advancement of Learning*, he explains that 'the wisdom of a lawmaker consisteth not only in a platform [model] of justice, but in the application thereof', and therefore those responsible for the law must

> tak[e] into consideration by what means laws may be made certain, and what are the causes and remedies of the doubtfulness and incertainty of law; by what means laws may be made apt and easy to be executed, and what are the impediments and remedies in the execution of laws; what influence laws touching private right of *meum* and *tuum* have into the public state, and how they may be made apt and agreeable; how laws are to be penned and delivered, whether in Texts or in Acts; brief or large; with preambles or without; how they are to be pruned and reformed from time to time; and what is the best means to keep them from being too vast in volumes or too full of multiplicity and crossness; how they are to be expounded, when upon causes emergent and judicially discussed, and when upon responses and conferences touching general points or questions; how they are to be pressed, rigorously or tenderly; how they are to be mitigated by equity and good conscience; and whether discretion and strict law are to be mingled in the same courts or kept apart in several courts; again, how the practice, profession, and erudition of law is to be censured and governed; and many other points touching the administration, and (as I may term it) animation of laws.[23]

Bacon catalogues questions about the organisation and expression of the law, the logical, systematic, and ethical execution of the law, and the governance or oversight of the 'practice, profession, and erudition [learning]' of the law. Any and all of these questions could be provoked in the course of defining, administering, witnessing or representing justice.

Much more revealing than Elton's portrait example is the analogy of gardening that was a regular feature of early modern legal and political rhetoric. The government and the law's representatives were hardly standing still; rather, they imagined themselves engaged in the backbreaking labour of 'weeding' the entire commonwealth, a labour that must be understood to include and to be predicated on the 'weeding' of the law itself. Unlike a standstill and, at the other extreme, unlike utopian proposals for radical change, the gardening analogy bespeaks a concentration on the needs of the present and the pragmatic nature of the work to be done in legal, political, and social maintenance. The nature and work of legal reform in regulating the governance of the commonwealth thus offer an institutional expression of the classical principle – moving from Aristotle, to Justinian, to Aquinas, and to early moderns like Thomas Elyot, Thomas Wilson, and Thomas Floyd – that justice entails 'a perpetual and a constant will'.[24] Legal reform was a virtuous habit, an office or duty, that underwrote the very existence of the commonwealth. It was the perpetual effort that enabled the status quo or the experience of local and national continuity.

The role and autonomy of legal officers in governance and legal professionals in everyday transactions made the integrity of officers, lawyers, processes and instruments a popular source of concern and criticism, from above and below, from inside and outside the legal profession. As Alison Chapman writes, 'a deep respect for lawyers and jurists coexisted in the English consciousness with an equally deep suspicion of them'.[25] Raising similar questions about 'the state of the law and law enforcement' as 'privy councillors, judges and parliamentary committees', this critique can be described as an extension of the analytical life of legal reform and legal culture. Prest explains that legal historians have nevertheless 'long tended to discount evidence of popular dissatisfaction with the ethical standards of early modern lawyers and law courts, as stemming from a combination of ignorance, antiprofessional animus, and moralistic naïveté'.[26] He argues instead that a continuity existed between professional and popular critiques, especially when legal errors and abuses were perceived to stem from 'human weaknesses'. Making a similar case, Chapman points to Thomas Egerton's speech in the 1601 parliament, in which he 'called for a bill that would cap the rising numbers of solicitors, men whom he called "Vipers of the Commonwealth"'.[27] In the writings of the sixteenth-century legal scholar and practitioner, William Lambarde, Prest uncovers a '[l]egally literate appraisal of this (highly unsystematic) legal system' that mirrors the popular opinions dismissed by historians: 'Lambarde's surviving discussions of the law and its institutions are frequently concerned to identify, condemn, and propound remedies for the moral failings of individual legal practitioners and functionaries.'[28] In his account of 'The offences of publike persons' from the *Archeion, or, A Discourse Upon the High Courts of Justice in England*, for instance, Lambarde identifies 'the misdemeanours of publike men, and *Officers*, that [are] forged out of *fraud*, and *wilinesse*'.[29] Lambarde was 'a qualified barrister . . . unusually well placed to evaluate the operational strengths and weaknesses of the common law'.[30] At the same time that his critique reflects the depth of his experience and expertise, it also echoes popular sentiment that was a function of widespread participation in the justice system. The ability and responsibility to critique law and governance was a feature of early modern culture that cut across professional and social distinctions. While the coterie works of Inns-of-Court writers featured in Part I of this book may emphasise aspects of the law that the upper ranks of the legal-political system were in a position – indeed, had a duty – to repair, nevertheless, the plays by Shakespeare that are analysed in Part II testify to the broad appeal of the topic of legal reform: *Measure for Measure* and *The Winter's Tale* were played on the popular stage and at court.

The phenomenon of legal reform in early modern England has also been overlooked because of modern disciplinary boundaries. As it is reconstructed in this study – as it was envisioned by authorities, articulated in parliamentary sessions and performed by officers – the topic necessarily straddles legal and political history. The fact that the law was a 'hallmark of politics in the early modern period', however, is 'virtually ignored by those who profess an interest in early modern government'.[31] The chasm that exists between these two fields means that legal reform has gained a footing in neither. The division between legal and political history has been duplicated in many interdisciplinary studies by literary historians. For instance, literary historians focusing on early modern politics have ignored lawmaking and legislative reform in parliament. Oliver Arnold has taken to task the new historicists, so widely influential within late-twentieth and early twenty-first-century political literary studies, for marginalising parliamentary history: 'the new historicist map of early modern political culture has very seldom stretched beyond crown and court', with the result that the field has 'discovered the crackle of art and psychic complexity in Elizabeth's speeches and James's many writings, but this ocean of parliamentary discourse remains unexplored'.[32] The neglect of parliamentary speeches means that a substantial source of political rhetoric rests unparsed, as Brian Vickers, Kevin Sharpe, and Peter Mack have all complained.[33] It also means that the discourse on legal reform contained in these speeches has gone unnoticed. The next section of this chapter modestly amends this picture through a close reading of the extensive comments on legal reform that were voiced in the numerous eloquent and influential parliamentary speeches of Nicholas Bacon.[34] Martin describes '[t]he exhortations of [Lord Keepers] to successive parliaments about the need for disciplined, uniform and equitable exercise of justice throughout the country' as 'a clear example of the Privy Councillors' attention to the practical difficulties of governance'.[35] Bacon not only established legal reform as an ongoing priority within governance, but his rhetoric set a precedent for his Elizabethan and Jacobean successors. I have adopted Bacon's division of legal reform into the 'perfection' and 'execution' of the law for the structure of this book. These two branches or stages of legal reform were reworked through individual literary writers' perspectives and purposes.

Perfection

In *The Arte of English Poesie*, published in 1589, ten years after Nicholas Bacon's death, George Puttenham defends the use of rhetorical figures in public speeches by referring the case to 'them that knew Sir Nicholas Bacon, Lord Keeper of the Great Seal . . . and have bene conversant with [his] speaches made in the Parliament house and Star Chamber. From whose lips I have seen to proceed more grave and natural eloquence than from all the orators of Oxford or Cambridge.'[36] That 'natural eloquence' turns out to be the product of study. Puttenham goes on to paint a quaint tableau in which the Lord Keeper is spied in the solitary act of self-improvement, consulting his rhetorical textbooks:

> I have come to the Lord Keeper Sir Nicholas Bacon, and found him sitting in his gallery alone with the works of Quintilian before him; indeed, he was a most eloquent man, and of rare learning and wisedom, as ever I knew England to breed, and one that joyed as much in learned men and men of good wits.[37]

Nicholas's son, Francis, would later write that 'A mans nature is best perceived in privatnesse, for there is no affectation.'[38] Puttenham's sketch of the Lord Keeper derives its effect from the same premise. This method of revealing character, moreover, is employed to confirm the reliability of another. A grammar-school textbook in early modern England, Quintilian's *Institutio Oratoria* popularised the argument that only good men speak well and that good speakers must thus be good men.[39] In Puttenham's anecdote, Nicholas Bacon's reputation as a rhetorician is proven to be a reliable sign of his good character: the vignette of 'privatnesse' without 'affectation' corresponds with public impression. His studiousness proves his eloquence is 'naturall'; it is the refined or perfected expression of an excellent inner virtue. By devoting his contemplative time to Quintilian, the Lord Keeper commits himself to improving his efficacy in public life.[40] His contemplative life is justi-fied by its application to public service/speaking, and his active life is virtuously directed by the wisdom of classical authority.

Puttenham's anecdote provides an introduction not only to the Elizabethan reputation and legacy of Nicholas Bacon as a rhetorician and statesman, but also to the rhetorically trained mentality that was sensitive to the relationship between form and character. In his opening and closing parliamentary speeches, the Lord Keeper rhetorically divided the work of legal reform into, first, the evaluation and revision of the law's form and content, and, second, the monitoring and correc-tion of the officers in charge of the law's execution. From his speeches, we can extract historical terms for a discussion of legal reform as well as historical anxieties over the operation of the law. His remarks, con-sistent throughout his long career, provide a frame of reference through which we can interpret literary works that focus on the problematics of legal reform. Parliamentary speeches and practice have yet to receive sustained scrutiny within the field of early modern law and literature. T. E. Hartley reminds us, however, that the work of parliament was legal reform: 'when we speak of Parliament as a legislative body we should define its task as one of legislative *review*', a process that entailed 'the rejection of bills, or existing acts, as well as the acceptance of newly proposed laws. It could also involve the confirmation, or rejection, of current statutes.'[41] To recover 'the working principles' of parliamentary legal reform, moreover, Hartley suggests studying the formulaic ceremo-nies and speeches that took place at the beginning of each session.[42]

In his opening speech to the very first Elizabethan Parliament, Nicholas Bacon enumerated the 'matters and causes' upon which the Houses should 'consulte'. Among the members' primary functions were 'the well making of lawes' and 'the reforming and removing of all enormities and mischeifes that doe, or might, hurte or hinder the civill orders or pollicies of this realme.' He went on to provide a checklist for parliamentarians to be used, much like the topics of rhetorical invention, to generate a comprehensive enquiry into the condition of the laws. The Houses were to ascertain where new laws were required: 'what thinges by private wealthe's devise have bene practized and put in ure within this realme, contrary or hurtefull to the common wealthe of the same, for which noe lawes be yet provided.' Members were to review the current laws' performance: whether they were 'sufficient to redresse the enormityes they were mente to remove'. They were to consider further the ethical, equitable character of the laws: 'whether any lawes be to severe and to sharpe or to softe and to gentle'. Does the law suit the crime, and does it provide an example or caution to others? Finally, they were to consider whether the laws suited the times: 'whether any lawes made but for a tyme be meete to be continued for ever, or any made to be perpetuall and yet meete to be continued but for a tyme or presently to cease'. Notwithstanding his careful analysis of the legislator's function, Bacon ensures comprehensiveness by extending this section of his remarks to provide for the unknown or unforeseen. 'To be short', he summarised, 'you are to consider all other imperfeccions of lawes made and all the wantes of lawes to be made, and thereupon to provide their meetest remedyes respecting the nature and qualitie of the disorder and offence, the inclination and disposition of the people, and the manner of the tyme.'[43]

As Peter Mack observes, Nicholas Bacon's opening remarks provided 'a general pattern for formal speeches on the government side', not only throughout his own career in parliament, but also for successive Lord Keepers and Lord Chancellors.[44] Most notably, John Puckering, Thomas Egerton and Francis Bacon would re-energise the first Elizabethan Lord Keeper's emphasis on legal reform at the end of the sixteenth century and into the seventeenth. They would extend its principles and its terms beyond parliamentary sessions and throughout their legal-political work and speeches. While Egerton would encourage parliament to 'prune' – that is amend and abridge – the laws rather than make new ones, he would also direct his reforming energies toward the officers, organisation and fees of the courts of Chancery and Star Chamber.[45] Francis Bacon was a consistent advocate for reform throughout his legal-political career, explaining in 'A Proposition to His Majesty ... Touching the Compiling and Amendment of the Laws of England' (1616/17):

> I speak only by way of perfiting [the laws] ... what I shall propound is not to the matter of the laws, but to the manner of their registry, expression, and tradition: so that it giveth them rather light than any new nature.[46]

Bacon's focus on the 'manner' of the law – its accurate and consistent recording ('registry'), its unambiguous wording ('expression') and its organised transmission to succeeding generations of legal professionals ('tradition') – reflects his orderly and rhetorical approach to reform. Here, as in his father's opening speeches to parliament, perfecting the law is represented as 'a matter of order and explanation [rather] than of alteration'.[47]

While Nicholas Bacon's parliamentary speeches emphasise the role of the magisterial class in legal reform, his son Francis would envision systemic legal reform driven by monarchal leadership. Reform needed royal backing if it were to succeed, just as his schemes for the advancement of knowledge, including the establishment of libraries and gardens, were imagined as royal works.[48] Francis would write numerous commendatory passages praising Elizabeth and James for their improvements to the law and governance in the texts in which he advanced schemes for greater reform. In *Maximes of the Common Lawes*, a work that 'create[s] new and better rules under the guise of restatement', he praises the Queen for using her authority to 'give unto your lawes force and vigour' and being 'carefull of their amendment and reforming'.[49] In 'An Offer to King James of a Digest to be Made of the Laws of England', Bacon not only flatters his prince but also cautions him about the dangers of neglecting the state of the law. He likens the making of good laws to a father's testament that provides for the future of his children and the neglect of the law to a father's neglect of the future:

> Princes that govern well are fathers of the people: but if a father breed his son well, or allow him well while he liveth, but leave him nothing at his death, whereby both he and his children, and his childrens children, may be the better, surely the care and piety of a father is not in him complete.[50]

Moving from the microcosm to the macrocosm, Bacon presents the results of legal reform as the proper inheritance of the English people: 'I have commended [the laws of England] before for the matter, but surely they ask much amendment for the form; which to reduce and perfect, I hold to be one of the greatest dowries that can be conferred upon this kingdom.' The writer's choice of analogy is bitterly ironic, since Nicholas Bacon died unexpectedly before making provisions for his last child, reversing Francis's financial circumstances and redirecting the course of his career. Francis expected his sovereign to read personal experience into the political analogy – that of James himself, whom 'God hath blessed . . . with posterity',[51] as well as his own well-known family history.

Nicholas and Francis Bacon described the future perfection of the law as the responsibility of the present sovereign, statesmen, legislators, judges, and magistrates, which could be achieved through processes that looked 'not to the matter of the laws, but to the manner'. Francis's great professional and socio-political rival, Edward Coke, is instead identified with a historicising rhetoric through which the law's contemporary faults were characterised as deviations from a superior legal tradition. However innovative they may in fact have been, his own judgements and theories were strategically depicted as the restoration of a common law 'which hath beene refined and perfected by all the wisest men in former succession of ages and proved and approved by continuall experience to be good & profitable for the common wealth'.[52] A key feature of Coke's common-law ideology, the characterisation of reform as the law's restoration, also encouraged rhetorical and literary comparisons of Elizabeth I to the classical goddess of justice, Astraea. The Queen's reign was compared to Astraea's return to earth that, according to Virgil, was supposed to inaugurate a new Golden Age by restoring justice to mankind.[53] Astraea is discussed in greater detail in the following chapters on Spenser's *Faerie Queene* and Donne's 'Satyre V', while Coke's contribution to legal-political controversy is treated in the final chapter on *The Winter's Tale*. Perfection and restoration were the bywords of a discourse that helped regulate the so-called living law. This discourse was actively circulated through legal-political treatises, speeches, literary writings, and other communications in an attempt to protect the common good and the legal-political status quo.

Even though the 'nature' (the matter or substance) of the law was supposed to remain unaffected by reform efforts, the law's perfection was still urgently advocated by its proponents for the very reason that the system's potential for justice was at stake. Condensing the number of laws through amendment and abridgement, for instance, was repeatedly promoted for the sake of English subjects and legal professionals alike. In his opening remarks to the third Elizabethan parliament, Nicholas Bacon instructed the members, 'yow are to looke whether there be too many lawes for any thinge, which breedeth soe many doubtes that the subiect somtime is to seeke howe to observe them and the counsellor howe to give advise concerninge them' (*PPE* 1: 137–9). In the eighth parliament (1593), Lord Keeper Puckering cautioned members, 'not to spend the tyme in devising of new lawes and statutes; wherof there is already so great store . . . that . . . it were more convenient by abridgment and explanacion to make them lesse difficill for the practise of them, then by addicion of newe, to increase the danger of the quiet subiect' (*PPE* 3: 18). In the same session Francis Bacon sat for Middlesex. In the earliest surviving fragment from his parliamentary speeches, he finds an opportunity to support Puckering's opening remarks and to echo his own father's: 'scarce a whole year would suffice, to purge the statute-book [or] lesson the volume of laws; – being so many in number that neither common people can half practice them, nor the lawyer sufficiently understand them'.[54] In this parliamentary mantra, reiterated by legal authorities and statesmen concerned with the integrity of governance and the maintenance of the common weal, justice is contingent upon the system's power to represent and communicate itself accurately, efficiently and effectively to professionals and non-professionals alike.

At the same time, the repetitive concerns expressed in the opening speeches to successive Elizabethan parliaments also testified to the law's continuing *im*perfection. On its own, legislative review was insufficient to the task of reform. Part I of this study focuses on the institutional improvisations that developed to compensate for the law's ongoing imperfections. In chapters on the 1594–5 Gray's Inn Christmas revels and John Donne's 'Satyre V', I examine the statute proviso that built exceptions directly into new law, the general pardon statute that released subjects from the penalties of so-called 'snaring' statutes, the equitable extension of the reason or spirit of the law that adjusted justice for novel or exceptional cases, and the structure of legal-political representation that overcame the limitations of a centralised government and the absence of regular oversight for the innumerable officeholders throughout the country. These activities entailed ongoing efforts to reform, revise, restore or correct the law in response to the exigencies of the present. They required a high degree of initiative and competence on the part of magistrates. In the literary representations of these activities, therefore, the question of reform inevitably raises the question of the character – the integrity and skill – of the officers in charge of reforming and executing the law.

Execution

The law's perfection was a key feature of the Elizabethan Lord Keeper's parliamentary script that reminded members of their duties and of their sovereign's conditional sanction of the Houses' activities. In his speech at the close of Parliament, however, Nicholas Bacon's focus shifted from the reform of the law to the reform of those in charge of its execution, or from rhetorical to ethical criticism. '[T]he good governaunce of the subjecte at home, the lackes and defaultes whereof', the Lord Keeper explained, 'standes altogether eyther in the imperfeccion of lawes or els in the fearefullnes, sloughtfullnes or corrupcion of temporall officers that ought to see to the due execucion of them' (*PPE* 1: 82–3). As Hartley points out, the effective administration or enforcement of the law was a 'constant preoccupation' of the Lord Keepers and Lord Chancellors of Elizabeth's reign, and Nicholas Bacon's most eloquent parliamentary rhetoric was inspired by this topic.[55] In his closing remarks, Bacon addressed parliament not as the country's political representatives, but as a gathering of the magnates and magistrates with the individual responsibility of disseminating law and order at the local level. His tone dramatically shifted to address this new audience that his own speech effectively summoned. Rhetorical questions, analogies, and colloquial interjections of 'trowe you' and 'Surely, surely' (absent from his opening speeches) bespeak his familiarity with this version of his audience as well as the vehemence of his remarks. The ceremonious appeal to duty in the opening speeches gave way to an appeal to reason and common sense, an inclusive strategy designed to placate listeners he was about to criticise scathingly. While he would go on to enlarge the scandals typical of local officers, at the same time he implicitly and explicitly suggested that he was preaching to the choir: 'And like as this is not saide to those that bee good, so is this and much more to bee saide and donne against those that bee ill' (*PPE* 1: 192).

Bacon's comments on the 'due execucion' and the 'due administra-cion of justice' (*PPE* 1: 50) were, in fact, much more extensive than those on legislative reform or review. The reason for this is straight-forward enough. The making and reforming of laws is an enormous waste of time and resources if they are not afterwards enforced: 'all theise labours, travailes and paines taken . . . all the charge susteined by the realme about the making of [laws] is all in vaine and labor lost without the due execucion of them' (*PPE* 1: 191). In *The Education of a Christian Prince*, Erasmus attributes the observation to Aristotle, who explained 'that it is useless to establish good laws if there is no one who will labour to uphold what has been well established; indeed, it sometimes happens that the best established laws are turned to the total ruin of the state through the fault of the magistrates.'[56] Bacon's closing speeches entered a heightened analogical mode when he considered this waste: 'it hath bynn saide, a law without execucion it is but a bodie without life, cause without an effect, a countenance of a thinge and in deed nothinge' (*PPE* 1: 191). He repeatedly developed comparisons with unused implements, including an unlit torch, unused garden tools and unread books.[57] These analogies would be repeated in speeches by suc-ceeding Lord Keepers and Chancellors.

Legal authorities – real and fictional alike – depicted the lack of execution and law enforcement as the ultimate sin of omission, or the most offensive form of negligence, because of the socially destructive consequences. '[T]he making of lawes without execucion doe verie much harme', explained Bacon, 'for yt breedes and bringes forth contempt of lawes and lawe-makeres and all magistrates, which is the verie founda-cion of all misgovernance.' Bad justices are thus 'the very occasioners of all injuries and injustice and of all disorders and unquietnes in the com-mon-wealth' (*PPE* 1: 191). In the third scene of *Measure for Measure*, Shakespeare's Duke of Vienna makes the same argument in more suc-cinct terms. Echoing Bacon's comparison of 'a law without execucion' to 'a bodie without life', the Duke explains, 'our decrees, / Dead to infliction, to themselves are dead', with the result that, 'Liberty plucks Justice by the nose, / The baby beats the nurse, and quite athwart /

Goes all decorum.' '[W]e bid this be done', he concludes, 'When evil deeds have their permissive pass, / And not their punishment.'[58] In Book V of *The Faerie Queene*, 'The Legend of Artegall, or of Justice', a poem I return to in the next chapter, Spenser's version of the argument is conveyed through a very different tone:

> For vaine it is to deeme of things aright,
> And makes wrong doers justice to deride,
> Unlesse it be perform'd with dreadlesse might.
> For powre is the right hand of Justice truely hight.[59]

Legislative reform was an act of legal-political decorum or prudence in which the form, content and expression of the law was measured against current public need and common and legal definitions of justice: MPs were asked 'to consider . . . the nature and qualitie of the disorder and offence, the inclination and disposition of the people, and the manner of the tyme' (*PPE* 1: 34–5). The reformation of officers, on the other hand, measured the corrosive effects of human action or inaction on the forms and force of the system.

In his closing speeches to parliament, Bacon's remarks progressed from a general account of the problem of execution to a detailed picture of the types of offending officers. In the process, he evoked figures who would be right at home in the collections of character essays that multiplied at the turn of the century and that typified and satirised empirical observations of human nature and social conduct. He divided his subject matter into descriptions of slothful, 'uncareful' and finally hypocritical justices, 'the better to provide a remedie against this mischeife' (*PPE* 1: 191). He began his ethical or character criticism by attacking the 'slougthfull' justices who 'will never creepe out of their dores to any courte . . . for the due administracion thereof, excepte they be drawne thereto by some matters of their owne, nor cannot endure to have their eares troubled with hearinge of controversies of their neighbours for the good appeasinge of the same.' The 'uncareful' justice is equally to blame. '[H]ow', asks the Lord Keeper, 'can the uncareful man that maketh noe accoumpt of any of the common causes of his countrie but respecteth onely his private matters and commoditie become a diligent searcher out, follower and corrector of felons, murderers, and such like common enemyes to the common wealthe?' Only motivated to perform their official, statutory duties as magistrates when it is in their self-interest, these figures make a virtue out of their vice by adopting the guise of quiet men: 'such careles and slouthful men doe dayly . . . cloke these their faultes with the title of quietnes . . . where in very deed they seeke only ease, profitt and pleasure to them selves, and that to be sustayned and borne by other men's cares and labours as drones doe among bees' (*PPE* 1: 50).

These justices, however, pale in comparison with the 'monsterous disguisinge' of the ultimate hypocrite who deliberately breaks the very laws he was meant to enforce. Bacon concludes his legal sermon with an emphatic denunciation of local officers who twist the legal system into an instrument for personal profit:

> Is it not (trowe you) a monsterous disguisinge . . . to have hym that should by his othe and dutie set forthe iustice and righte, againste his othe and dutie offer iniurge and wronge . . . sweyinge of juryes accordinge to his will, acquiteinge some for gayne, inditeinge other for mallice, bearing with him as his servante, overthrowinge the other as his enemye, procuringe all questmongers to be of his liverye or otherwise in his daunger, that his winkes, frowninges and countenances may direct all inquestes? Surely, surelye, it is true that thease be they that be subverters and perverters of all lawes and orders, yea, that make dayly the lawes that of their owne nature be good to become instrumentes of all iniurye and mischiefe . . . theas be those whom, if yee cannot reforme for their greatnes, yee ought heere to complayne of for their evillnes.[60]

The Lord Keeper's comments reveal the anxieties of central government over local officeholders' unsupervised exercise of authority and influence. At the same time that this vividly enargic account suggests that no illicit practices pass unobserved, the 'winkes' and 'frowninges' of justices were precisely the kinds of signs that the Queen and her chief statesmen and legal ministers could not personally witness. This limitation of central government inspired Bacon's most ambitious proposal for legal reform, a system of regular provincial visitations to evaluate the performance of local officers (*PPE* 1: 83). As an advisor to James I, to his favourites and as Lord Chancellor, his son Francis would take pains to advocate and institute the investigation of local officers as a vital function of the Assize judges who were already responsible for holding court throughout the country during law-term vacations. These authorities, if put to the task, could be 'the best intelligencers of the true state of the Kingdom, and the surest means to prevent or remove all growing mischiefs within the body of the Realm.'[61] In Chapter 4, I argue that the Assize judges' responsibility for the oversight of local justice informs the structure and ethics of *Measure for Measure*.

Lorna Hutson has brought to the attention of literary scholars the unique participatory structure of the English legal system that relied on officers and jury members drawn from nearly every level of society to fulfil their sworn duties without much legal expertise and without much intervention from the authorities at Westminster. This historical insight overturns earlier Foucauldian and new historicist interpretations of socio-political subversion-containment processes that were premised on a division between the identities and interests of the state or the law and the people.[62] As the above speeches suggest, however, the structure of the English system, so dependent as it was on individual initiative, skill and virtue, inevitably heightened anxieties (from above and below) over the character of legal representatives. Character criticism, disseminated through the tiers of the justice system in charges to parliament, judges, juries, officers and courtrooms of public spectators and refracted in sermons and literature, encouraged self-awareness in officers and scrutiny by the English public. Governors 'by their pre-eminence they sit . . . on a pillar on the top of a mountain,' Elyot wrote, 'where all the people do behold them, not only in their open affairs, but also in their secret pastimes, privy dalliance, or other improfitable or wanton conditions: which soon be discovered by the conversation of their most familiar servants.'[63] Because titles came not only with official responsibilities but also with a ready audience, legal and political representatives had the further obligation to portray the exemplary subject. 'The due *observation* of the said Lawes doth generally without any limitation or exception concerne all', Coke explained in the Preface to the fourth volume of his *Reports*, '[b]ut principally Princes, Nobles, Judges, and Magistrates, to whose custody & charge the due execution (the life and the soule of the Laws) is committed; for that they in respect of their places are more eminent & conspicuous then other men.'[64]

The topic of legal reform bifurcates into the perfection of the organisation, expression and content of the law, and its ethical execution by motivated officers. The semantic range of 'perfection', however, forestalls any absolute division. In his 1612 essay 'Of Dispatch', Francis Bacon equates perfection with execution in his analysis of business – the business of parliamentary committee work in particular, according to Karl R. Wallace: 'There bee three parts of businesse; the preparation, the debate, or examination, and the perfection. Whereof, if you looke for dispatch, let the midle onely be the worke of many, and the first and last the worke of few.'[65] The *Dictionarium Linguae Latinae et Anglicanae* and *A World of Words* both define 'perfection' as 'a full dispatching and atchieving of a matter', while in his *Glossographia*, Thomas Blount defines 'achievement' as 'the performance or accomplishment of any gallant exploit, a bringing to perfection'.[66] Perfection, then, commonly denoted the most complete realisation of something: in the case of business or gallant exploits, it meant the successful execution of an intention or plan; in the case of a skill, language, art or memorised play text, complete proficiency; in the case of plants or bodies, complete ripeness or maturity.[67] Effective execution turns out to be the empirical expression of perfection. Thus to construe reform as a matter of perfecting the law is to continually tie form, language, ideals and ideology to execution, dispatch, practice and performance. And thus, while this project breaks down into two sections on perfection and execution, they inevitably interpenetrate.

This Introduction has sought to historically define the scope of early modern legal reform and its field of study. The next chapter offers a close reading of Book V of Spenser's *Faerie Queene*, which represents the reformation of law in terms of both its equitable correction and its administration. The Knight of Justice, Artegall, corrects regional law and governance across a number of historical allegories that most frequently allude to the sixteenth-century English efforts to colonise Ireland. Yet his methods and success are called into question not only through his defeat in combat by Radigund, but also through his rescue that is accomplished by his fiancé. As Britomart travels back through Faerieland, retracing the knight's steps in order to liberate him from thralldom to the Amazon, we discover that the countryside has not been subdued in the wake of his reformation of justice. Britomart's re-enactments of the knight's battles re-present the activities of legal reform and governance as ongoing tasks requiring consistent magisterial presence and attention. In killing Guizor's brothers on the same bridge where Artegall previously fought Pollente, she illuminates the limits of the knight errant as a delivery system for lasting order and corrects the kind of inconsistency in legal administration that was targeted frequently in treatises on the reformation of Irish governance. In her defeat of Radigund, Britomart corrects the relationship between the magistrate's private passions and the execution of public justice that was impaired when Artegall's pity directed him to spare the Amazon's life in battle. Most significantly, Britomart's own pity for the people of Radigone motivates the equitable restoration of an older legal-political system to the occupied city. Her efforts advance a form of rule that is historically legitimised and that reflects the nature or character of the population. The successful reformation of justice figured throughout Britomart's contribution to the Book, however, is ultimately undone in the final episode, in which Artegall is forced to return to the Faerie court after Irena is restored to power but before her territory can be reformed. In those final moments, Spenser presents the botched English or monarchal intervention in Ireland as deforming the instruments of reform. I have positioned this chapter at the beginning of the book not only for chronological reasons, but because the matter introduces a number of topics and contexts that will be developed at greater length in the studies that follow, including legal education, Aristotelian legal equity, historical reasoning, itinerant or peripatetic justice and character criticism.

Part I then focuses on literary representations of the law's imperfections and their corrections by writers on the inside of the legal profession and close to the culture of the royal court. Chapter 2 examines the *Gesta Grayorum*, an account of the 1594–5 Christmas revels at Gray's Inn, one of the English common-law societies and education institutions. The Christmas revelers mounted a large mock court and the elaborate entertainments for their fictional Prince of Purpoole were performed by and before a community of Inn members and associates that included common-law students, legal professionals, courtiers, parliamentarians, and statesmen. In their abridged parliament, they mock the general pardon that compensated for the snaring statutes that had accrued over the course of the sixteenth century. These kinds of statutes, which turned subjects into unintentional lawbreakers, found their way into Shakespeare's comedies and John Donne's satires. In parodying the terms and structure of the Elizabethan general pardon, the revelers target a significant legal-political device that publicly forgave select statutory infractions and broadcasted the sovereign's merciful character. The revellers' proceedings deliberately compromise not only the corrective powers of legislation but also trials in order, ultimately, to display the performers' talents for the principal governing task of socio-political maintenance that was accomplished through reforming operations. Francis Bacon's subsequent orations on government redirect the course of the entertainments away from the comical errors of lawmakers and legal representatives toward the industrious, systematic reform of the fictional state. Bacon's writings on legal reform were remarkably consistent, not to mention copious, throughout his long legal-political career. But they began to take shape in the late 1580s and 1590s, when his position and influence as a parliamentarian and as a legal authority solidified. He would not write 'A Proposition ... Touching the Compiling and Amendment of the Laws of England', which systematically reimagined the organisation of English law, until 1616/17; nevertheless, his early works, such as his orations for the Gray's Inn revels, demonstrate a similar commitment to the perfection of the law.

Chapter 3 examines John Donne's 'Satyre V', which applies the social and ethical reforming energy of the satiric genre to the need for system-wide legal reform in England. The piece is a tribute to his employer, the Lord Keeper Thomas Egerton, who was lauded for his integrity and commitment to reforming the financially exploitative aspects of legal process, particularly in the Court of Chancery. Central to Donne's satiric critique of the law is his attack on the excesses within the legal-political system that have been generated by the offences of suitors and legal professionals alike. The analysis is complicated, however, through the evocation of corrective strategies that instrumentalise excess: equity (in Chancery and practices of statute interpretation), legal and political representation and secretarial service. Grown from individual infractions into a source of systemic disorder, the excesses of suitors and legal professionals need to be checked through the processes that the speaker characterises as 'knowing' and 'weeding'. The weeding or expunging of abuse depends on the knowledge of its existence first circulating through the legal-political hierarchy. That circulation of knowledge, in turn, is dependent upon an extensive network of the queen's legal counsellors, representatives and servants who, in common political idiom, were also characterised as another type of excess, as the numerous eyes and ears of the body politic. These representatives are themselves a source of the problem and impede the flow of information and justice that they were initially created to facilitate. Donne exploits traditional legal-political analogies to illuminate the tensions in a system that both functioned and was forestalled by excess. His analogical style self-consciously imitates the statute interpretation strategies and principles outlined in Egerton's own treatise, *A Discourse upon the Exposicion [and] Understandinge of Statutes*, the earliest known English treatise on the topic. Analogy was at the heart of sixteenth-century methods of statute interpretation, according to which judges were to extend the sense or spirit of the law to cover novel cases on the grounds of likeness. In this way the exception was reabsorbed within the rule. Analogical extension, the discovery or generation of similitude and agreement, was thus pivotal to equitable justice. Equity, however, could also be overextended and the law stretched beyond recognition. While identifying the system's weaknesses, therefore, Donne's analogical style also invites suspicion; the reader's literary scrutiny is thereby engaged in the same legal-political surveillance needed 'to know and weed out'.

Linking the chapters in this section is a concern with excess – rhetorical, poetic, ethical, and legal. Excess is not only the instrument or result of the abuse of the legal system, but it is repeatedly one of the established rhetorical and representational instruments for addressing or mitigating the law's inherent or structural imperfections. Both chapters of Part I are also concerned with statute form and equitable interpretation strategies. Statute law was of immense professional and socio-political interest to the Inns of Court students (including Bacon and Donne) who would have attended the formal lecture series on statutes delivered by senior Inn members. Through these 'readings', statute interpretation skills were associated with professional advancement and authority. The literary works in Chapters 2 and 3 are even more closely linked by the creative identification and correction of the law's imperfections that showcased the refined legal-political skills of writers in pursuit of office and favour. The ambitions of these wits required the careful negotiation of encomium and critique within dramatic and literary performances that mimicked legal-political practice. In the mock general pardon statute of the Gray's Inn revels and in the analogical style of Donne's 'Satyre V', a mastery of legal and literary forms asserts a phantom professional and socio-political power. In multiple ways, then, the representation of legal reform in these works intentionally draws attention to the speaker or writer: reform proves inseparable from the character and competence of the reformer.

Part II examines the centrality of the reformation of legal officers and legal administration to Shakespeare's *Measure for Measure* and *The Winter's Tale*. Performed at court and on the public stage before a broad social spectrum, these plays bridged the elite–popular divide through the representation of law and justice. Given the extensive participatory nature of the English justice system, most London playgoers would have had a relationship to the law regardless of their relationship to the central powers and politics that preoccupied the writers and audiences or readers of the Gray's Inn revels and 'Satyre V'. 'If we accept that Shakespeare's public audience comprised a fairly broad cross section of London's population', Victoria Hayne writes, 'then a substantial proportion of the audience must themselves have been actual or eligible participants in the law-enforcement process, serving their turns as members of the watch, headboroughs, constables, members of a jury, justices of the peace, etc.'[68] Those who weren't eligible for office-holding still may have been a plaintiff, defendant or witness in a civil or criminal case. Shakespeare's plays were written with not only officeholders in mind, but also the English public, which held common beliefs about the responsibility of subjects and officeholders to the common good and the common peace. It was an era, as Ethan H. Shagan writes, with a 'stark absence of any ethics that was not at heart about the maintenance of the public order'.[69]

In Chapter 4, I argue that *Measure for Measure* is patterned on the cyclical structure of the Assize sessions, through which judges from Westminster presided over trials in counties throughout England. Convening twice a year, the court produced a repeating representation of central authority that shaped the countryside's legal and social calendar until the later twentieth century. Most importantly, by the end of the sixteenth century, the Assize judges had acquired the responsibility for the oversight of local justice. During the court sessions, officers could be publically exposed and shamed for corruption. The first scene of *Measure for Measure*, in which the Duke departs from Vienna leaving it in the hands of his substitute Angelo, parallels the Assizes' dissolution and withdrawal from county life. Likewise, the last scenes of the play, which chart the Duke's return to Vienna and resumption of power, resemble the court's grand return to the counties. The extraordinary circumstances that ignite the play plot, then, the Duke's sudden and mysterious departure, in fact made sense in relation to a regular feature and experience of the national legal system. Between these two coordinates of the Duke's departure and return, or during the invisible part of the Assize system, the strengths and weaknesses of the local officers are exposed and finally officially recognised in the open-air hearing that concludes the play. The structure of the play thus frames a process of local intelligence-gathering and public revelation that was specifically associated with Assize judges. We watch as Angelo and Escalus, acting like justices of the peace for their county, attempt to put the Duke's commission into execution, to put policy into local practice. Just as important as the revelation of his deputies' characters, however, is that of the Provost. Preserving the certainty and force of the law along with the lives of Viennese subjects, the Provost executes his function with consideration for the social pressures that have triggered the legal action at hand. His professional decorum, especially in his treatment of Pompey, is the immediate model for the Duke's own schemes and rear-rangement of relationships in the final scene. The reformation of local justice thus hinges on the meeting of Duke and Provost, which is enabled through the Assize-like structure of the play. This reading of *Measure for Measure* emphasises the play's relationship to a native, longstanding institution of the English common law whose cyclical process achieved a flexibility and responsiveness to social conditions that was increasingly exploited at the end of Elizabeth's reign and the beginning of James's. To use Bradin Cormack's words, the Duke's method of legal reform offers 'the possibility of finding within law the mobility that . . . we may too easily locate only in the phantasm of a "life" beyond law'.[70]

The last chapter shifts focus from local governance to national law and politics. While the reform of justice in *Measure for Measure* results from the Provost and the Duke's labour-intensive and improvisational interventions in the lives of subjects and in the legal process, I argue that justice in *The Winter's Tale* is restored through the more careful obser-vance of the boundaries between legal and political power. Chapter 5 examines the character of the 'oracle of the law' within legal and literary writings contemporaneous with Shakespeare's *The Winter's Tale*. The epithet signified a legal expert and wise counsellor who cultivated authority through deliberative and self-presentation practices that invited comparison with the rhetorical and performance style of the oracles of antiquity. While the judiciary advanced its own oracular image through professional practices, this same kind of oracle was repeatedly depicted as a recognisable social type in the character essay collections that were increasingly published in the early seventeenth century. The legal-political connotations of 'oracle' facilitate a new reading of *The Winter's Tale*, in which Apollo's supernatural oracle evokes human judicial figures. While Apollo's oracle makes only a brief appearance in the trial scene, nevertheless its influence pulses throughout the play via its representatives, Camillo and Paulina, whose strategies and counsel ultimately ensure that the oracular prophecy is fulfilled. Through these human oracles, I argue, the play is infused with the explosive tensions between the sovereign and the judiciary in early seventeenth-century England, through which the King's prerogative and the jurisdictions of courts came into question. The arguments between King Leontes and his oracular, judicial counsellors dramatise the competing claims to legal authority and administration expressed by proponents of absolute monarchy and of the common law. While the historical conflict resulted in Edward Coke's removal from the bench and the Privy Council in 1616, Shakespeare's play concludes by accommodating monarchal and common-law ideology in a final scene that cleanly divides the function and jurisdiction of the sovereign from those of the judge while respecting the necessary contributions of each. The legal-political reconciliation that I find in Shakespeare's play is in keeping with David Chan Smith's recent re-evaluation of Coke's earlier practice that sought 'to maintain both the prerogative and the rights of the subject'.[71]

Notes

1. John Brewer and John Styles (eds), *An Ungovernable People: The English and Their Law in the Seventeenth and Eighteenth Centuries* (London: Hutchinson, 1980).
2. Barbara Shapiro, 'Law Reform in Seventeenth Century England', *American Journal of Legal History* 19.4 (1975), p. 281.
3. See Julian Martin's chapter on 'A Statesman's Responsibility', which describes Thomas Cromwell as a model for Elizabethan statesmen, in *Francis Bacon, the State, and the Reform of Natural Philosophy* (Cambridge: Cambridge University Press, 1992). See also G. R. Elton's numerous works on Thomas Cromwell, reform and government in the earlier sixteenth century, including *English Law in the Sixteenth Century: Reform in an Age of Change* (London: Seldon Society, 1979); *Reform and Reformation: England, 1509–1558* (Cambridge, MA: Harvard University

26   *Legal Reform in English Renaissance Literature*

Press, 1977); *Reform and Renewal: Thomas Cromwell and The Common Weal* (Cambridge: Cambridge University Press, 1973); *Reform by Statute: Thomas Starkey's Dialogue and Thomas Cromwell's Policy* (London: Oxford University Press, 1968); and *The Tudor Revolution in Government: Administrative Changes in the Reign of Henry VIII* (Cambridge: Cambridge University Press, 1953).

4. On synchronic affinities and diachronic projects in early modern English literature, see Colin Burrow, 'Reading Tudor Writing Politically: The Case of *2 Henry IV*', *Yearbook of English Studies* 38 (2008), pp. 234–50.

5. See Cynthia Herrup, *The Common Peace: Participation and the Criminal Law in Seventeenth-Century England* (Cambridge: Cambridge University Press, 1987); Lorna Hutson, *The Invention of Suspicion: Law and Mimesis in Shakespeare and Renaissance Drama* (Oxford: Oxford University Press, 2007); Martin Ingram, *Church Courts, Sex, and Marriage in England, 1570–1640* (Cambridge: Cambridge University Press, 1988); Barbara Shapiro, 'Classical Rhetoric and the English Law of Evidence', in Victoria Kahn and Lorna Hutson (eds), *Rhetoric and Law in Early Modern Europe* (New Haven: Yale University Press, 2001), pp. 54–72, and *Probability and Certainty in Seventeenth-Century England: A Study of the Relationships between Natural Science, Religion, History, Law, and Literature* (Princeton: Princeton University Press, 1983).

6. Martin, *Francis Bacon*, pp. 103–4. Steve Hindle and Anthony Fletcher have illuminated 'the conflation of judicial and administrative functions within early modern government' (Hindle, *The State and Social Change in Early Modern England, c.1550–1640* (Basingstoke: Palgrave Macmillan, 2000), pp. 3, 30). See Anthony Fletcher, *Reform in the Provinces: The Government of Stuart England* (New Haven: Yale University Press, 1986)). W. J. Jones explains that 'the justices [of the peace, working at the local level] were regulating the structure of government as established under the Tudors' ('The Crown and the Courts in England, 1603–1625', in Allen D. Boyer (ed.), *Law, Liberty, and Parliament: Selected Essays on the Writings of Sir Edward Coke* (Indianapolis: Liberty Fund, 2004, p. 289)).

7. Francis Bacon, *Of the Advancement and Proficience of Learning or the Partitions of Sciences*, trans. Gilbert Wats (Oxford, 1640), pp. 436–7.

8. Hindle, *The State and Social Change*, p. 9.

9. On the early modern legal development of the concepts of 'mischief' and 'inconvenience', see Judith H. Anderson, *Reading the Allegorical Intertext: Chaucer, Spenser, Shakespeare, Milton* (New York: Fordham University Press, 2008), pp. 168–82; and Bradin Cormack, *A Power to Do Justice: Jurisdiction, English Literature, and the Rise of Common Law, 1509–1625* (Chicago: University of Chicago Press, 2007), pp. 173–6. Cormack describes English law as 'fundamentally improvisational, unfolding into doctrine only as and through practice' (*A Power to Do Justice*, p. 1). While this is an eloquent characterisation of the long-term development of the law, through which legal theory and principles developed from common law practice, my focus on legal improvisation has a very different orientation. The institutionalised improvisations I describe were calculated to compensate for the law's weaknesses while inhibiting innovation or the creation of new or erroneous precedents or principles.

10. Martin, *Francis Bacon*, p. 8.
11. The religious Reformation was a 'reformation' to the extent that it was understood as a return to, and restoration of, the primitive church by Protestant theologians and writers like John Bale, for example, whose *King Johan* 'reflect[s] the revised historiography of the English Reformation' and expresses the desire for 'a pure and reformed Church restored to the idealism of its earliest and most glorious period' (Vincent Gillespie, 'Monasticism', in Brian Cummings and James Simpson (eds), *Cultural Reformations: Medieval and Renaissance in Literary History* (Oxford: Oxford University Press, 2010), pp. 497).
12. 'reform, v.1.', *OED Online* (Oxford University Press, September 2016).
13. Martin Ingram, 'Reformation of Manners in Early Modern England', in Paul Griffiths, Adam Fox and Steve Hindle (eds), *The Experience of Authority in Early Modern England* (New York: St. Martin's Press, 1996), p. 52.
14. Martin, *Francis Bacon*, p. 9.
15. Hindle, *The State and Social Change*, p. 178.
16. Andrew Hadfield, 'Introduction', in Edmund Spenser, *The Faerie Queene: Book Six and the Mutabilie Cantos*, ed. Andrew Hadfield and Abraham Stoll (Indianapolis: Hackett, 2007), pp. xii, viii.
17. Hindle, *The State and Social Change*, p. 177.
18. Shapiro, 'Law Reform', p. 281.
19. Wilfrid Prest, 'William Lambarde, Elizabethan Legal Reform, and Early Stuart Politics', *Journal of British Studies* 34.4 (1995), p. 478.
20. Elton, *English Law in the Sixteenth Century*, p. 12.
21. A. K. R. Kiralfy, 'Law Reform by Legal Fictions, Equity and Legislation in English Legal History', *American Journal of Legal History* 10 (1966), p. 3.
22. Nancy L. Matthews, *William Sheppard, Cromwell's Law Reformer* (Cambridge: Cambridge University Press, 1984), pp. 1–2. On legal reform in the seventeenth century see Anthony Fletcher, *Reform in the Provinces: The Government of Stuart England* (New Haven: Yale University Press, 1986); Barbara Shapiro's articles, 'Codification of the Laws in Seventeenth Century England', *Wisconsin Law Review* 2 (1974), pp. 428–65, 'Law Reform in Seventeenth Century England', *American Journal of Legal History* 19.4 (1975), pp. 280–312, and 'Sir Francis Bacon and the Mid-Seventeenth Century Movement for Law Reform', *American Journal of Legal History* 24.4 (1980), pp. 331–62; and Donald Veall, *The Popular Movement for Law Reform, 1640–1660* (Oxford: Clarendon Press, 1970).
23. Francis Bacon, *The Advancement of Learning*, in *Francis Bacon: A Critical Edition of the Major Works*, ed. Brian Vickers (Oxford: Oxford University Press, 1996), p. 287.
24. Thomas Floyd, *The Picture of a Perfit Common wealth* (London: 1600), pp. 174–5.
25. Alison Chapman, 'Milton and Legal Reform', *Renaissance Quarterly* 69 (2016), p. 538.
26. Prest, 'William Lambarde', p. 478. See also Wilfrid R. Prest, 'Judicial Corruption in Early Modern England', *Past and Present* 133 (1991), pp. 67–95.
27. Chapman, 'Milton and Legal Reform', p. 539.

28. Prest, 'William Lambarde', pp. 466–7.
29. William Lambarde, *Archeion, or, A Discourse Upon the High Courts of Justice in England* (London, 1635), pp. 82–3.
30. Prest, 'William Lambarde', p. 466.
31. J. G. A. Pocock, Gordon Schochet, and Lois G. Schwoerer, 'Introduction', in David Armitage (ed.), *British Political Thought in History, Literature and Theory, 1500–1800* (Cambridge: Cambridge University Press, 2006), p. 16; Hindle, *The State and Social Change*, p. 13. The notable exceptions to this rule are Hindle, *The State and Social Change*, and Christopher W. Brooks, *Law, Politics and Society in Early Modern England* (Cambridge: Cambridge University Press, 2008).
32. Oliver Arnold, *The Third Citizen: Shakespeare's Theater and the Early Modern House of Commons* (Baltimore: Johns Hopkins University Press, 2007), pp. 24–6. On Shakespeare's access to information about parliament procedure and business, see Arnold, *The Third Citizen*, pp. 20–4.
33. Brian Vickers complains that 'a full examination' of Francis Bacon's parliamentary speeches is 'yet to be performed' ('Bacon and Rhetoric', in Markku Peltonen (ed.), *The Cambridge Companion to Bacon* (Cambridge: Cambridge University Press, 1996), p. 207). Kevin Sharpe observes that, '[r]emarkably, no historian of parliament studies the speeches as a rhetorical performance, as an act intended to persuade and constructed with (different) auditors and conventions of persuasion in mind' (*Remapping Early Modern England: The Culture of Seventeenth-Century Politics* (Cambridge: Cambridge University Press, 2000), p. 15). See also Peter Mack's chapters on 'Political Argument' and 'Elizabethan Parliamentary Oratory' in *Elizabethan Rhetoric: Theory and Practice* (Cambridge: Cambridge University Press, 2002).
34. On Nicholas Bacon's life and career, see Robert Tittler, *Nicholas Bacon: The Making of a Tudor Statesman* (London: J. Cape, 1976) and 'Education and the Gentleman in Tudor England: The Case of Sir Nicholas Bacon', *History of Education* 5.1 (1976), pp. 3–10; and John Campbell, *The Lives of the Lord Chancellors and Keepers of the Great Seal of England*, vol. 2 (London, 1846).
35. Martin, *Francis Bacon*, p. 105.
36. George Puttenham, *The Arte of English Poesy*, ed. Frank Whigham and Wayne A. Rebhorn (Ithaca: Cornell University Press, 2007), pp. 223–4. On Nicholas Bacon's rhetoric, see Patrick Collinson, 'Sir Nicholas Bacon and the Elizabethan *Via Media*', *Historical Journal* 23 (1980), pp. 255–73; Elizabeth McCutcheon, *Sir Nicholas Bacon's Great House Sententiae* (Amherst: English Literary Renaissance Supplements, III, 1977); and R. J. Schoek, 'Rhetoric and Law in Sixteenth-Century England', *Studies in Philology* 1 (1957), pp. 110–27.
37. Puttenham, *The Arte of English Poesy*, p. 224.
38. Francis Bacon, 'Of Nature in Men', *The Essaies of Sr Francis Bacon Knight, the Kings Solliciter Generall* (London, 1612), p. 155.
39. See Chapter 1 of Book 12, in Quintilian, *The Orator's Education, Volume V: Books 11–12*, ed. and trans. Donald A. Russell, Loeb Classical Library 494 (Cambridge, MA: Harvard University Press, 2002).
40. On the relationship between rhetoric and public life, see R. S. White,

Natural Law in English Renaissance Literature (Cambridge: Cambridge University Press, 1996), pp. 81–2. See also the rest of Puttenham's chapter on 'How our writing and speeches public ought to be figurative, and if they be not do greatly disgrace the cause and purpose of the speaker and writer', in *The Arte of English Poesy*, pp. 223–6.

41. T. E. Hartley, *Elizabeth's Parliaments: Queen, Lords, and Commons, 1559–1601* (Manchester: Manchester University Press, 1992), p. 19. In the sixteenth century, Thomas Smith explained the function of parliament by detailing the activities of legislation and legal reform:

> The Parliament abrogateth olde lawes, maketh newe, giveth orders for thinges past, and for thinges hereafter to be followed, changeth rightes, and possessions of private men, legittimateth bastards, establisheth formes of religion, altereth weightes and measures, giveth formes of succession to the crowne, defineth of doubtfull rightes, whereof is no lawe alreadie mads, appointeth subsidies, tailes, taxes, and impositions, giveth most free pardons and absolutions, restoreth in bloud and name as the highest court, condemneth or absolveth them whom the Prince will put to that triall . . . (*De Republica Anglorum*, ed. Mary Dewar (Cambridge: Cambridge University Press, 1982), p. 78)

Smith was considered one of three Elizabethan parliamentary theorists, along with William Lambarde and John Hooker (see D. M. Dean and N. L. Jones, 'Introduction', in D. M. Dean and N. L. Jones (eds), *The Parliaments of Elizabethan England* (Oxford: Basil Blackwell, 1990), p. 2).

42. Hartley, *Elizabeth's Parliaments*, p. 19.

43. T. E. Hartley (ed.), *Proceedings in the Parliaments of Elizabeth I*, vol. 1 (Wilmington, DE: M. Glazier, 1981), pp. 34–5. Hereafter this text is cited parenthetically by *PPE* followed by the volume and page number.

44. Mack, *Elizabethan Rhetoric*, p. 229.

45. Simonds D'Ewes, *A Compleat Journal of the Votes, Speeches and Debates, Both of the House of Lords and House of Commons Throughout the Whole Reign of Queen Elizabeth, of Glorious Memory* (London, 1693), p. 524.

46. Francis Bacon, 'A Proposition to His Majesty by Sir Fancis Bacon . . . Touching the Compiling and Amendment of the Laws of England', in Francis Bacon, *The Works of Francis Bacon*, ed. James Spedding, Robert Leslie Ellis and Douglas Denon Heath, Vol. 13 (London, 1872), p. 63. Elsewhere, notably in the Preface to his *Maximes of the Common Lawes*, Bacon articulates a more complex relationship between form and content. Perfecting the form of the law *does* result in changes in the substance and practice of the law, presumably another stage of the law's refinement. He writes that a professional repays the gains derived from his profession by adding to the discipline: 'thereby not onely gracing it in reputation and dignity, but also amplifying it in perfection and substance'. Clearing uncertainties in the law will result in 'the amendment in some measure of the very nature and complection of the whole law'. Nevertheless, even in the *Maximes*, Bacon still insists that 'you have here a worke without any glory of affected noveltie' (*The Elements of the Common Lawes of England* (London, 1630), sig. B2², C1ʳ). This text is hereafter cited by *Maximes*.

47. Bacon, 'A Proposition', p. 66. See Glenn Burgess's discussion of Francis Bacon's *De Augmentis Scientiarum* and 'A Proposition' in *The Politics of the Ancient Constitution: An Introduction to English Political Thought, 1603–1642* (University Park: Pennsylvania State University Press, 1993), pp. 54–7.

48. See, for example, the speech of 'The Second Counsellor, Advising the Study of Philosophy' in his device for the Gray's Inn Christmas revels of 1594–5 (*Gesta Grayorum: or, The History of the High and Mighty Prince, Henry Prince of Purpoole ... Who Reigned and Died, A.D. 1594* (London, 1688)); Bacon, *The Advancement of Learning*, p. 174; the essays 'Of Building' and 'Of Gardens' in *The Essayes or Counsels, Civill and Morall*, ed. Michael Kiernan (Oxford: Oxford University Press, 1985); and Martin, *Francis Bacon*, p. 163. On Bacon's ideas on the royal authorisation of the law, see also Richard Helgerson, *Forms of Nationhood: The Elizabethan Writing of England* (Chicago: University of Chicago Press, 1992), p. 75.

49. Daniel R. Coquillette, *Francis Bacon* (Stanford: Stanford University Press, 1992), p. 36; Bacon, *Maximes*, sig. A3^{r-v}.

50. Francis Bacon, 'An Offer to King James of a Digest to be Made of the Laws of England', *The Works of Francis Bacon*, vol. 4 (London, 1826), p. 375. This text is hereafter cited by *Digest*.

51. Bacon, *Digest*, p. 380.

52. Edward Coke, *The Selected Writings of Sir Edward Coke*, ed. Steve Sheppard, vol. 1 (Indianapolis: Liberty Fund, 2003), p. 95. On the use of 'custom' as an argument for poetic, legal and political innovations, see Stephanie Elsky, '"Wonne with Custome": Conquest and Etymology in the Spenser–Harvey *Letters* and *A View of the Present State of Ireland*', *Spenser Studies* 28 (2013), pp. 165–92.

53. On the Astraea/Elizabeth I connection, see Francis Yates, *Astraea: The Imperial Theme in the Sixteenth Century* (London: Routledge & Kegan Paul, 1975), pp. 29–87. See also Spenser's representation of Astraea in *The Faerie Queene*, discussed in Chapter 1 below, and see Donne's in 'Satyre V', discussed in Chapter 3 below.

54. Quoted in Coquillette, *Francis Bacon*, p. 29.

55. Hartley, *Elizabeth's Parliaments*, pp. 33–4.

56. Desiderius Erasmus, *The Education of a Christian Prince*, trans. and ed. Lisa Jardine (Cambridge: Cambridge University Press, 1997), p. 91.

57. See, for example, *PPE* 1: 49.

58. William Shakespeare, *Measure for Measure*, in *The Norton Shakespeare*, ed. Stephen Greenblatt, Walter Cohen, Suzanne Gossett, Jean E. Howard, Katherine Eisaman Maus and Gordon McMullan, 3rd edn (New York: W. W. Norton, 2016), 1.3.27–39.

59. Edmund Spenser, *The Faerie Queene*, ed. A. C. Hamilton, revised 2nd edn (London: Routledge, 2013), 5.4.1.

60. *PPE* 1: 50. See the same comments made in the Lord Keeper's speech at the close of the third parliament (*PPE* 1: 192).

61. Francis Bacon, 'A Letter of Advice, Written by Sir Francis Bacon to the Duke of Buckingham, when He Became Favourite to King James', in *The Works of Francis Bacon*, ed. James Spedding, Robert Leslie Ellis and Douglas Denon Heath, vol. 13 (London, 1872), p. 19.

62. See Lorna Hutson, 'Rethinking the "Spectacle of the Scaffold": Juridical Epistemologies and English Revenge Tragedy', *Representations* 89.1 (2005), pp. 30–58; and her *The Invention of Suspicion*.

63. Thomas Elyot, *The Book Named the Governor*, ed. and intro. S. E. Lehmberg (London: Everyman's Library, 1962), p. 97.

64. Coke, *Selected Writings*, p. 1: 99.

65. Karl R. Wallace, 'Discussion in Parliament and Francis Bacon', in Brian Vickers (ed.), *Essential Articles for the Study of Francis Bacon* (Hamden, CT: Archon Books, 1968), p. 206. Francis Bacon, 'Of Dispatch', in *The Essaies of Sr Francis Bacon Knight, the Kings Solliciter Generall* (London: 1612), pp. 74–5.

66. John Florio, 'Perfettione', in *A World of Words* (London: 1598), p. 268; Thomas Thomas, 'Perficio', in *Dictionarium linguae Latinae et Anglicanae* (London: 1587), sig. Vv4^r; Thomas Blount, 'Achievment', in *Glossographia: or A Dictionary, Interpreting all such Hard Words* (London, 1656).

67. 'perfection, n.', *OED Online* (Oxford University Press, September 2016).

68. Victoria Hayne, 'Performing Social Practice: The Example of *Measure for Measure*', *Shakespeare Quarterly* 44.1 (1993), p. 27.

69. Ethan H. Shagan, *The Rule of Moderation: Violence, Religion and the Politics of Restraint in Early Modern England* (Cambridge: Cambridge University Press, 2011), p. 9.

70. Cormack, *A Power to Do Justice*, p. 2.

71. David Chan Smith, *Sir Edward Coke and the Reformation of the Laws: Religion, Politics and Jurisprudence* (Cambridge: Cambridge University Press, 2014), p. 4. Smith situates his argument in relation to Charles Gray, 'Reason, Authority, and Imagination: The Jurisprudence of Sir Edward Coke', in Perez Zagorin (ed.), *Culture and Politics from Puritanism to the Enlightenment* (Berkeley: University of California Press, 1980), pp. 25–66, and Janelle Greenberg, *The Radical Face of the Ancient Constitution: St Edward's 'Laws' in Early Modern Political Thought* (Cambridge: Cambridge University Press, 2001). For Law and Literature studies that present legal ideology and authorities in opposition to monarchal and absolutist agendas, see Andrew Zurcher, *Shakespeare and Law* (London: Methuen Drama, 2010) and Paul Raffield, *Images and Cultures of Law in Early Modern England: Justice and Political Power, 1558–1660* (Cambridge: Cambridge University Press, 2004).

Chapter 1

'Perpetuall Reformation' in Book V of Spenser's *Faerie Queene*

Like other literary texts examined in this book (including Donne's 'Satyre V' and Shakespeare's *Measure for Measure* and *The Winter's Tale*), Spenser's 'Legend of Artegall, or of Justice', Book V of *The Faerie Queene*, has historically suffered from critical disapproval and even neglect. The poetry has been found deficient on various formal grounds and excessive in its representation of violence. The brutal and mass violence depicted within Book V's historical allegories, especially those that represent the sixteenth-century English colonisation of Ireland, are frequently read as doing irrevocable harm to Artegall's claim to the title, Knight of Justice. It creates an ethical paradox for the national epic, which self-consciously proclaims its intention to represent and instill virtue, and ultimately implicates the author himself. C. S. Lewis famously identified Spenser's personal ethical failure – he was an agent, apologist and benefiter of colonialism – as the root cause of Book V's aesthetic failures: 'Spenser was the instrument of a detestable policy in Ireland, and in his fifth book the wickedness he had shared begins to corrupt his imagination.'[1] More recently, criticism has probed the ways in which literary forms and traditions enabled Spenser's support for and representations of colonial oppression in Book V and in his political treatise, *A View of The Present State of Ireland*, that was composed in the same period. In *A View*, Irenaeus presents a 'sharpe course . . . for the bringing under of those rebels of Ulster and Connaught' that would 'prepar[e] a way for their perpetuall reformation'.[2] Ciaran Brady argues that the treatise's 'dialogue form, like the metaphors, the antiquarian discussions and the superficial logistical proposals . . . [were] exploited to allow Spenser to retain the mantle of the conscientious humanist scholar while he urged a brutal and desperate policy.' 'The Legend . . . of Justice' shares a number of tensions with *A View*. Through poetry, Book V likewise attempts to 'provide a moral justification for the relentless use of force and terror in bringing Ireland to order'.[3]

My own reading of the poem foregrounds the representation of governance as a form of 'perpetuall reformation' that entails consistent, insistent, endless attention, and that also therefore links political conditions with the strength of legal-historical continuity. The violent erasure of wrongdoers and wrongdoing, Book V reveals, is not merely individually and nationally traumatic, but altogether futile if it is not accompanied by the ongoing reformation – the maintenance and adjustment – of law and governance. One of the traditional critical dissatisfactions with Book V centres on the fact that Artegall's justice is 'inconclusive', in Judith H. Anderson's words.[4] As Andrew Hadfield points out, 'Book Five . . . is the first book in which the Knight, Artegall, is actually prevented from completing his quest by Gloriana, the Faerie Queen'.[5] In this chapter, I argue that Artegall's quest is not simply unfinished but, rather, endless, and that the justice that hinges on ongoing reform emerges in contrast to the historically destructive pattern of erratic English magisterial assertiveness and retreat in sixteenth-century Ireland. The methods of legal reform and the vision of reformed colonial order in Book V, moreover, are shaped substantially by English legal culture. As Andrew Zurcher explains, 'the failure to consider Spenser's native legal and political context has led to a number of fundamental misapprehensions about The Faerie Queene' and that 'nowhere is this more true than in Book V' in which 'the language of Spenser's narratives "Of Justice" . . . suggest[s] the relevance of contemporary English legal practice and theory to [his] understanding of justice.'[6] Spenser's poetic analysis of legal reform, I argue, refracts the common law's absorption of the historical reasoning found within the Aristotelian tradition on justice and legal equity, especially in Britomart's extensive contribution to the Book.

I read Artegall and Britomart as persona allegories for the definition of justice that descends from The Nicomachean Ethics, according to which

> the just man is said to be a doer, by choice, of that which is just, and one who will distribute either between himself and another or between two others not so as to give more of what is desirable to himself and less to his neighbour (and conversely with what is harmful), but so as to give what is equal in accordance with proportion . . .[7]

This definition, transmitted through Aristotle's text as well as those of Justinian and Aquinas, made its way into the treatises of sixteenth-century English writers such as Thomas Elyot, Thomas Wilson and Thomas Floyd in a more succinct formula: 'justice' was Englished as 'a perpetual and a constant will, yeelding every one his owne by even portion'.[8] Artegall evokes the principle of proportionality within the decrees and administration of justice. Proportionality comes into view through the difference in his judicial response to private injury and to public threat in the first two cases of Sir Sanglier and Pollente. This early distinction establishes the significance of legal reform as the focus of the Knight of Justice's endeavours. Rather than the resolution of private disputes, the majority of Artegall's adventures involve the correction of regional and frontier law and governance. This pattern culminates in the restoration of Irena to her throne in Canto 12. Before he can reach the princess, however, the Knight of Justice himself needs to be reformed and restored to his own office. In Canto 5, Artegall is taken prisoner by Radigund after he fails to decapitate her beautiful head in single combat. Britomart is then called upon by Artegall's groom, Talus, to liberate her fiancé from thraldom to the Amazon. As she retraces the knight's route through Faerieland to the city of Radigone, we discover that the countryside has not been subdued in the wake of Artegall's reformation of justice. Britomart's re-enactments of the knight's battles, on Pollente's bridge and with Radigund, re-present the activities of legal reform and governance as ongoing tasks. She thereby reforms and exemplifies the other part of the popular definition of justice, the 'perpetual and . . . constant will' to do justice.[9] After she slays the Amazon, Britomart's pity is directed toward the subjects of the city of Radigone and motivates the equitable reinstatement of a law that is historically legitimised and that accords with the character of the nation. Her reforms are ultimately refracted in Artegall's restoration of the princess Irena, through which the Knight of Justice comes closest to embodying constancy in the form of perpetual magisterial presence and re-education. Instead, however, Artegall is called back to the Faerie court 'ere he could reforme [Irena's realm] thoroughly'.[10]

Artegall's Division of Justice

At the beginning of Canto 4, Spenser linguistically enacts the complexities of the law's organisation and administration.[11] The opening lines are reminiscent of Nicholas Bacon's description of the perfection and the execution of the law within the parliamentary speeches that were quoted in the Introduction. The making and reforming of laws is an enormous waste of time and resources, he explained, if they are not afterwards implemented: 'all theise labours, travailes and paines taken . . . all the charge susteined by the realme about the making of [laws] is all in vaine and labor lost without the due execucion of them.'[12] Spenser draws a similar distinction between the production of what he terms 'True Justice' and its enforcement:

> Who so upon him selfe will take the skill
> True Justice unto people to divide,
> Had neede have mightie hands, for to fulfill
> That, which he doth with righteous doome decide,
> And for to maister wrong and puissant pride.
> For vaine it is to deeme of things aright,
> And makes wrong doers justice to deride,
> Unlesse it be perform'd with dreadlesse might.
> For powre is the right hand of Justice truely hight.
>
> (5.4.1)

While the stanza as a whole is clearly organised by this basic distinction between judgement and enforcement, ambiguities surface within the first two lines as the reader tries to make out what it means exactly to 'divide' 'True Justice' and the most likely referent of 'Who'. The verb more commonly used to describe the determination of legal judgements in Book V is 'deal', used twelve times, while 'divide' appears only twice. The distinction employed in Spenser's stanza and in Bacon's parliamentary speech constitute examples of logical division, as it is described in *The Rule of Reason*. Thomas Wilson writes that, 'As a definicion . . . doeth declare, what a thyng is, so the division sheweth, how many thynges are conteined in the same.' The first example that he offers of division can be found within his account of the device itself: 'A division, is either the dividyng of a worde, or of a thing'. In the opening of Canto 4, we are invited to divide the word 'divide' 'into every severall significacion that he hath'.[13] The verb had connotations related to early modern logical, rhetorical, pedagogical and legal culture. To 'divide' 'True Justice' was not only to determine and deliver a judicial resolution that must subsequently be enforced, but also to present an argument or oration on moral philosophy. The initial referent may as easily be the poet himself, who aims 'to fashion a gentleman . . . in vertuous and gentle discipline', as a hypothetical magistrate.[14] The stanza begins in a vein that is reminiscent of the epic speaker's conventional complaint about the inadequacy of his humble talents to represent his elevated theme: 'Who so upon him selfe will take the skill / True Justice unto people to divide, / Had neede have mightie hands . . .' The performance of justice is thus a more expansive exercise in the opening of the stanza, where it embraces instruction in virtue, than in the conclusion, where it is reduced to the 'dreadlesse might' and 'powre' required to enforce positive law. The progression from instruction to enforcement re-enacts in miniature the mythical shift in the nature and organisation of justice that takes place between the

Golden and Iron Ages, and that is represented at greater length in the Proem and Canto 1 of Book V.

While 'Spenser's description of the age of Saturn follows Ovid's carefully', Hadfield observes that the Elizabethan poet adapts his model by making 'the concept of justice ... a key element of the Golden Age, rather than a later development to cope with the degeneration of the world.'[15] In the time before the 'powre' to enforce the law was required, the Goddess of Justice's primary function was pedagogical. In Canto 1, we learn:

> For Artegall in justice was upbrought
> Even from the cradle of his infancie,
> And all the depth of rightfull doome was taught
> By faire Astraea, with great industrie,
> Whilest here on earth she lived mortallie.
> For till the world from his perfection fell
> Into all filth and foule iniquitie,
> *Astraea* here mongst earthly men did dwell,
> And in the rules of justice them instructed well.
>
> (5.1.5)

All men were just in the mythical past not simply because of their uncorrupted nature, but because of the goddess's instruction in virtue, through which all men could perfect their nature. This education is presented in an idyllic setting, far removed from the punishments of the sixteenth-century courtroom and classroom alike.[16] In the Proem, we are invited to imagine Justice overseeing a feast rather than convening a trial. '[D]uring *Saturnes* ancient raigne,' the speaker explains, 'Justice sate high ador'd with solemne feasts, / And to all people did divide her dread beheasts' (5.Proem.9). Since 'no man was affrayd / Of force, ne fraud in wight was to be found' (5.Proem.9), it makes sense to read the 'dred beheasts' of the Goddess as preventive directives, similar to those found in early modern discourses on justice, law, and good governance. The preventive force of instruction is highlighted in the section 'On Enacting or Emending Laws' of Erasmus's *Education of a Christian Prince*: 'It is ... a mistake to think that the laws should ... merely give orders and not instruction; on the contrary, they should be concerned to deter men from law-breaking more by reasoning than by punishments.'[17] The principle of prevention was also evident in English treatises on the practical administration of local justice. In his manual for Justices of the Peace, for instance, Michael Dalton explains that 'The conservation of this Peace' involves 'preventing', 'pacifying' and 'punishing': 'But of the three, the first, the preventing ... is most worthy to be commended to the care of the Justices of Peace.'[18] In Spenser's version of the Golden

Age, Astraea provides preventive instruction in a virtue that every man successfully manifests, precluding the need for legal enforcement and therefore officers.

The education of Artegall as a magistrate or the Knight of Justice, then, is an innovation that marks the mythical evolution of justice from the training of all men in the virtue to that of an elite governing class authorised to represent and enforce the law. The preventive 'dread beheasts' at Astraea's feast are transformed into Artegall's 'dreadfull heast' that is supported by 'might':

> Thus she him trayned, and thus she him taught,
> In all the skill of deeming wrong and right,
> Untill the ripenesse of mans yeares he raught;
> That even wilde beasts did feare his awfull sight,
> And men admyr'd his overruling might;
> Ne any liv'd on ground, that durst withstand
> His dreadfull heast, much lesse him match in fight,
> Or bide the horror of his wreakfull hand,
> When so he list in wrath lift up his steely brand.

(5.1.8)

These opening scenes of instruction establish the education of the magistrate as the guarantee of justice in a fallen world. They also establish the magistrate himself as the first object of improvement. Artegall's progression in his office is tacked onto his growth from boy to man, joining but also distinguishing his public and personal identities and bringing into question the relationship between the two as the Book begins. The magistrate's maturation and reformation, meanwhile, will be signalled by a return to study in the last episode, when Artegall nearly completes his quest, as I will discuss in the final section below.

One of the initial tests of Artegall's judgement involves the distinction between private and public offences and the proportional response required by each. In his very first 'inquest', the knight condemns Sir Sanglier, who has killed his own lady and kidnapped a more appealing one that was travelling with a nameless squire. Through Artegall's intervention, the living lady almost meets the same fate as the dead one in a Solomonic test that would have literally divided and distributed her among the two men who desire her (5.1.26). Perceiving the squire's willingness rather to part from his love than to have his love parted, however, Artegall rules in the young man's favour. Sir Sanglier is forced to restore the lady he has stolen and is sentenced to wear the head of his own dead mistress against his breast for a year. In Canto 2, however, the narrative shifts focus from corrective justice to legal reform. The relative leniency of Sanglier's sentence is replaced by a scale of punishment that is correlated with the threat posed to the common good by Pollente and Munera's offences. Pollente and his groom extort fees from and kill travellers who wish to cross a bridge – both rich and poor are affected, we're told, suggesting the comprehensive victimisation of the commonwealth – while his daughter Munera hoards the growing ill-gotten fortune in her castle (5.2.6). Artegall 'undid the evil fashion, / And wicked cust019omes of that Bridge refourmed' by turning their punishment into a form of deterrence. While Pollente's groom 'of evil guize' is killed instantly by the Knight of Justice, both father and daughter suffer death and dismemberment. Their severed body parts are displayed as warnings for future magistrates (5.2.19, 5.2.26). Pollente's head is mounted on a pole

> Where many years it afterwards remayned,
> To be a mirrour to all mighty men,
> In whose right hands great power is contayned,
> That none of them the feeble overren,
> But alwaies doe their powre within just compasse pen.
>
> (5.2.19)

If 'Artegall is a notably brutal governor' in this second case, writes Hadfield, it is 'precisely because the law is under threat and with it the very possibility of order'.[19]

The 'mirrour' of the severed head provides 'a warning which recalls Spenser's citation of Machiavelli in *A View* ... that the magistrate's abuse of power should incur draconian penalties', according to Hadfield.[20] At the end of his extended discussion of martial and magisterial misconduct in his political treatise, Spenser writes, 'this (I remember) is worthily observed by Machiavel in his discourses upon Livie, where he commendeth the manner of the Romans government, in giving absolute power to all their Councellors and Governours, which if they abused, they should afterwards dearely answere' (*A View* 160). While Spenser may directly conjure Machiavelli's warning to frontier governors in the conclusion to *A View*, the same principle is also elaborated on at length in Erasmus's account of magisterial corruption in *The Education of a Christian Prince*, a text that employs examples that more closely resemble the contents of Book V. 'Many laws have been introduced quite justifiably but have been put to the worst uses by the corruption of officials,' Erasmus writes; 'there is nothing so pernicious as a good law diverted to evil purposes.' To illustrate this 'deeply rooted ... evil' that requires 'the more thoroughly [to] be extirpated', he offers a case that mirrors the corruption of tolls that is represented in the Pollente episode:

> It was a good idea, in days gone by, to provide officials on the frontiers of states to supervise imports and exports, to ensure, of course, that merchants

and travellers could come and go free from the fear of bandits . . . But nowadays the traveller is held up at every turn by these customs duties, visitors are
harassed, merchants are fleeced, and there is no longer any word of protect-
ing them although the tolls increase from one day to the next. In this way the
purpose for which the institution was first established has been totally lost,
and what was a sound practice when introduced has been turned into utter
tyranny by the fault of those who administer it.[21]

The original intention of the law is upended by the form of its present
execution, which has 'grown up almost everywhere' and is 'now firmly
established by long custom'.[22] Historical progress is represented as a function of corruption within this ubiquitous phenomenon, just as it is in the
account of the transition from the Golden to the Iron Age in the Proem and
Canto 1 of Book V. Within the Pollente episode, a structural weakness or
imperfection within the phenomenon of positive law becomes visible: the
vulnerability of legal administration to the officer's self-interested abuse of
authority or power that is the corollary to the potential for perfection that
is imagined in the scenes of instruction. By identifying the episode with this
perennial problem that was introduced along with the office or jurisdiction
of the magistrate, the kind of legal reformation that is required also comes
into focus. This potential for abuse cannot be eliminated from the execution of justice; it can only be monitored and regulated through the careful
selection and correction of individual magistrates.

Since the legal-administrative problem identified by the poem is
subject only to regulation rather than complete removal, we should be
deeply suspicious of the exaggerated conclusiveness that characterises
the end of this episode. Not only are the corrupt magistrates killed, but
Talus goes on to destroy the ill-gotten riches and to obliterate Munera's
castle.

> Thereafter all that mucky pelfe he tooke,
> The spoile of peoples evill gotten good,
> The which her sire had scrap't by hooke and crooke,
> And burning all to ashes, powr'd it downe the brooke.

> And lastly all that Castle quite he raced,
> Even from the sole of his foundation,
> And all the hewen stones thereof defaced,
> That there mote be no hope of reparation,
> Nor memory thereof to any nation.

(5.2.27–8)

Unlike the body parts that are instrumentalised to publicise the punishment for crimes against the commonweal, the riches and the castle, the
inspiration and the instrument of injustice, are so thoroughly erased that
they leave no signs, neither to warn nor to tempt others. According to the

prevailing interpretation of this scene, 'Spenser's use of Artegall/Talus
. . . represent[s] the interdependence of justice and force; allegorically it
renders the argument in *A View* that English sovereignty depends on a
military suppression of native Irish power.'[23] By 'remmoving all those
inconveniences, and new framing (as it were) in the forge, all that is worne
out of fashion', as Irenaeus recommends in the political treatise, Artegall
and Talus clear the way for 'faire means and peaceable plotts to redresse
the [realm]' (*A View* 91). On this reading, the episode would represent – to
Spenser and his first readers – an early example of Artegall's perfection of
justice. Katherine Eggert contends that in cantos 1 through 4, 'Artegall's
doome extends even to narrative itself, as with the end of each canto an
episode in his travels is firmly and finally concluded', in contrast with
the pattern of narrative irresolution that she tracks throughout the prior
Book.[24] As I will argue, however, the possibility and the value of erasure
will be called into question when we return to the bridge with Britomart,
whose role will emphasise reform through legal-historical continuity.

In an intricate argument about this episode, Bradin Cormack asserts
that Spenser allegorises the displacement of Irish customary law by
statute law that, through its interpretation, functions as a vehicle for
coercion. The English colonial practice of statutory interpretation is represented as analogous to allegorical practice itself, 'revealing to and concealing from the understanding'.[25] 'Artegall aims to produce a political
culture', Cormack writes, 'through the simultaneous memorialization
and erasure of an (Irish) customary past.' If 'Artegall's justice imprints
the landscape with significant [i.e. signifying] absences,' I argue that the
most important one turns out to be that of the magistrate himself.[26] The
Knight of Justice quickly moves on from the bridge ('unto his former
journey he retourned' (5.2.28)). This is a mistake in governance pointed
to repeatedly throughout *A View*. As Irenaeus explains, 'the presence
of the Governour is . . . a great stay and bridle unto those that are ill
disposed', and 'the Irishman (I assure you) feares the Government no
longer then he is within sight or reach' (*A View* 126, 127). As conclusive
as the scene initially appears, the violent obliteration of corrupt officers,
custom, coin and castle turns out to be a dangerously incomplete policy
and story once the reforming magistrates depart. This only becomes
evident, however, once we return to the scene with Britomart and Talus.

Britomart's Legal Constancy

When applied to human affairs, 'division' typically indicates '[t]he fact
of being divided in opinion, sentiment, or interest; disagreement, vari-

ance, dissension, discord'.[27] In 'A Treatise of Monarchy', Fulke Greville writes that Astraea's departure from earth and the consequent transition from natural to positive law ('To Mans Laws which but corrupt reason be') results in the separation and the divisiveness of entire peoples: 'After which Change, men have liv'd more divide / By Laws, then they at first by Language were'.[28] The positive law is necessitated by and helps formalise Iron Age difference and discord. The negative connotation of 'divide' is only latent in Spenser's idea of 'divid[ing]' 'True Justice' that appears at the beginning of Canto 4; however, the potential for magistrates to precipitate disorder as well as order is subsequently revealed in Book V through the travels of Britomart and Talus. On their way back through Faerieland to rescue Artegall from his Amazon captor, these two must disperse rebellious energies that have grown up after, and even as a result of, Artegall's reformation of law and justice. In the process, Britomart not only re-performs the knight's former adventures and redistributes his original judgements, but her efforts also improve upon Faerieland justice by establishing administrative continuity and a form of legal equity through which historical law is made compatible with the novel case and the nation. Britomart's judicial achievements are the result of the hybrid identity she assumes in Book V, as both the Knight of Justice and Constancy, a virtue closely related to chastity but charged with the regulation of the emotions. Because of her personal and magisterial constancy, Britomart's anger and pity are able to inspire action that corresponds with the requirements of public justice.

The first scene that she re-enacts in Book V is the fight on Pollente's bridge. In Canto 6, the aged knight Dolon mistakes the Knight of Chastity for that of Justice on the evidence of her travelling companion, 'that yron page . . . / Which still was wont with Artegall remaine' (5.6.34). Britomart thus becomes the target of revenge plots designed by Dolon and his living sons:

> He had three sonnes, all three like fathers sonnes,
> Like treacherous, like full of fraud and guile,
> Of all that on this earthly compasse wonnes:
> The eldest of the which was slaine erewhile
> By *Artegall*, through his owne guilty wile;
> His name was *Guizor*, whose untimely fate
> For to avenge, full many treasons vile
> His father *Dolon* had deviz'd of late
> With these his wicked sons, and shewd his cankred hate.

> (5.6.33)

Despite Artegall and Talus's best efforts at the reformation of the bridge, the removal of one source of disorder has led to the emergence of another. From Guizor's death grow three more disruptive bodies, those of his father and two remaining brothers. Neither the preventive dictums emblematised by Pollente and Munera's body parts nor the policy of violent erasure has resulted in lasting order. Disorder is thereby realised as a perpetual potential that necessitates ongoing magisterial vigilance and involvement. Britomart is initially responsible for reforming justice here by establishing continuity in legal administration. She thus embodies the general principle of justice as 'a perpetual and a constant will', according to the frequently regurgitated formula.

Britomart's reiterative judicial action on the bridge corrects the kind of inconsistency in legal administration that was targeted frequently in sixteenth-century treatises on the reform of Irish governance. In his 'Conjectures' on the state of Ireland, for example, Edward Walshe argued that

> it were most necessary to reduce the proceadinges of Yrlande to some rule or orders that shulde be observed from one Deputy to an other ... For it is certayne that the confusion of opinions and thapplienge of ... services and treasures apon every newe Judgement was and shalbe a continuall labarinth And yf this were ons concluded then eviry niewe deputy shulde begyn where the former deputy made an ende and so some goode shulde be done wheras hitherto it hath ben otherwyse And eviry newe Deputy sekinge a singular waye moche confusion hath happened.[29]

Walshe's account of legal uncertainty as a function of system-wide accident and disorder within Irish governance is redescribed as a function of corruption in *A View*, composed fifty years later. Through the voice of Irenaeus, Spenser depicts a chain of governors sabotaging each other's attempts at legal reform in the quest for reputation and reward:

> For this ... is the common order of them, that who commeth next in place, will not follow that course of government, how ever good, which his predecessors held, either for disdaine of himselfe, or doubt to have his doings drowned in another mans praise, but will straight take a way quite contrary to the former ...

According to Irenaeus's interlocutor, Eudoxus, the schemes and negligence of Deputies are major contributors to Ireland's 'continuall wretchedness'. Magistrates who attempt to undercut the reputation of their predecessors and successors are an 'inconvenience [that] were well looked into' because the 'malady' is 'more hardly to be redressed in the governor then in the governed' (*A View* 90–1). Whether by accident or design, English governance amounted to a 'discontinuous sequence of independent and short-lived programmes' for the reformation of Ireland, in Brady's words. It 'succeeded only in precipitating a general alienation amongst all of the island's communities . . . all were united in a profound mistrust of Tudor reform as mediated through the plans of the viceroys in Dublin castle.'[30]

Britomart's achievement extends beyond administrative to legal continuity. At the same time that the limitation of the initial scope and enforcement of Artegall's justice is revealed through the Dolon family's plot, the same justice is also redressed through the way in which it is re-enacted by Britomart. Through its repetition, Artegall's judgement is newly legitimised as the beginning of a pattern in a progressive legal history. On 'that perillous Bridge, / On which *Pollente* with *Artegall* did fight', Britomart encounters and kills Dolon's remaining sons. She disposes of the brothers every bit as easily and ruthlessly as Artegall had disposed of Guizor:

> She stayd not to advise which way to take;
> But putting spurres unto her fiery beast,
> Thorough the midst of them she way did make.
> The one of them, which most her wrath increast,
> Uppon her speare she bore before her breast,
> Till to the Bridges further end she past,
> Where falling downe, his challenge he releast:
> The other over side the Bridge she cast
> Into the river, where he drunke his deadly last.

(5.6.39)

Britomart transforms the original outcome into a judicial tradition or practice that accommodates emergent circumstances and legal cases. She thereby begins to function as the representative or judge of at least one form of equity long before she comes across Isis Church.

Near the end of Book V of *The Nicomachean Ethics*, Aristotle defines equity as the 'correction of legal justice'. Such equity is the result of an interpretative process, he argues, that bridges the gap between the general wording of the law and the particulars of individual cases through the imaginative reconstruction of the lawmakers' original intentions:

> [A]ll law is universal but about some things it is not possible to make a universal statement which shall be correct . . . the error is not in the law nor in the legislator but in the nature of the thing, since the matter of practical affairs is of this kind from the start. When the law speaks universally, then, and a case arises on it which is not covered by the universal statement, then it is right . . . to say what the legislator himself would have said had he been present, and would have put into this law if he had known.[31]

While Aristotle stresses the diversity of human actions as the cause of the law's limited descriptive power, that diversity is necessarily, in part, a function of time. This method of interpretation reinforces the legitimacy of positive law by construing both its historical authority and its relevance to the present. As Mark Fortier explains, 'the answer one arrives at will not be one that the lawmaker originally and specifically formulated, but one the imaginary lawmaker is made to formulate after the fact.'[32] Aquinas extended the concept of legal equity further by arguing that 'the lawgiver's intention is presumed to have been guided by the "collective welfare" (*communis utilitas*)'. The collective welfare, in turn, was to be determined by the political ruler, who would appeal to natural law, or a higher principle, to resolve the case.[33]

Alan Cromartie traces the development of legal equity in medieval and early modern English thought through Sir John Fortescue, who isolates the king as the source of equitable judgements because it belonged to his singular power to correct the law when exceptions were discovered. But Fortescue identifies the common good with 'the sanctity of private property', thus the monarch's equitable decisions were justified on the grounds that they fulfilled, rather than overturned, the common law's function. In the 1520s and 1530s, Christopher St German published Latin and English versions of a treatise that presented 'a new attitude that tended to sever equity from kingship'.[34] Drawing on the medieval work of Jean Gerson, St German's *Dialoge in Englisshe, bytwyxte a Doctour of Dyvynitie and a Student in the Lawes of Englande* also established a place for equity within the interpretation of every law: 'equitie must alway be observed in every lawe of man and in every generall rewle therof . . . Lawes covet to be rewled by equitie.'[35] He thus 'assimilat[ed] the use of *epieikeia* to ordinary common law judicial reasoning'.[36] The 'stunning revolution in the provision of equitable justice in England' that began with the writings of St German culminated in the famous collection of law reports by Edmund Plowden, first published in 1571.[37] Cromartie writes that 'the way in which [Plowden] characterized the hermeneutic task [of equity] appeared to exclude the idea of *external* correction'.[38] In a response to Ernst Kantorowicz's influential critique of Plowden's *Commentaries* as 'the final emanation of a nearly vanished political theology' of the king's two bodies, Lorna Hutson argues that the famous collection of law reports was more historically significant for establishing within English common law 'an Aristotelian theory of equitable interpretation'.[39] By the end of the sixteenth century, the lawmakers' intentions were equated with the common good that, in turn, was defined to reflect present needs by the common law judiciary in their equitable interpretations of statutes.[40] Legal equity is perhaps the only dimension of the early modern 'culture of equity' that has not yet been mined for a close reading of Britomart, who is directly, repeatedly but still opaquely identified with equity in Book V.[41] Yet the logic of legal equity shapes her entire contribution. While the Dolon family's plot was clearly unanticipated by Artegall and Talus, Britomart resolves the present case in a way that links it with the past execution of justice.

The same historical logic that structured the equitable interpretation of specific cases was writ large in the concept of 'artificial reason', through which the common law's relationship to the entire nation was imagined. In contrast to the persistent complaints and suspicions of deputies in Ireland, judges in England were idealised in legal writings for their professional commitment to the transmission and perpetuation of historical law and order. With characteristic hyperbole, John Davies wrote in the preface to his early seventeenth-century collection of Irish case reports that 'there are no Judges in any State or Kingdome under the Sunne, that do more reverence the opinions & Judgements of their predecessors then the Judges of England have ever done'.[42] The judiciary's deference to past legal authorities was a distinguishing feature of the professional practice of 'artificial reasoning' that was held to have ensured the historical persistence of the English common law as well as its continuing relevance. Edward Coke provided the most famous definition of 'artificial reasoning' in the first volume of his *Institutes of the Laws of England*:

> The common Law it selfe is nothing else but reason, which is to be understood of an artificiall perfection of reason, gotten by long study, observation, and experience . . . [B]y many succession of ages it hath been fined and refined by an infinite number of grave and learned men, and by long experience growne to such a perfection, for the government of this Realm . . .[43]

While Coke was inconsistent on a number of professional and historical topics across his many writings, his comments here argue that the 'refine[ment]' of the law, achieved through the 'perfection' of the professional deliberation of many judges, has resulted in the law's continuing suitability 'for the government of this Realm'. Professional and antiquarian accounts of legal history employed the language of 'reason' and 'custom' to craft accommodations of these two forces – continuity and change – that were essential to the law's claims to facilitate justice in contemporary cases, for contemporary England. According to Glenn Burgess, 'the common lawyers habitually saw the common law as a set of rules that was constantly changing. Historical evolution was at the heart of the common law. Historical evolution provided the major ground for the defence of English law in terms of being immemorially fitted to the needs of the nation.'[44] In the re-performance of the Pollente episode, Britomart's association with legal equity is established; in the re-performance of the Radigund episode, she will apply the same principle of resuscitating historical law to craft justice not in a particular case, but for the current population of the newly liberated city.

The concept of 'artificial reason' provided a defence against incursions into the common law jurisdiction from external forces (such as the monarch, parliament, and the church, none of whose agents met the qualifying conditions to speak the law), while the professional 'perfection of reason, gotten by long study, observation, and experience' also provided a defence against the individual judge's weak or corrupt reason and passions. According to numerous characterisations in medieval and early modern writings, Andrew Zurcher explains, common law judges 'applied established maxims, precedents, and statutes in a process strictly controlled by custom and usage'.[45] But by accommodating discretionary thinking within the interpretation of cases and the common good, both legal equity and artificial reasoning opened a space for the individual judge's contribution to the execution and development of law. Coke idealises this contribution in his formulation of artificial reasoning above, but the fictional Irenaeus addresses the problem of the judge's human frailty in *A View*: 'it is dangerous to leave the sence of the law unto the reason or will of the judge, who are men and may bee miscarried by affections, and many other meanes' (*A View* 40). In Book V of *The Faerie Queene*, Artegall's misplaced pity toward Radigund, which results in an injustice to the city of Radigone as well as his own imprisonment, represents the perennial threat and the dangerous consequences of magisterial passion within a 'judge-centered, ethical jurisprudence'.[46] Pity, however, is not vilified so completely within Book V as John D. Staines maintains in his reading of Artegall's behaviour.[47] Instead, I argue that Spenser follows Aristotelian tradition again and allegorises the regulation, rather than the erasure, of emotions through Britomart's quest. Subtending her legal equity and artificial reasoning is an emotional life whose ends are coordinated with those of public justice.

As Kathy Eden has demonstrated, Aristotle understood equity to be the product of a process of reasoning that was supported by 'the proper emotional responses'.[48] In another synthesis of Aristotle's commentary on equity and the emotions, Eugene Garver explains the productive contribution of the emotions within all deliberation. Emotion focuses our attention on particulars as the objects of thought; therefore, 'emotion completes reasoning by making it particular enough to have something definite to do.' Thus the emotions are not only capable of altering judgements but they enable them in the first place. By springing from our experience of particulars and by guiding thought toward specific actions, the emotions are also necessarily political: they are 'modes of involvement . . . with a practical world constituted by relations with other people'.[49] The two emotions that come to the fore in Britomart's quest to recover her fiancé are anger and pity, both of which are defined by Aristotle as responses to injustice. Anger is 'an impulse, accompanied by pain, to a conspicuous revenge for a conspicuous slight directed without justification towards what concerns oneself or towards what concerns one's friends', while pity is 'a feeling of pain caused by the sight of some evil, destructive or painful, which befalls one who does not deserve it'.[50] Through the alternation of anger and pity, in response to the correct objects for deliberation and action, Britomart is able to reform Artegall's justice. While the Stoic tradition (a common focus of criticism on the representation of violence in Book V) advocated the suppression or erasure of emotions, Britomart's are regulated through the virtue of constancy, which, in Spenser's text, guides the magistrate's emotions toward the common good.

Through Britomart's participation in Book V, constancy emerges as the virtue that correctly directs the officer's emotions and that ultimately enables equitable judicial practice. The law's historical continuity and reform ultimately rest upon the 'constancie of our Judges', to use John Davies' words.[51] Thomas Floyd's Aristotelian definition of justice concludes with an account of the supplementary virtues required for its performance that emphasises constancy from different angles. Justice is

> a perpetual and a constant will, yeelding every one his owne by even portion wherein prudence, magnanimity, and constancy, as assistants or gards, are requisit: the one to distinguish lawful things from unlawful: the other, not to be daunted or held backe by any sinister chaunce: the third . . . to persevere in yeelding justice.[52]

The passage begins and ends with forms of constancy, as a 'perpetual and a constant will' to distribute justice to all and as the 'persever[ance]' to distribute justice continually. According to Thomas Elyot, constancy not only undergirds justice but all virtue by subduing the passions: 'that man which in childhood is brought up in sundry virtues, if either by nature, or else by custom, he be not induced to be alway constant and stable, so that he move not for any affection, grief, or displeasure, all his virtues will shortly decay.' While 'to governors nothing is more proper than to be in their living stable and constant', he goes on to explain that inconstancy is associated especially with children and women, and therefore, 'in rebuking a man of inconstancy, [we] call him a childish or womanly person.' Artegall's thraldom through women's clothes and work is particularly apt, then, since his romantic and judicial constancy intersect and simultaneously waver when he fails to decapitate Radigund in response to the beauty of her face. Elyot concedes in a bad joke, however, that 'some women nowadays be found more constant than men' and 'specially in love towards their husbands; or else might there happen to be some wrong inheritors.'[53]

Through constancy, Britomart is able to redefine the objects of anger and pity within Book V, reforming Artegall's justice in Radigone and correcting the relationship between the judge's passions and the law. But why is the Knight of Chastity from Book III called upon to represent constancy in the 'The Legend of Artegall or of Justice'? Amelia A. Zurcher explains the historical overlap and distinction between chastity and constancy in early modern English culture and romance:

> Constancy frequently takes an object . . . and so can be formulated as a will toward something, in opposition to chastity's logic of withholding – a distinction that in this period was generally understood to prove an ethical advantage for constancy . . . [T]he constant woman . . . increased her ties to the public realm, by functioning as quasi-private support for a man who was in the public eye. Female chastity in early modern England, in contrast, was often condemned as a perverse, selfish, and fruitless withdrawal from social obligation . . . For this reason, chastity in the Renaissance . . . tended to slide into constancy, the classic example being Spenser's Britomart, Knight of Chastity, whose adventures are all aimed toward the clearing of a symbolic space for union with Artegall.[54]

On this account, Britomart's constancy in Book V is easily imagined as a form of reformed chastity, a response to Astraea's own 'perverse . . . withdrawal' not only from the public sphere (she first retreats to a cave with the child Artegall) but ultimately from the earth itself.

In Book V, the female knight's magisterial and romantic constancy are mutually enabling throughout her quest for revenge. By executing Guizor's brothers without hesitation, she looks equally like the learned, experienced, mechanistic judge, dispensing the 'True Justice' that is determined through the professional habit of artificial reasoning, *and* like a jealous lover driven by impulsive rage. Instead of undermining public justice, as Floyd and Elyot's treatises and Artegall's thraldom warn that it may, Britomart's emotional life is persistently aligned with its requirements. Through her revenge, Spenser transforms personal desire into a force that motivates and even legitimises the execution of the positive law. This is less counterintuitive if we consider Derek Dunne's powerful corrective to 'the stale binaries of Law/Revenge' that have been disseminated in early modern literary criticism primarily through studies of revenge tragedy. 'The divine sanction of vengeance is one of the cornerstones of early modern law,' he writes, 'which metes out punishment according to retributive principles.'[55] In a printed Assize sermon on the 'Prohibition of Revenge', William Westerman explicates Paul's command, '*Avenge not your selves (dearely beloved) but give place unto wrath: for it is written: vengeaunce is mine, and I will repaye, sayth the Lord.*' The biblical interdiction, Westerman explains, is restricted to private acts of revenge, because the Lord's vengeance is carried out on earth by magistrates:

> The *Revenge* therefore that is by this *Prohibition* removed, is *private*; such as receiving injuries offered without *right*, repayeth them againe without *Law*. The revenge, & redresse of wrongs warranted unto us, is the wrath & vengeance of the Lord: either mediatly to be executed by his Ministers ordayned to take vengeaunce of evill doers: or else immediatly by the Lord himselfe, where the sword of the Magistrate is too short, or the hand too slack, to smite the malefactor.[56]

In his character sketch 'Of the Good Magistrate', Joseph Hall writes that the magistrate's 'sword hath neither rusted for want of use, nor surfeteth of blood, but after many threats is unsheathed, as the dreadfull instrument of divine revenge'.[57] Through such writings, revenge is located within – rather than in competition with – the law when it is carried out by the magistrate. Spenser's poem sets up the same contrast between private and public revenge. The story of Guizor's family can be redescribed as a story of private revenge that is pitted against the agent, Britomart/Artegall, of public revenge. In his pity toward Radigund, Artegall fails to enact the public revenge that was required of him.[58] By contrast, Britomart's character aligns passion and self-interest with the demands of public justice. By allegorising legal reform through Britomart's quest for revenge, Spenser is able to model a constructive version of the inescapable intersection between character and public office.[59]

Upon hearing from Talus that Artegall has been overcome by a woman, Britomart arms and departs with the iron groom for Radigone, while 'in her thought did hide / The felnesse of her heart' that was 'right fully bent / To fierce avengement of that womans pride, / Which had her Lord in her base prison pent' (5.6.18). Invited by Dolon, a benign-seeming older knight, to rest at his castle, she refuses to remove her armour before bed, 'For she had vow'd, she said, not to forgo / Those warlike weedes, till she revenge had wrought' (5.6.23). Her rage increases after her narrow escape from the unsuccessful night attack by Dolon's sons that leaves her 'wondrous wroth, and inly burning, / To be avenged for so fowle a deede' (5.6.31). Britomart's passion builds throughout her appearances in Book V, cresting finally in her defeat of Radigund, when the female knight corrects Artegall's emotional-judicial error and kills the Amazon usurper:

> [Radigund] being layd, the wrothfull Britonesse
> Stayd not, till she came to her selfe againe,
> But in revenge both of her loves distresse,
> And her late vile reproch, though vaunted vaine,
> And also of her wound, which sore did paine,
> She with one stroke both head and helmet cleft.
>
> (5.7.34)

The female knight's sensitivity to personal taunts and wounds implicates a personal, and even petty drive. In this moment, her wrath seems to represent an extreme that counters Artegall's leniency or misguided pity. Ultimately, however, these hints allow Spenser to gesture toward the dangerous and perennial potential of judicial passion while foregrounding reformed judicial conduct. (From a plot perspective as well, if Britomart were *too* perfect in the role of judge, she would replace rather than reform and restore her fiancé.) Britomart's personal revenge is in defence of the representative of justice, Artegall; it is thus necessarily public revenge, and Radigund meets the same severe fate as other offenders who threaten the common good.

Britomart's sense of office, her mindfulness of the common good, surfaces unequivocally in her emotional and behavioural transition that follows. Focusing on Artegall's behavior in Book V, Staines argues that Spenser offers a wholehearted Stoic repudiation of pity as *misericordia*, as the perverse extension of mercy or *clementia* that results in injustice, before it is resuscitated as an aspect of courtesy in Book VI.[60] I argue instead that the function and value of pity is reformed within Book V through the representation of Britomart's inner life that evokes Aristotle's definition of the emotion, according to which pity is properly excited by injustice and motivates its correction. After taking revenge upon Radigund, Britomart's pity is excited by the suffering of Radigund's former subjects. As the Amazon's subjects retreat, Talus begins a 'piteous slaughter' of 'all that ever came within his reach', a violence that serves no military, political, or legal function (5.7.35). Jessica Wolfe reads Talus as 'an allegorical embodiment of Stoicism taken to a disturbing and at times absurd extreme'. She writes, '[w]hile Artegall is all too easily mollified by his adversaries, Talus clearly solves the juridical challenges posed by the miscarriage of the affections in that he is not a man but an automaton.' If, as Wolfe argues, 'Book V weighs the ethical and political liabilities of both rigor and mercy' through the representation of Talus and Artegall, I argue that Britomart emerges as a *via media* between the two.[61] The female knight's emotional response to the senseless carnage results in the restraint of her own rage and power, before she turns to Talus and, for the first time in the Book, he is checked:

And now by this the noble Conqueresse
Her selfe came in, her glory to partake;
Where though revengefull vow she did professe,
Yet when she saw the heapes, which he did make,
Of slaughtred carkasses, her heart did quake
For very ruth, which did it almost rive,
That she his fury willed him to slake:
For else he sure had left not one alive,
But all in his revenge of spirite would deprive.

(5.7.36)

Hadfield argues that Britomart evokes here the principle or lesson of restraint symbolised by Pollente's head on a pole.[62] She orders Talus to contain his 'powre within just compasse' just as he is on the brink of again performing an act of erasure like that which characterised the treatment of Munera and her castle – this time on a much grander scale – and that has already proven to be an inadequate policy for reforming order. Instead of pursuing the erasure of the present population, we are subsequently told that Britomart restores a historical patriarchal order to the city and that the subjects are required to pledge allegiance to Artegall (5.7.43). The equitable practice that generated legal continuity on Pollente's bridge Britomart here extends to the reformation of an entire city. By reinstating a historical legal order that has 'growne to such a perfection, for the government of this Realm', her actions embody the logic of artificial reason, with its regard for historical continuity and the contemporary nation.

Many critics have tried to account for 'Britomart's ... perplexing subjugation of women to men's rule'.[63] Brian C. Lockey has argued that the city's reformation confirms 'a traditional conception of justice comprised of a patriarchal regime that subordinates women based on the doctrine of natural law'. By realigning positive with natural law, Britomart adopts a form of equity that 'involved a correction of the existing human law, in cases where following the law itself would result in injustice'. He writes that since this definition of equity, deriving from the natural law tradition, 'was seen as originating in the sovereign's power of administering justice outside of the ordinary channels, it was often associated with the sovereign's power of prerogative.' The same reasoning structured the natural law justification of conquest, through which the sovereign's right to overrule law that produces injustice legitimises colonial invasion and violence.[64] Andrew Zurcher employs a similar understanding of equity when he writes that the episodes of Book V 'contribute to Spenser's representation of equity as an imperial type of justice, a corrective principle intervening from outside, to improve local or legal justice.'[65]

Yet Britomart's intervention offers more challenges to than support for the logic and ethics of equity and conquest, as described by Lockey. In this specific episode, male governance is emphasised as a historical phenomenon, and nature here stands neither for human nature nor natural law, but for the nature or character of a people. In *De republica anglorum*, Thomas Smith uses clothing as a simile to illustrate the conventional political idea 'That the Common Wealth or Policie Must Be According to the Nature of the People': 'as ye would putt a garment fyt to a man's bodie . . . so the bodie politique is in quiet, and findeth ease, pleasure and profit' when the form of government conforms to 'the nature of the people'.[66] In a mirroring of Artegall and the other prisoners' restoration to their male attire and status, Britomart returns Radigone to a previous rule of law that is legitimised as historical and whose historical continuity is solidified through its newly asserted relationship to the present; it is a rule of law understood to be more *suit*able to the population:

> So there a while they afterwards remained,
> [Artegall] to refresh, and [Britomart's] late wounds to heale:
> During which space she there as Princes[s] rained,
> And changing all that forme of common weale,
> The liberty of women did repeale,
> Which they had long usurpt; and them restoring
> To mens subjection, did true Justice deale:
> That all they as a Goddesse her adoring,
> Her wisdome did admire, and hearkned to her loring.
>
> (5.7.42)

Spenser earlier dubs Britomart a 'noble Conqueresse' only to strike through that title: she acts as the law's representative rather than its source. Instead of exercising a sovereign power to *over*rule the Amazon's law, moreover, it is her restoration and championing of the city's own political order and legal system that precipitates her sovereign and finally divine status – an apotheosis that is depicted as a function of the people's good will, just like that described earlier of Osyris and Isis in Canto 7 (5.7.2–3). Because she 'did true Justice deale' through her reformations while 'she there as Princes rained', the people of Radigone, 'as a Goddesse her adoring, / Her wisdome did admire, and hearkned to her loring' (5.7.42). Britomart is conveniently removed from the scene,

Astraea-like, so that Artegall can come back into focus as the Knight of Justice; she transforms back into the Knight of Chastity as her active role in the public sphere evaporates or transforms into lore. Britomart's success in Book V is refracted in Artegall's reformed emotional constancy, which is subsequently on display in the trial of Duessa in Canto 9. There, the knight's 'constant firme intent' and 'zeale of Justice' do not waver in the face of multiple direct appeals to his pity, including Duessa's face. Instead, his resolute judgement prevents Arthur's passions from leading the proceedings astray (5.9.46, 49).

Britomart's constancy results in legal administrative consistency and directs her emotions toward the objects of the common good, enabling equitable accommodations between law and nation that in turn generate legal historical progress. Through her role in Book V, Spenser poetically surmounts the 'insurmountable theoretical problem for the English in Ireland [that] was the lack of fit between the Irish and an English customary law they resisted as the chief sign of the colonizing presence'.[67] In the opening pages of *A View of the Present State of Ireland*, Irenaeus explains to Eudoxus the reason for his 'dislike' of the laws of England, which are 'not so meete for that realme of Ireland, and not onely the common Law, but also the Statutes and Actes of Parliament': 'lawes ought to be fashioned unto the manners and conditions of the people, to whom they are meant, and not to be imposed upon them according to the simple rule of right' (*A View* 19–20). Through Britomart, English colonial imposition is figured instead as legal historical restoration. It is an ideal, derived from English common law thought and practice, that Spenser is unable to realise within his political treatise. Irenaeus finally offers the now infamous compromise that justifies violent overrule in Ireland: 'sithence wee cannot now apply lawes fit to the people, as in the first institutions of common-wealths it ought to bee, wee will apply the people, and fit them unto the lawes, as it most conveniently may bee' (*A View* 135).[68]

The Restoration of Irena and the Unfinished Reformation of Ireland

In Book V, the knight errant's episodic adventures emerge as a figure for short-lived and distracted justice, whose limitations are revealed when Britomart retraces Artegall's steps. The re-performance of the scene on Pollente's bridge makes clear that the conclusion of the original episode in Canto 2 was in fact inconclusive, and that its poetic resolution was an unacknowledged paradox: 'Sir Artegall undid the evill fashion, /

And wicked customes of that Bridge refourmed. / Which done, unto his former journey he retourned' (5.2.28). As the female knight's participation demonstrates, the restoration of justice requires no end to the maintenance of justice. There is no moving on from reform, not if it is responsible for the establishment of legal historical continuity and present order. As the question of Artegall's own maturation as a magistrate seems to approach resolution, with the apparent success of his quest in the final episode, judicial constancy, or the division of true justice through perpetual reformation, takes the form of a return to study. After the princess Irena is rescued and restored to rule, Artegall takes to his desk instead of his horse:

> During which time, that he did there remaine,
> His studie was true Justice how to deale,
> And day and night employ'd his busie paine
> How to reforme that ragged common-weale . . .

$$(5.12.26)$$

The perpetual departure of the knight errant, 'pricking' on yet another 'plaine', is finally superseded by the image of continual magisterial presence and the continual monitoring and improvement of the judge's knowledge and performance of his office through re-education. The image of the studious judge recalls the opening scenes of instruction, in which the magistrate's character was identified as the precondition for justice in the Iron Age. It is also the same idealised image of the studious judge that we saw in the Introduction, in George Puttenham's anecdote of Nicholas Bacon, in which the Lord Keeper is spied in the solitary occupation of reading a rhetorical manual, revealing his virtuous character through the devotion of his leisure time to a form of self-improvement that contributes to his public life. Spenser's judge studying 'How to reforme that ragged common-weale' is also the one perfecting his skill in the artificial reason of the common law that harmonises historical law with the contemporary nation and that is reflected in Britomart's reformation of Radigone. Since the nature of the people is subject to historical change, the education that enables the law's equitable adjustment to the common good must also be an unending pursuit. Re-presented in Canto 12 as an ongoing project, the magistrate's education enables the regular monitoring of his relationship to and execution of his office in the context of this historical flux.

The enterprise of reformation through re-education is cut short, however, when Artegall is called back to Gloriana's court and his travels are reignited. The knight is compelled to give up the comprehensive reformation of Irena's domain in a stanza that is frequently taken as a specific and piercing denunciation of Elizabeth's recall of Arthur Grey, Lord Deputy of Ireland and Spenser's erstwhile patron.[69]

> But ere he could reforme it thoroughly,
> He through occasion called was away,
> To Faerie Court, that of necessity
> His course of Justice he was forst to stay,
> And *Talus* to revoke from the right way,
> In which he was that Realme for to redresse.
> But envies cloud still dimmeth vertues ray.
> So having freed *Irena* from distresse,
> He tooke his leave of her, there left in heavinesse.
>
> (5.12.27)

'The Faerie Queene promises to save Irena from the tyranny which threatens the latter's rule (and, of course, her own as well),' writes Hadfield, 'but she is actually seen to be threatening that stability in her premature recall of the means of implementing justice.'[70] Tobias Gregory points out, however, that 'Spenser does not attribute Artegall's recall to the command of Gloriana but offers only non-explanations: "through occasion", "of necessitie". Our sense is only that "occasion" has more to do with Faery Court than with Grantorto.'[71] Thus Artegall's recall not only evokes Arthur Grey's in 1582, 'but also suggests the general ills of revolving-door government' that resulted from Tudor policy in sixteenth-century Ireland.[72] Having 'freed Irena from distresse', we're told that Artegall's unwilling departure produces her new plight of 'heavinesse'.

On his return to court, the knight is confronted with the figures of Detraction, Envy and the Blatant Beast, who transform the role of character criticism within the poem. The ending of Book V pivots between two images of the magistrate, as a perpetual student of virtue and equitable reform and as the perpetual subject of slanderous attack; it distinguishes between one form of character criticism that is an instrument for the analysis and reformation of law and justice and another form that is legally and politically de-formative. This contrast provides a final refraction of the historical moment in which Spenser wrote. Brady describes the way magisterial character, or rather reputation, determined the financial support and success of sixteenth-century reform programmes in Ireland. At the English Court

> the quality of each governor and his policy tended to be assessed not by any objective standard of competence, but by the current political standing of the faction or interest group to which the governor himself belonged. Thus personalised, reform policies became subject to a barrage of criticism and abuse, sometimes acute but more often of an irrelevant and quite slanderous nature,

and each policy, whatever its independent merits, rested in constant danger of random discontinuity and sudden death.[73]

The link between reform and reputation is explicitly made in *A View*, when Eudoxus worries that 'the thorough prosecuting of that sharpe course which [Irenaeus has] set downe for the bringing under of those rebells of Ulster and Connaught, and preparing a way for their perpetuall reformation' will 'haply, by any such sinister suggestions of crueltie and too much blood-shed ... be overthrowne, and all the coste and labour therein imployed bee utterly lost and cast away' (*A View* 105–6). Spenser's efforts to use his writings to repair Arthur Grey's reputation for 'crueltie and too much blood-shed' have long been acknowledged, but the elements from the Lord Deputy's career that have been detected in the treatise and the poem are held in common with a number of other Tudor governors. They are all present, for example, in Henry Sidney's 'memoir' of his earlier three terms as Lord Deputy of Ireland. Sidney's text reads like a real-life romance, in which he is on the constant move from one Irish crisis to another, distracted from his primary intentions no less frequently than Artegall.[74] He is repeatedly called away before he feels his reforms can take shape and effect. There is even a great rescue in Cork, 'where at that time lay a full noble and virtuous lady, the wife of Sir Warham St Leger, whom the citizens were sometimes in consultation and consideration to deliver to James FitzMaurice, which he earnestly, and with great threats required.'[75] Like Irena, the lady is rescued in the nick of time.[76] Despite Sidney's lengthy, expensive, and dangerous service to the queen, he was, like Grey, subject to recall and to character-wounding criticism at the English royal court.[77] Indeed, the denigration of his reputation is easily interpreted as a pretext for denying reimbursement. Sidney, Grey, and others were menaced by the same forces as those personified by Detraction, Envy and the Blatant Beast that attack Artegall on his way back to Gloriana's court.

Spenser's representation of legal reform introduces a number of topics that will be developed further in the chapters that follow. In Part I, legal education and the sixteenth-century transformation of legal equity will come into greater focus through studies of the 1594–5 Christmas revels at Gray's Inn and John Donne's 'Satyre V'. In Part II, itinerant justice and character criticism will be recovered as effective instruments of legal reform within Shakespeare's plays, *Measure for Measure* and *The Winter's Tale*. And constancy, too, will resurface as an important virtue for understanding female characterisation in Shakespeare's late romance.

Notes

1. C. S. Lewis, *The Allegory of Love: A Study in Medieval Tradition* (New York: Oxford University Press, 1958), p. 349.
2. Edmund Spenser, *A View of the State of Ireland*, ed. Andrew Hadfield and Willy Maley (Oxford: Blackwell, 1997), p. 105. I use the more common title for this treatise, *A View of the Present State of Ireland*. Hereafter this edition will be cited parenthetically.
3. Ciaran Brady, 'Spenser's Irish Crisis: Humanism and Experience in the 1590s', *Past and Present* 111 (1986), pp. 41, 18.
4. Judith H. Anderson, '"Nor Man It Is": The Knight of Justice in Book V of Spenser's *Faerie Queene*', *Publications of the Modern Language Association* 85.1 (1970), p. 65. See also Anderson's 'Spenser's *Faerie Queene*, Book V: Poetry, Politics and Justice', in Michael Hattaway (ed.), *A Companion to English Renaissance Literature and Culture* (Malden, MA: Blackwell, 2000), pp. 195–205.
5. Andrew Hadfield, 'Introduction', in Edmund Spenser, *The Faerie Queene: Book Six and the Mutabilie Cantos*, ed. Andrew Hadfield and Abraham Stoll (Indianapolis: Hackett, 2007), p. vii.
6. Andrew Zurcher, *Spenser's Legal Language: Law and Poetry in Early Modern England* (Cambridge: D. S. Brewer, 2007), p. 125.
7. Aristotle, *The Nicomachean Ethics*, trans. David Ross, J. L. Ackrill and J. O. Urmson (Oxford: Oxford University Press, 1998), p. 121.
8. Thomas Floyd, *The Picture of a Perfit Common Wealth* (London: 1600), pp. 174–5.
9. On persona allegory in *The Faerie Queene*, see Elizabeth Fowler, 'The Failure of Moral Philosophy in the Work of Edmund Spenser', *Representations* 51 (1995), pp. 47–76.
10. Edmund Spenser, *The Faerie Queene*, ed. A. C. Hamilton, revised 2nd edn (London: Routledge, 2013), 5.12.27. All further quotations to *The Faerie Queene* are to this edition and cited parenthetically by book, canto and stanza numbers.
11. Canto 4 is the end of the first section of Book V that, according to Michael O'Connell, allegorises 'the scope of the common law' ('*The Faerie Queene*, Book V', in A. C. Hamilton (ed.), *The Spenser Encyclopedia* (Toronto: University of Toronto Press, 1997), p. 281).
12. T. E. Hartley (ed.), *Proceedings in the Parliaments of Elizabeth*, vol. 1 (Wilmington, DE: M. Glazier, 1981), p. 191.
13. Thomas Wilson, *The Rule of Reason, Conteinyng the Arte of Logike* (London, 1563), p. 14^v–15^r.
14. Edmund Spenser, 'A letter of the Authors expounding his *whole intention in the course of this worke: which* for that it giveth great light to the Reader, for the better understanding is hereunto annexed', in *The Faerie Queene*, ed. A. C. Hamilton, revised 2nd edn (London: Routledge, 2013), p. 713.
15. Andrew Hadfield, *Edmund Spenser's Irish Experience: Wilde Fruit and Salvage Soyl* (Oxford: Clarendon Press, 1997), pp. 148–9.
16. On the role of punishment and pedagogy in Book V, see Jeff Dolven, *Scenes of Instruction in Renaissance Romance* (Chicago: University of Chicago

Press, 2007), pp. 207–37, and 'Spenser's Sense of Poetic Justice', *Raritan* 21.1 (2001), pp. 127–40. On Astraea's educational role imagined through the context of early modern wardship, see Judith Owens, 'Warding off Injustice in Book Five of *The Faerie Queene*', in Donald Beecher, Travis DeCook, Andrew Wallace and Grant Williams (eds), *Taking Exception to the Law: Materializing Injustice in Early Modern English Literature* (Toronto: University of Toronto Press, 2015), pp. 204–24.

17. Desiderius Erasmus, *The Education of a Christian Prince*, trans. and ed. Lisa Jardine (Cambridge: Cambridge University Press, 1997), p. 80.

18. Michael Dalton, *The Country Justice, Conteyning the Practise of the Justices of the Peace out of Their Sessions, Gathered for the Better Helpe of Such Justices of Peace as Have Not Beene Much Conversant in the Studie of the Lawes of This Realme* (London, 1618), p. 7. See also Virginia Lee Strain, 'Preventive Justice and *Measure for Measure*', in Kevin Curran (ed.), *Shakespeare and Judgment* (Edinburgh: Edinburgh University Press, 2017), pp. 21–44.

19. Hadfield, *Edmund Spenser's Irish Experience*, p. 157.

20. Hadfield, *Edmund Spenser's Irish Experience*, p. 160.

21. Erasmus, *The Education of a Christian Prince*, pp. 86–7. Erasmus goes on to offer another example of a law, 'established in days gone by', according to which 'property washed ashore from a shipwreck should be held by the prefect of the sea . . . so that they could prevent it being seized by the wrong people', which resembles the episode of the two brothers in Canto 4 of Book V of *The Faerie Queene*. In the dismemberment of the offenders, Bradin Cormack reads an allusion to 'a mode of historical poetry alternative to [Spenser's] own allegory – namely, the mirror literature exemplified by William Baldwin's *Mirror for Magistrates* (1559) and, in Ireland, by John Derricke's 1581 work, *The Image of Ireland*' (Cormack, *A Power to Do Justice: Jurisdiction, English Literature, and the Rise of Common Law, 1509–1625* (Chicago: University of Chicago Press, 2007), p. 170).

22. Erasmus, *The Education of a Christian Prince*, p. 86.

23. Cormack, *A Power to Do Justice*, p. 165.

24. Katherine Eggert, *Showing Like A Queen: Female Authority and Literary Experiment in Spenser, Shakespeare, and Milton* (Philadelphia: University of Philadelphia Press, 2000), p. 38.

25 Cormack, *A Power to Do Justice*, p. 172.

26. Cormack, *A Power to Do Justice*, p. 176.

27. 'division, n. 4', *OED Online* (Oxford University Press, September 2016).

28. Stanzas 242 and 244 of Fulke Greville, 'A Treatise of Monarchy', in *The Remains of Sir Fulk Grevill, Lord Brooke: Being Poems of Monarchy and Religion* (London, 1670), p. 65.

29. Edward Walshe, 'Edward Walshe's "Conjectures" Concerning the State of Ireland [1552]', D. B. Quinn (ed.), *Irish Historical Studies* 5 (1946–7), p. 317.

30. Ciaran Brady, 'Court, Castle, and Country: The Framework of Government in Tudor Ireland', in Ciaran Brady and Raymond Gillespie (eds), *Natives and Newcomers: Essays on The Making of Irish Colonial Society, 1534–1641* (Dublin: Irish Academic Press, 1986), pp. 47–8.

31. Aristotle, *Nicomachean Ethics*, p. 133.

32. Mark Fortier, *The Culture of Equity in Early Modern England* (London: Routledge, 2005), p. 66.

33. Alan Cromartie, '*Epieikeia* and Conscience', in Lorna Hutson (ed.), *The Oxford Handbook of English Law and Literature, 1500–1700* (Oxford: Oxford University Press, 2017), pp. 325, 326.

34. Cromartie, '*Epieikeia* and Conscience', p. 328.

35. Christopher Saint German, *Here after followeth a Dialoge in Englisshe, bytwyxte a Doctour of Dyvynitie and a Student in the Lawes of Englande* (1531), sig. D2^r.

36. Cromartie, '*Epieikeia* and Conscience', p. 334.

37. Zurcher, *Spenser's Legal Language*, p. 125.

38. Cromartie, '*Epieikeia* and Conscience', p. 334.

39. Lorna Hutson, 'Not the King's Two Bodies: Reading the "Body Politic" in Shakespeare's *Henry IV*, Parts 1 and 2', in Victoria Kahn and Lorna Hutson (eds), *Rhetoric and Law in Early Modern Europe* (New Haven: Yale University Press, 2001), p. 168; Lorna Hutson, 'Imagining Justice: Kantorowicz and Shakespeare', *Representations* 106.1 (2009), p. 132.

40. Hutson, 'Not the King's Two Bodies', p. 175.

41. In *The Culture of Equity*, Mark Fortier identifies five definitions of equity within the critical tradition of Book V, finding fault with the explanatory powers of each: 'equity as the mitigation of the rigours of the law' (p. 116); as the restraint of leniency (p. 117); as an imperfect force for justice in a fallen world (p. 119); as an amorphous idea that can be appropriated to defend power (p. 120); and as an amorphous, unresolved idea that contributes to the shabbiness of the Book (p. 121). 'What must lie at the basis of any reading of *The Faerie Queene*', writes Fortier, 'is an awareness of the complex strains of equity informing the poem' and potentially generating contradictions (p. 120). He admits that 'the complexities of Spenser's allegory make it difficult to sustain the simple association of Artegall with justice and Britomart with equity', which his own reading proposes (p. 117). Andrew Zurcher identifies Artegall with the equity of Chancery and his groom, Talus, with the mechanistic rigour of the common law (*Spenser's Legal Language*, pp. 138–9).

42. John Davies, *Le Primer Report des Cases & Matters en Ley Resolves & Adjudges en les Courts del Roy en Ireland* (Dublin, 1615), p. 5^r.

43. Edward Coke, *The Selected Writings of Sir Edward Coke*, ed. Steve Sheppard, vol. 2 (Indianapolis: Liberty Fund, 2003), p. 701. Coke is often portrayed as the champion of an unchanging, immemorial common law, but this famous quotation on artificial reason charts two kinds of progress: the refinement of the individual judge's abilities through study and experience, and the refinement of the law itself through the collective work of generations of legal authorities. For a more extended discussion of artificial reason, see Chapter 5 on *The Winter's Tale* below.

44. Glenn Burgess, *The Politics of the Ancient Constitution: An Introduction to English Political Thought, 1603–1642* (University Park: Pennsylvania State University Press, 1993), pp. 71–2.

45. Zurcher, *Spenser's Legal Language*, pp. 138–9.

46. Fowler, 'The Failure of Moral Philosophy in the Work of Edmund Spenser', p. 65.

47. John D. Staines, 'Pity and the Authority of Feminine Passions in Books V and VI of *The Faerie Queene*', *Spenser Studies: A Renaissance Poetry Annual* 25 (2010), pp. 129–61.

48. Kathy Eden, *Poetic and Legal Fiction in the Aristotelian Tradition* (Princeton: Princeton University Press, 1986), p. 61.

49. Eugene Garver, *Aristotle's Rhetoric: An Art of Character* (Chicago: University of Chicago Press, 1994), pp. 116, 112.

50. Aristotle, *Rhetoric*, in *The Rhetoric and the Poetics of Aristotle*, intro. and trans. Edward P. J. Corbett (New York: Modern Library, 1984), pp. 113, 92.

51. Davies, *Le Primer Report des Cases*, p. 4ᵛ.

52. Thomas Floyd, *The Picture of a Perfit Common Wealth* (London, 1600), pp. 174–5.

53. Thomas Elyot, *The Book Named the Governor*, ed. S. E. Lehmberg (London: Everyman's Library, 1962), pp. 206–7.

54. Amelia A. Zurcher, *Seventeenth-Century English Romance: Allegory, Ethics, and Politics* (New York: Palgrave Macmillan, 2007), p. 69.

55. Derek Dunne, *Shakespeare, Revenge Tragedy and Early Modern Law: Vindictive Justice* (Basingstoke: Palgrave Macmillan, 2016), pp. 17–19.

56. William Westerman, *Two Sermons of Assise: The One Intituled; A Prohibition of Revenge: The Other, A Sword of Maintenance* (London, 1600), pp. 1, 3–4.

57. Joseph Hall, *Characters of Vertues and Vices: In Two Bookes* (London, 1608), p. 62.

58. Brian C. Lockey argues that, in his pursuit of Radigund, Artegall 'seems to misunderstand his role as the more limited one of taking revenge for the personal affront made to fellow knights' ('"Equitie to measure": The Perils of Imperial Imitation in Edmund Spenser's *The Faerie Queene*', *Journal for Early Modern Cultural Studies* 10.1 (2010), p. 56).

59. Lockey, '"Equitie to measure"', p. 56.

60. Staines, 'Pity and the Authority of Feminine Passions', pp. 134–5.

61. Jessica Wolfe, *Humanism, Machinery, and Renaissance Literature* (Cambridge: Cambridge University Press, 2004), pp. 204, 209, 210.

62. Hadfield, *Edmund Spenser's Irish Experience*, p. 168.

63. Andrew Majeske, *Equity in Renaissance Literature* (London: Routledge, 2006), p. 94. While the discourse on the complications of gender in this section of the poem is especially rich on the topic of male and female rule, it has little to say about the ramifications of Britomart's decision to *return* or *restore* Radigone to male rule.

64. Lockey, '"Equitie to measure"', pp. 57, 58–9.

65. Zurcher, *Spenser's Legal Language*, p. 139.

66. Thomas Smith, *De Republica Anglorum*, ed. Mary Dewar (Cambridge: Cambridge University Press, 1982), pp. 62–3. As Elizabeth Fowler points out, '[i]t was a commonplace of political thought that the form of government should be matched with the nature of the people' ('The Failure of Moral Philosophy', p. 53).

67. Cormack, *A Power to Do Justice*, p. 175.

68. For an account of the historical evolution of 'convenience' from a techni-

cal to a more general legal sense, see Cormack, *A Power to Do Justice*, pp. 174–5.

69. 'The allegory is a clear defence of Lord Grey's deputyship in Ireland, as has long been recognized', writes Hadfield, in *Edmund Spenser's Irish Experience*, pp. 154–5.

70. Hadfield, *Edmund Spenser's Irish Experience*, p. 154.

71. Tobias Gregory, 'Shadowing Intervention: On the Politics of *The Faerie Queene* Book 5 Canto 12', *English Literary History* 67. 2 (2000), p. 382.

72. Gregory, 'Shadowing Intervention', p. 383.

73. Brady, 'Court, Castle, and Country', p. 43.

74. See, for example, Henry Sidney, *A Viceroy's Vindication? Sir Henry Sidney's Memoir of Service in Ireland, 1556–1578*, ed. Ciaran Brady (Cork: Cork University Press, 2002), pp. 45, 47, 52, 53, 70–1.

75. Sidney, *Memoir*, p. 64. See also Wallace T. MacCaffrey, 'Sidney, Sir Henry (1529–1586)', *Oxford Dictionary of National Biography* (Oxford University Press, 2004; online edn, January 2008).

76. Gregory, 'Shadowing Intervention', pp. 378–9.

77. Sidney, *Memoir*, p. 57.

Part I

Perfection

Chapter 2

Snaring Statutes and the General Pardon in the *Gesta Grayorum*

The four Inns of Court evolved in the fourteenth century into the educational institutions and societies of the English legal profession.[1] These communities provided easy access to the central legal courts, the royal court and the entertainments of London and its suburbs. In addition to, or instead of, the formal training that they could receive in the law, gentlemen's sons used their time at the Inns to cultivate the knowledge, skills and manners necessary for movement within elite sociopolitical spheres. By the turn of the seventeenth century, Inns members resided, studied, dined, conducted business, nurtured literary tastes and talents, and organised grand revels together, collectively forming one of the richest 'socioliterary environments' in the period.[2] Studies have traditionally assessed the literary output of the Inns in terms of their members' relationships to the royal court or the monarchy. Arthur Marotti's study of this coterie culture in the 1590s emphasises the competition among members who vied for the limited opportunities for advancement that emanated outward from Elizabeth's court.[3] Such aspirations resulted in literary works and performances, like the Gray's Inn Christmas revels that are the focus of this chapter, that 'reinforced the connections between the Inns and the royal court, the participants demonstrating their interest in and knowledge of their culture's central political institution', and that 'highlight[ed] the intentions of Gray's Inn revelers as aspiring courtiers who looked to the monarch and to her officers for preferment'.[4] While Marotti considers the literary effects of anxieties related to the dearth of opportunities for individual gallants, Paul Raffield considers instead the controversial extension of the royal prerogative in the same period and reads the same revels as an oppositional response from the English legal profession. Through the establishment of their own fictional commonwealths at Christmas, '[t]he legal profession sought a new Utopia in which the sovereignty of common law was acknowledged by subject and ruler'. Each Inn was transformed into 'an independent state, whose practices reflected the artificial reason and unchanging perfection of common law', whose 'ancient provenance [was] prior to and independent of the royal prerogative'. These mythological realms emphasised 'the practice of "ancient" English custom at the Inns' that countered 'the abuse of executive power by unaccountable instruments of government'.[5]

Marotti's account of the Inns writers' subject positions and Raffield's ideological reading, I argue, do not adequately reflect the more characteristic diversity of the Gray's Inn Christmas revels of 1594–5, which are preserved in an anonymous text from 1688. Presumably narrated by one of the participants, the *Gesta Grayorum* recounts the elaborate festivities that lasted from December to February, and that involved a mock coronation, an abridged parliament, a trial, a play performance, processions through London, orations, masques, dances, and other devices. Such an undertaking was only possible because Inns members could wield multiple skill sets and identities related to various legal and public offices. The writers, performers and audience members of the revels included common law students and authorities as well as parliamentarians and other statesmen, men of diverse ages whose participation within the legal-political hierarchy was varied and extensive. Before they could establish and represent a uniform, communal, ideological identity, the revels were, first and foremost, a testament to Inns members' professional and political elasticity. Elasticity and inventiveness were essential magisterial virtues in a system in which most agents were unsupervised for most of the time, and in which, therefore, critique was persistently expressed through the self-reflexive terms of legal reform. The potential for arbitrary rule was inscribed in all office-holding, not only or even primarily in the monarchy, so that the parody of legal-political misconduct must first reflect back upon the revellers themselves, the fictional lawmakers and political leaders, and raise questions of self-governance. How perfect are the fictional laws and customs that they create, and how well are they executed? We are invited to ask and answer such questions through the evaluation of the performance recorded in the *Gesta Grayorum*, in which references are made to the 'promise', 'reputation', and 'honour' of the performers that rested on the increased, satisfied or thwarted 'expectations' of their distinguished audience members. A pattern of 'credit' won, lost, and regained functions as an overarching plot that incorporates error into the performance and highlights the revellers' improvisational flair for correcting it.

Michelle O'Callaghan argues that '[t]he revels are utopian both in their projection of an artificial city-state and generically, in that, like More's *Utopia*, they belong to a humanist tradition of *lusus*, of learned

play.' As learned play, the revels sought 'to open spaces for improvisation and creative manoeuvre within established discourses and ceremonial forms' that would permit 'dissonant voices' to be heard.[6] I want to
push back on the idea that such spaces had to be introduced into the
law, through play or any other external mechanism. Instead, I argue that
structurally open spaces provided the invitation to learned play, and that
it was the mastery, reform and regulation of the law's open spaces
that ultimately provided the pedagogic rationale of the Inns revels.
Literary and theatrical exercises enabled the Inns member to present
himself in the role of governing and reforming agent, concerned with the
perfection and execution of the law and with the regulation of self and
other. The Gray's Inn revellers would constantly negotiate the fine line
between impressive display and ignominious conduct in a form of sport
that continually highlighted the actual stakes of governing. Done right,
the festivities would showcase a mastery of legal-political forms and
discourse that the revellers were able to wield for their sport – a grand,
collaborative expression of *sprezzatura*. Done wrong, the festivities
would insult officials and the Queen's court, cause disorder at the Inns
and in affiliated London communities, and damage the Inn's reputation
in a particularly memorable fashion. This chapter supports these claims
by taking a fine-grain approach to several features of the Gray's Inn
Christmas revels, including the parliament, the trial, the performance
of *The Comedy of Errors*, and Francis Bacon's orations on the art of
government.

   It is perfectly understandable if modern readers of the *Gesta Grayorum*
have overlooked the general pardon statute as an especially improbable
part of the revellers' fictional government. But the statute – which at
various times included the forgiveness of offences ranging from the vio-
lations of regulatory statutes, to heresy, to homicide and treason – was
indeed ratified in nearly every Elizabethan parliament. It provided one
of the most significant institutional responses to pervasive anxieties over
the condition and application of the statute laws. The pardon's rhetoric,
legal writings and literature from the period all represent the English
subject as unjustly 'snared' by statute. These fears resonate especially in
several of Shakespeare's comedies and John Donne's *Satyres* that I also
discuss below. Through the tactical parliamentary extension of royal
mercy, the Elizabethan general pardon was intended to mitigate the
dangers that the law itself posed to the English people. At the same time,
the pardon's contents also provided direction for the local execution of
law and social policy. During the revels, these two faces of the pardon
come into focus. At Gray's Inn hall, the form of the general pardon
explodes with excesses that invert and subvert its regulatory utility,

exposing an internal clash between the universal extension of royal mercy and the simultaneous extension of the law and the state into every aspect of the subject's life. The relationship between lawmaker and legal instrument dramatises a structural threshold within the system where formal flexibility equally enabled and jeopardised the law's integrity and functionality.

If the mock parliament ultimately supports Raffield's reading that the revels are imbued with anxiety and reactions to a threateningly expansive royal prerogative, they are also imbued with a sensitivity to lawmakers' own role as facilitators or inhibitors of that expansion. The revellers take sharp aim at themselves and their own profession through their general pardon and in the subsequent mock trial or 'law sports'. The subsequent orations on government, attributed to Francis Bacon, strategically redirect the course of the entertainments away from the comical errors of lawmakers and legal and political officers, and raise the more general question about good governance by outlining a plan of systemic reform for the fictional state. The Christmas revels thus approach the problem of legal reform repeatedly and from several angles and, in the process, they shape misrule into a mode of serious analysis. As Natalie Zemon Davis writes, 'Misrule can have its own rigour and can also decipher king and state.'[7] The revels' distortion and perfection of the law's forms and instruments ultimately point to the officer's or statesman's character as the enabling or limiting condition of an effective justice system. The performance of disorder enabled the display of the skills in self-regulation and self-governance demanded by a justice system that relied on the largely independent workings of officers. The entertainments for the fictional Prince of Purpoole presented Innsmen not as Utopian ministers, but as England's future legal authorities, statesmen and courtiers, through representations of the crucial governing processes of identifying and reforming legal, political and personal errors.

Snaring Statutes

In the Introduction to this book I examined a number of quotations from parliamentary speeches that argued for law reform rather than lawmaking. Here, I want to return to the same kind of source in order to put more pressure on the types of laws that were thought to need reform. By the end of the sixteenth century, the expansion of statute law had become a major concern for legal-political authorities, who feared its impact on the average English subject and on the legal professional charged with interpreting or applying the law. A thorough knowledge of the system was impeded by the sheer volume of legislation. Numerous Elizabethan parliamentary speeches and legal reform tracts, several of which are quoted in the Introduction, also addressed the danger posed by laws that were no longer appropriate or just either in terms of the infraction they targeted or the punishment they prescribed, laws that were largely forgotten through disuse, and laws, old or new, that were too convoluted to be understood, obeyed, or imposed. These 'snaring' statutes constituted a significant failure of the law to protect the English subject's life, property and rights. Many of Francis Bacon's parliamentary speeches and legal reform writings shed light on the reality of these 'swarving [snaring] penalties that lye upon many subjects'.[8] In a House of Commons speech from 1601, he argued 'for the repeal of divers statutes, and of divers superfluous branches of statutes . . . The more laws we make the more snares we lay to trap ourselves'. And again, in 1607, he complained that 'this continual heaping up of laws without digesting them maketh but a chaos and confusion, and turneth the laws many times to become but snares for the people.'[9]

While statute law in general threatened to turn the average subject into an unintentional offender, the penal laws in particular left the subject especially vulnerable to inequitable penalties. It was a topic that would inspire a powerful rhetorical response from Bacon throughout his legal-political career. In cautioning judges against 'hard constructions and strained inferences' in legal interpretations, he warned that 'there is no worse torture then the torture of lawes; specially in case of Lawes penall':

> [Judges] ought to have care that that which was meant for terrour, be not turned into rigour; and that they bring not upon the people that shower whereof the Scripture speaketh; *Pluet super eos laqueos* : For penall lawes pressed, are a showre of snares upon the people.[10]

And later, in 'A Proposition to His Majesty . . . Touching the Compiling and Amendment of the Laws of England', Bacon vividly imagines the potential of dormant statutes to transform into mechanisms of oppression during 'bad times', or under pressure from some kind of social, political or economic crisis: 'there are a number of ensnaring penal laws, which lie upon the subject; and if in bad times they should be awaked and put in execution, would grind them to powder.'[11] Nor was Bacon alone in his concern with the state of these laws. His professional and socio-political rival, Edward Coke, similarly worried that 'certaine of our penall statutes . . . time hath antiquated as unprofitable, and remaine but as snares to intangle the subjects withall.'[12] Barbara Shapiro and Julian Martin both report that '[s]peeches which deplored the confusion produced by the tangle of penal laws' were made throughout the 1590s and 1601 parliaments.[13]

Both popular and coterie literary works from the period mobilise snaring statutes and the widespread anxieties over the dangerous imperfections of the law. Shakespeare adopts the snaring statute as a plot device in no fewer than four comedies. He repeatedly introduces unknown as well as unjust laws that infuse his materials with a tragic potential. While he does not reproduce the contents of the historic laws, he does represent the way they could suddenly come into existence for a community and the way they had to be accommodated as part of a new social reality. Through these plot devices, positive law is aligned with the unpredictable and with reversals of fortune. In *The Merchant of Venice*, Portia stuns the courtroom not only by winning Antonio's case but by producing a second, life-threatening law that targets Shylock instead of the merchant. Through this so-called alien statute, Shylock's life is placed at the Duke's mercy for the attempted murder of a Venetian citizen; the moneylender is stripped of his resources and religion. If at first ensnarement is presented as the potential of private contracts, it resurfaces at the end of the play as a social threat through its association with public justice. The legal treatment of Shylock problematises the end of the play, disrupting the spirit of inclusion and forgiveness typically attributed to the resolution of comedy. The other Shakespeare examples, however, begin with a snaring statute that is essential to the plot. Most obviously, the conflict of *Measure for Measure* grows out of the Duke's decision to 'awake' an 'antiquated' penal law that punishes fornicators with death: one of the 'strict statutes and most biting laws . . . Which for this fourteen years we have let slip'.[14] The play raises explicit questions about the ethical and efficacious use of 'terrour' versus 'rigour' in the application of the law. The plots of *A Midsummer Night's Dream* and *The Comedy of Errors* are likewise propelled toward two kinds of beheadings simultaneously, execution and marriage, because of a snaring statute. In all four of the plays mentioned, Shakespeare's focus turns from the statute itself to its execution, to the need for regulation within legal practice or for discretion in those who invoke or administer the law.

In *A Midsummer Night's Dream*, the main plot is launched when Egeus 'beg[s] the ancient privilege of Athens' that enables him to 'dispose' of his daughter Hermia to the man of his choice or else send her to death, 'according to our law / Immediately provided in that case' (1.1.41–5). '[A]ncient' may be read to signify a law of long, established and therefore just use. But it seems more likely that its antiquity signals that it is out of use and has been forgotten by most. Alternatively or additionally, Egeus takes a law that was 'meant for terrour' and threatens to apply it with 'rigour' in an attempt to legally surprise and entrap his own daughter. If at first the Athenian law seems too harsh, the source of injustice is quickly relocated within the father's strict interpretation. Egeus himself is faulty in his own understanding or presentation of the law. Duke Theseus reveals that the father has ignored, forgotten or was never familiar with a certain celibacy provision. As Theseus explains, if Hermia refuses to marry Demetrius, she must 'die the death', or 'abjure / For ever the society of men' (1.1.65–6). Theseus' contribution transforms Egeus's tragic statute into a tragicomic one that embodies the potential for reversals of fortune through three alternatives: Demetrius, death, or life without death (as the result of the nun's spiritual devotions and as the result of a life without orgasms). Through the piecemeal, dialogic recovery of the details of the 'ancient privilege of Athens', Shakespeare's text releases the uncertainties of legal process that resulted from the half-known, half-understood contents of statute law. By aligning positive law with the unpredictable forces of accident and fortune in *A Midsummer Night's Dream*, this reading challenges the critical tradition that cites the law as one of the primary means through which Athens is established as the rational, rule-driven, well-ordered social world in contrast to the magical disorder of the forest. The distinction between city and forest diminishes substantially, as does the authority of all things 'ancient'.

In *The Comedy of Errors*, Shakespeare encloses the Roman new comedy plot that derives from Plautus's *Menaechmi* within a frame narrative in which Egeon of Syracuse arrives in Ephesus only to be arrested and condemned to death under a newly enforced law. Aggressions between the two states have reignited because of the Duke of Syracuse's decision to enforce an old decree against Ephesian merchants, some of whom have already been executed. We're never told directly why the Duke of Syracuse has suddenly decided to rigorously impose this old law, but his action pits the interests of the state treasury against the interests of commerce. In the Duke of Ephesus's opening speech we learn that Syracuse recently 'sealed his rigorous statutes' with the 'bloods' of Ephesian merchants, 'our well-dealing countrymen' who 'want[ed] gilders to redeem their lives', suggesting that Syracuse is primarily interested in the large financial penalty. By awaking and enforcing the antiquated law that dates from a period of open hostilities (of 'mortal and intestine jars' (1.1.11)) between the two states, Syracuse prompts a mirror response from Ephesus. 'It hath in solemn synods been decreed' on both sides to stop all trade, and anyone discovered in the other's territory is to be put to death, 'Unless a thousand marks be levied / To quit the penalty and ransom him' (1.1.21–2). '[B]ad times' in international relations have brought down 'a showre of snares upon the people' in both states. The frame narrative establishes the unusually tight timeline for a Shakespearean plot: the conflicts and confusions introduced by the presence of two pairs of identical twins in Ephesus must be resolved before the end of day, when Egeon will be executed unless his lost sons are discovered and can pay the statute's fine.

The first lines of the play are Egeon's, and he uses them not to protest the extremity of the law in which he's become entangled or the injustice of his sentence, but to acquiesce in his own death: 'Proceed . . . to procure my fall', he tells the Duke, 'And by the doom of death end woes and all' (1.1.1–2). He goes on to provide, not a defence speech, but a long narrative of his life of misfortune, in which he has apparently been forever separated from his wife and twin sons. His death sentence is merely the last accident among many. To Egeon, it is the end of his personal tragedy and he welcomes such a death as the inevitable conclusion to the pattern of his life. The early modern audience member, however, might recognise Egeon's tale instead as an unfinished romance that is subject, generically, to reversals and restorations as much as to tragic or near-tragic misfortunes. From this perspective, the snaring statute and the death sentence become an episode and not an inevitable conclusion to the tale. Positive law is again aligned with the forces of chance, with the uncertain and unpredictable in human life. Built into the antiquated law itself is the potential for one more reversal of fortune that the depressed Egeon wishes to escape: the Syracusan in Ephesus may avoid the death penalty if he or his friends can produce a thousand marks. The laws used to produce mixed-mode effects within these comedies have been overlooked as artificial plot devices, devoid of probability or mimesis. Redescribed as snaring statutes, however, they come to represent the phenomenon of the startling materialisation of laws and legal penalties that was historically experienced as an imminent possibility within early modern English life.

In John Donne's *Satyres*, composed and privately circulated in the 1590s and influenced by the culture of Lincoln's Inn, the subject's personal vulnerability to snaring statutes is contrasted with the legal, political, and social pre-eminence signalled by statute-writing. In satires II and IV in particular, statutes emerge as an expression and statute-writing as a practice of the authentic or fully realised legal, political, and social power to which the satiric speaker and his coterie audience of young gallants aspire. Statutes are not mentioned until the last two lines of 'Satyre II', but they conclude a catalogue that progresses from the least to the most effective forms of writing. Poets, playwrights and those 'who write to lords, rewards to get . . . like boys singing at doors for meat', are all outdone by barristers like 'Coscus', who are becoming rich by buying up the property of 'heirs melting with gluttony'.[15] Although Coscus will soon 'compass all the land / From Scots to Wight, from Mount to Dover strand' through legal 'parchments . . . large as his fields' (ll. 77–8, 87), the last two lines of the poem present statute-writing as a superior form of legal-political power and as a weapon that could, if deployed correctly, forestall the progress and success of Coscus and his kind. The poem concludes with the courtier-speaker's complaint that 'my words none draws / Within the vast reach of th'huge statute laws' (ll. 111–12), equating the splenetic and detailed description of human faults and legal abuses found in satire with the matter of legislation. Indeed, both satirist and legislator enjoyed a privileged liberty of speech and a 'vast reach' when it came to the criticism of social, economic and political conditions, as well as the morality of personal conduct. The 'reformation of manners' was a preoccupation of each.[16] That the Satirist's words are *not* statutes, however, reveals their poetic impotence; he is, in the end, one more of those poets who are 'poore, disarmed . . . not worth hate' (l. 10). His complaint becomes one last refraction of his personal, social, economic and finally political marginalisation. Nevertheless, the speaker succeeds here in breaking down the binary opposition between gallant and lawyer that structures the rest of the poem, and with it the seemingly inevitable degeneration of the former's lifestyle and influence that correlated with the gains in the latter's. Studies on the Inns of Court emphasise social and class tensions between gentlemen's sons (who treated the Inns as finishing schools that would prepare them for life and service at the royal court) and serious law students (who were pursuing advancement through a profession).[17] Donne's speaker disrupts this dynamic by introducing a third term in the form of a hypothetical legislator, a position to which the gallant may still aspire. Although his words are not law, the speaker suggests that his credentials as a satirist qualify or prepare him for the job of legal reformer in the future. Donne increases the stakes of his satire by projecting the tensions among Inns students onto an arena of national legal-political consequence.

'Satyre IV' likewise ends with an expression of the speaker's desire to see his verse adopted as a form of law ('some wise men shall, / I hope, esteem my writs canonical' (ll. 243–4)), here registering his frustrated ambition and worsening circumstances despite (or as a direct result of) his progress from the Inns of Court milieu to the royal court. The comparison drawn between satire and statute in 'Satyre II' blows up into outright competition in 'Satyre IV', in which the speaker paints himself and his fellow wits as unfairly targeted by the law or as hapless subjects stumbling unintentionally into trouble. We hear of 'Glare', who went

To'a mass in jest, catched, was fain to disburse
The hundred marks which is the statute's curse,
Before he scapt . . .

                                                            (ll. 8–11)

A joke is taken too seriously, and statutory regulations impinge upon the gallants' penchant for (harmless?) jests and caprice. Glare's case is then compared to that of the speaker, whose 'destiny' finds him guilty of the 'sin' of going to the royal court and punishes him as if he were 'As vain, as witless, and as false as they / Which dwell at Court, for going once that way' (ll. 11–16). The law (man-made statute and destiny's) is unable to discriminate between irony and earnestness in the way that a witty satirist can. The satirist's judgement is more refined or subtle, and therefore potentially more equitable – or corrupt – than the law. The speaker implicitly defends Glare and himself based on their unserious intentions and the fact that their offences are isolated incidents, in light of which their respective punishments are excessive and unjust: Glare must dole out a hundred marks and the speaker, we discover, is shadowed at court by an insufferable parasite.

The speaker's so-called punishment quickly leads to more inadvertent offences, however, the longer he remains at court. Socially trapped by the parasite, he is forced to listen as his companion's conversation implicates him through gossip that rapidly progresses from 'trivial household trash' (l. 98) to outright slander. That slander, in turn, degenerates into a form of treason, exaggerating (one hopes) the ease with which an individual (merely visiting court, merely listening to the wrong person – and unwillingly) may accidentally come within the law's grasp, imagined here as a form of monstrous ingestion:

He [the parasite] like a priviledged spy whom nothing can
Discredit, libels now 'gainst each great man . . .
I, more amazed than Circe's pris'ners when
They felt themselves turn beasts, felt myself then
Becoming Traitor, and methought I saw
One of our giant Statutes ope his jaw
To sucke me in; for hearing him . . .

                                                            (ll. 119–33)

Given the new nature of his offence (treason) and the developing nature of his offensiveness (the speaker becomes characterised over the poem as a repeat offender), the speaker's punishment (the continued presence of this unshakable parasite) no longer seems unjust.

In order to uphold the fiction of the unfair law, the speaker reimagines his punishment as a fine so exorbitant that it would compensate not merely for a bad act or a bad character, but for original sin or the inherited weaknesses of human nature itself: 'since I am in, / I must pay mine and my forefathers' sin / To the last farthing' (ll. 137–9). But, we are told, 'th'hour / Of mercy' arrives, through which this incalculable fine is reduced to a comparatively negligible payoff (ll. 140–1). The parasite requests and receives money before finally moving on to prowl for more benefactors:

> ... He tries to bring
> Me to pay a fine to scape his torturing,
> And says, 'Sir, can you spare me' – I said, 'Willingly!' –
> 'Nay, sir, can you spare me a crown?' Thankfully I
> Gave it as ransom ...
> But he is gone, thanks to his needy want,
> And the prerogative of my crown ...
>
> (ll. 141–50)

The speaker can only escape the court parasite – and thus the jaws of 'giant Statutes' – through a 'ransom'. At the turn of the seventeenth century, a 'ransom' was an 'action or means of freeing oneself from a penalty; a sum of money paid to obtain pardon for an offense or imposed as a penalty ... a fine'. A 'ransom' was also, as it is today, a 'sum or price paid or demanded for the release of a prisoner or hostage'.[18] In Donne's 'Satyre IV', both senses of the word resonate to implicate the parasite's tenacious attachment to the speaker and the law's aggressive hold (through giant statute jaws) on the English subject. In Shakespeare's *Comedy of Errors*, Egeon needs one thousand marks 'To quit the penalty and ransom him' after breaking a law unintentionally and finding himself in short order arrested and sentenced to death. In both works, the word 'ransom' is suggestive of the alternatives of physical or financial duress awaiting the subject who has been snared by the law.

In 'Satyre IV', the speaker's 'ransom' is paid by 'the prerogative of my crown', playing on the name of the English coin, of course, but also comparing his release from the human leech's conversation to the Queen's mercy when it was extended to forgive statutory infractions or to rescue the subject from the law's unjust operations and fines. Despite the attention given to snaring statutes in the period, no system-wide overhaul – no amendment, abridgement, or explanation – of the laws was successfully achieved. Instead, the historical menace from such statutes was most successfully, or at least most publicly, offset by the Elizabethan general pardon that is carefully reproduced and parodied in the Gray's Inn Christmas revels. The revellers' mock pardon demonstrates the political potential of legislation that is only hinted at in

Donne's satires. Over-identifying with the snared subject, Donne's satiric speaker is unable to make the leap from versifying victim to legal reformer. With much more gusto, the revellers indulge downright in this legislative fantasy through their own version of the general pardon statute. Through their lists of the law's pardonable offences and the statute's exceptions, they display an acute knowledge of the structural and rhetorical dimensions of statute law, writing and interpretation that, in turn, would testify to their credentials as legal authorities and officeholders.

The General Pardon

The Gray's Inn revels are best known to literary historians for what was almost certainly the first performance of *The Comedy of Errors*.[19] According to the report in the *Gesta Grayorum*, the large crowd that had assembled for one of the evenings of entertainments would not make room for the professional actors onstage. The play could not be performed until the numbers were thinned by the departure of the contingent from the Inner Temple and not until dancing had exhausted some of the revellers' energies. The evening thus earned the nickname 'The Night of Errors'. The 'pattern of error and reform' that Andrew Zurcher identifies as a structural principle behind the revels, however, began before this famous debacle.[20] Though the Prince of Purpoole's rule was ostentatiously established with more than 140 followers in attendance on the very first 'grand night', the plans to hold a mock parliament, too, fell by the wayside as 'some special Officers' were missing 'without whose Presence it could not be performed'.[21] This excuse may in fact be pretence and may signal dramatic elision or compression that is intentionally or unavoidably clothed as disorganisation and error. Had the full parliament gone forward, a more ample representation of domestic issues might have complemented the later business on foreign affairs that is recorded in detail.[22] In any case, the organisers proceeded by enacting the two bills that every parliament ratified: 'The one was, a Subsidy of His Highness's Port and Sports. The other was [. . .] his gracious, general and free Pardon' (14). In actual parliaments these bills were drafted under the supervision of the Queen's learned counsel based on previous examples. The subsidy, the government's major source of tax revenue, was the primary reason for calling a parliament. After it was formally accepted at the end of a session, the general pardon was declared and operated most immediately as a kind of royal thanks. The pardon's tribute to the 'love' and 'affection' of the Queen's subjects was a decorous nod to their financial generosity.[23] This is the last we hear of the subsidy in the *Gesta Grayorum*, but the general pardon, including its formulaic preamble and conventional content, was diligently replicated by the revellers. Its lengthy provisions were read out by the Prince's Sollicitor and enclosed the subsequent entertainments within a parody of the statute's regulatory intention and language. In mocking this statute, the revellers (some of whom, including Francis Bacon, would have already served as MPs) targeted a measure that publicly compensated for the law's imperfections through the politically strategic extension of the Queen's clemency.

The preamble of the Elizabethan general pardon referred to the sovereign's 'm[er]cifull Disposicyon' toward her subjects, but this image of the queen was predicated on an unsettling universal characterisation of her subjects as not only 'lovinge' (loyal, dutiful), but also as legal offenders in need of a reprieve from legal punishment. The character of these offenders was mitigated, however, not only by their love for their sovereign but by the misfortune that triggered their entanglement with the law. They are presented as accidental transgressors, devoid of criminal intention, stumbling into trouble: 'Subject[es] have many and sundry waies by the Lawes and Statut[es] of this Realme, fallen into the daunger of div[er]se greate Penaltyes and Forfeytures ... wherewith her sayde Subject[es] stande now burthened and chardged.' The Queen's mercy, it is expected, will inspire not the reform of conscience so much as a more attentive consideration of the law's extensive stipulations: she is 'most graciouslie inclyned ... to dischardge some [part] of those greate Paynes Forfeytures and Penalties ... trustinge [her subjects] wilbe thereby the rather moved & induced from henceforthe more carefully to observe her Highnes Lawes and Statut[es], and to contynewe in theire loyall and due Obedience to her Ma[jesty].'[24] Speakers of the House traditionally thanked the Queen in return for her pardon during their closing speeches, assuring her that her subjects were 'most graciouslie incited (by this your Majestie's clemencie) to a more dilligent and carefull observacion of your Highnes' lawes then heretofore wee have accustomed'.[25] '[C]arefully to observe' the law is of course synonymous with obeying the law, but the phrasing of the statute preamble and the speaker's remarks implicate a legal system that required the subject's active ('dilligent and carefull') endeavour to keep clear of the law's punitive grasp. The general pardon's itemisation of forgivable offences thus exposed the system's failings more than the offender's. It was a tacit admission of and response to the law's continuing imperfections despite parliament's best legislative efforts.

While the rhetoric of the real statute's preamble expressed the hope

that the Queen's clemency would inspire the better attention and obedience to her laws, the enlarged list of pardonable offences and the tone of
linguistic and conceptual playfulness in the fictional Prince of Purpoole's
statute seemingly establish a culture of permissiveness. The list is organised by alliteration and rhyme more frequently than by legal categories
of offence. Thus alongside real and serious crimes are placed near- and
non-crimes: 'Frauds' are grouped with 'Fictions, Fractions, Fashions'
and 'Fancies', 'Conspiracies' with 'Concavities'. 'Suppositions' are
forgiven alongside 'Suppositaries' (22), recalling a very old joke from
George Gascoigne's *Supposes*, played at the Gray's Inn Candlemas
revels some thirty years earlier. The revellers' expanded list of pardonable offences parodies the rhetorical flare-ups evident in the speeches of
statesmen as well-respected as Nicholas Bacon who, in his first closing
speech to parliament, enlarged the role of magistrates in the following
terms: 'yee are to forsee the avoyding of all manner of frayes, forces,
ryottes and rowtes, and the discoveringe and revealinge in tyme of all
manner of conspiracyes, confederacyes and conventicles' (*PPE* 1: 49).
The revellers' statute mocks the lawyer's and the parliamentarian's well-
known tendency toward verbosity and synonymity in the vain pursuit
of comprehensiveness. In his study of 'the way in which the commons
debated the language of lawmaking itself', Seth Lerer tracks the critique of this kind of excessive amplification that was believed to breach
parliamentary decorum and threaten the effectiveness of legislation.[26]
Philip J. Finkelpearl writes that the revellers' statute was 'a gigantic, self-
defeating "amplificatio", a parody of the attempt of legal documents to
embrace all categories and possibilities'.[27]

Beyond its legal-political mimicry, however, the revellers' pardon
actually succeeds in generating an alarming form of legal comprehensiveness. The wordplay exposes the Prince's law as an instrument that
enables the state's ensnarement of the subject through the statute's
aggressive sprawl into the subject's life. The superficial linguistic associations among major, minor and imagined infractions (of decorum and
of law) position minor offences on a continuum with major felonies. As
with Donne's speaker in 'Satyre IV', who is caught up in the treasonous
slander of a court parasite, it is a slippery slope from the one kind of
offence to the other, greased by excesses of legal-political rhetoric. At the
same time that the mock pardon's rhetorical excesses apparently stress a
radical policy of permissiveness, that is, they also implicate the law's far-
reaching application to 'All, and all manner of' (22) subjects and their
activities. No aspect of public or personal behaviour – including one's
'Washings, Clippings and Shavings' (22) – was conceivably or actually
beyond the reach of legal regulation. The mock pardon overwrites the

law only to strategically illuminate the law's comprehensive jurisdiction over human conduct. Through their comical list of pardonable offences, then, the revellers bring the two faces of the general pardon – the lessening of the subject's statutory penalties and the increasing legal circumscription of the subject's life – into open conflict. The catalogue of pardonable offences is followed by satiric exceptions to the pardon that bring into focus the complexities of lawmaking in general and the distinct contradictions of a statute of general pardon in particular.

At the same time that the Queen's mercy ostensibly ransomed her subjects *en masse* through the general pardon, the same statute also defined the *un*pardonable through a list of exceptions, primarily serious felonies including rape, murder, counterfeiting and treason, through which the statute punished the deliberate transgressions of subjects and officers.[28] These offences were to receive the full prosecution and rigour of the law. Items were added to and dropped from the otherwise conventional list to reflect pressing social concerns identified by the crown or in parliament.[29] David Dean explains that the issues raised in failed bills initiated by MPs could resurface in this statute that was drawn up by government officials. He argues that this strategy allowed the government to inhibit debate on sensitive topics while still responding to MPs' (and by extension, the public's) concerns.[30] So-called sensitive topics often brought into question the jurisdiction or powers of parliament, for example, or the Queen's prerogative. The general pardon exceptions could also help reduce the amount of legislation that threatened to transform the legal system inadvertently or subversively and to increase the problem of snaring statutes. Most of the time, the trick to governing was to make existing law work for the commonwealth. Government policy and administration was largely a matter of selecting and emphasising particular statutes to construct a pattern for society to be disseminated via tiers of officials, judges and courts in localities throughout the country. The general pardon was one part of this gene therapy for the commonwealth that regulated the expression or suppression of aspects of the law to achieve the greatest possible social harmony.[31] Through the statute's lists of pardonable and unpardonable offences, judges and local officeholders were guided as to which infractions to forgive and which to prosecute; they were guided as to the execution of which laws within an overgrown system of statutes best reflected the central government's social policy. Despite its practical utility for magistrates, however, the general pardon introduced complications into the conventional statute form.

In his (serious, technical) *Reading of the Statute of Uses*, presented to the same community of Gray's Inn in 1600, Francis Bacon divided statutes into three parts:

> The statute consisteth . . . upon a preamble, the body of the law, and certain savings and provisoes. The preamble setteth forth the inconvenience; the body of the law giveth the remedy; and the savings and provisoes take away the inconveniences of the remedy.[32]

Legal reform in the shape of 'provisoes' was built into the lawmaking process to avert foreseeable disruptions attendant upon innovations:

> For new laws are like the apothecaries' drugs; though they remedy the disease, yet they trouble the body: and therefore they use to correct them with spices. So it is not possible to find a remedy for any mischief in the commonwealth, but it will beget some new mischief; and therefore they spice their laws with provisos to correct and qualify them.[33]

Bacon's elaboration of 'provisoes' is a function of his interest in legal reform and in method – legal, rhetorical, philosophical and scientific. In the Preface to *The Maximes of the Common Lawes* (contemporaneous with the revels) he would explain that his novel method for the 'cleere and perspicuous exposition' of legal rules entailed 'opening them with distinctions'.[34] A few years later in *The Advancement of Learning* he would criticise the traditional form of rhetorical induction, 'For to conclude upon an enumeration of particulars without instance contradictory is no conclusion, but a conjecture'.[35] As Daniel Coquillette writes, the 'final step of "negation" or "definition by exception" [that] was to become an important part of Bacon's philosophical method' was already present in his early legal works.[36] The statute form itself provided a model or an exemplar for Bacon's method. The statutes are larded with hypothetical clauses beginning with 'Provided that . . .' and 'Provided alwaies . . .' As with rhetorical amplification, however, these 'strings of qualifiers that distinguish the rhetoric of act and statute' incited anxieties about their potential to backfire. Lerer quotes a parliamentarian from 1571 who argues that provisos 'have bene oft the overthrow of that which was truly ment, wherein the cunninge adversary . . . subtilly insert more . . . to the hindrance of the whole.'[37] This potential for legislative confusion (accidental or deliberate) was augmented by the form of the general pardon. Conditional provisos can be found there as well, but they are overshadowed by the list of 'exceptions' through which synonym the statutory proviso functions expressly as negative definition and the statute explicitly doubles back upon itself. And, as with their take on parliamentary amplification, the Gray's Inn revellers' version of the proviso implicates what was 'truly ment' or enabled by the device on a political level.

The doubly corrective method of normal statute form – of remedy and proviso – was compounded in the general pardon. To begin with, the statute was an assertion of the sovereign's prerogative power, of her authority to designate the exception through merciful forgiveness, and the pardon was one enormous exception, ostensibly a universal liberation from the rule of law. Thus the statute's provisos constituted exceptions to an exception. This form is extra silly in the fictional pardon when the parodic exceptions are further qualified:

> *Except*, All such Persons as shall shoot in any Hand-Gun, Demy-Hag, or Hag-Butt, either Half-shot, or Bullet, at any Fowl, Bird, or Beast; either at any Deer, Red or Fallow, or any other thing or things, except it be a Butt set, laid, or raised in some convenient place, fit for the same purpose. (18)

Taken in a general sense, the provision amounts to a caution not to shoot unless you have a good shot. Taken in a technical or legal sense, the provision warns subjects that they are prohibited from hunting, unless of course it is legal. In the 1594–5 revels, the imaginary statute multiplies exceptions until the form collapses upon itself, inverting and reversing its apparent intention and exposing the problematics of the crown's improvisation on a legal form that cannot accommodate a general pardon without contradiction. The multiplying legal reversals participate in the same principle of comic complication that propels Shakespeare's cross-dressing heroines who are men playing women playing men. While Shakespeare's cross-dressings exploit and illuminate an initial reversal necessitated by the customary regulation of theatre, the revellers exploit and illuminate the reversals that structure the statute. They expose and mock its inversion of a basic legal intuition about the nature of rules through the very idea of a general pardon from the law. They expose and mock, too, the inversion of a legal and commonplace intuition about the nature of clemency effected by a general pardon that was, in reality, heavily restrictive.

Though the real provisos were supposed to qualify and refine new or amended legislation, the fictive exceptions ultimately undo the apparent magnanimity of Purpoole's statute. This is vividly evident in the last exception. While 'all, and all manner of Treasons, Contempts, [and] Offences' are initially forgiven, the Prince's Sollicitor concludes with a bald negation in which, 'All, and all manner of Offences, Pains, Penalties, Mulets, Fines, Amerciaments and Punishments, Corporal and Pecuniary, whatsoever' are finally excluded from the pardon (19). Once the reader gets past this blatant about-face in the statute's intention and function, a more technical sleight of hand becomes evident. Whereas the beginning of the statute emphasises the pardon of offences, the final exception emphasises the enforcement of punishments, particularly (though not exclusively) the pecuniary kind. If the real statute is presented as a generous release from the 'burthen' of 'greate Penaltyes and Forfeytures' inflicted for inadvertent infractions, here in the Prince of Purpoole's general pardon the penalties for those infractions still apply and with them – and this is the joke – the crown's income from the judicial process. K. J. Kesselring explains that Henry VIII's first general pardon proclamation was intended to allay public resentment inspired by the perception that Henry VII and his chief financial officers had exploited legal processes for profit at the expense of his subjects. Future pardons 'provided appropriate expressions of gratitude for taxation because the king willingly forfeited the financial proceeds of his justice' and 'freed people of the fines that potentially attended a host of business transactions and from the costs of often protracted litigation on these matters'.[38] *The Comedy of Errors*, Donne's *Satyres*, and the revellers' mock general pardon all gesture toward the financially exploitative dimension of statute law.

While all the Tudor monarchs except Mary enhanced their public image as merciful and magnanimous rulers through the general pardon, Elizabeth turned what had been an occasional measure into a regular feature of parliament and thus into a constituent component of the spectacle of her merciful persona.[39] In legal writings and in his first masque-like device, Francis Bacon links the Queen's virtue as a sovereign to the protection she provided subjects from excessive penalties and snaring statutes. In *Of Tribute; or, Giving That Which Is Due* (1592), the speaker, in 'Praise of His Sovereign', addresses, among other matters of state, the Queen's moderate methods of raising revenue: 'There shall you find . . . no extremities taken of forfeitures and penal laws, a means used by some kings for the gathering of great treasures . . . Yea further, there have been . . . a course taken by her own direction for the repeal of all heavy and snaring laws.'[40] In his Dedication to the Queen in *The Maximes of the Common Lawes*, he lauds the 'purpose for these many yeares, infused into your Maiesties breast, to enter into a generall amendment of the states of your lawes', including the removal of 'the swarving penalties that lye upon many subiects'. This project is 'greater than wee can imagine . . . of highest merit and beneficence towards the subject . . . because the imperfections and dangers of the lawes are covered under the clemency and excellent temper of your Majesties government.'[41] In the absence of systematic statute reform, the Queen's mercy, embodied in the general pardon, provided a necessary supplement to the law. The general pardon was presented as, in David Dean's words, 'an act of grace, a gift from the royal prerogative' for the benefit of her subjects whose welfare was threatened by the post-lapsarian system of man's laws.[42]

The members of Gray's Inn also used the general pardon as a form of self-promotion. As Michelle O'Callaghan explains, 'through parody and improvisation' the revellers 'asserted their mastery' over the institutions they fictionalised as well as over their own Inns.[43] Their compressed parliament advertised their ability to fit themselves into the system and roles of central power in a blatantly literal way. As substitutes for legal-political substitutes, as representations of representatives, they broadcasted their finesse as officeholders in a culture 'predispos[ed] to delegate authority'.[44] As mock lawmakers, they showed their commitment to the system's continuity through the reiteration and propagation of law. By focusing on the general pardon in particular, however, they presented themselves not only as lawmakers, but as law reformers or regulators. To achieve such authority or status entailed the discovery of the potential for error and exploitation in the very device used to publicly compensate for the law's imperfections. The reconstruction of the general pardon parodies the rhetoric, complications and contradictions of an improvisation of power through which the traditional statute form was manipulated to accommodate political ends that could, in reality, exploit the subject. By doing so, they implicated their own role in governance at least as much as the queen's. The revellers' rhetorical excesses ultimately highlight the unavoidable creative dimension of legal-political administration that resulted from the contribution of individuals making, interpreting, reproducing, distorting and reforming law. If the revellers' role as the law's regulators was established through the mock parliament, it was critiqued and corrected after the next 'grand night', when they became the source of disorder.

Vile Confederates in a Culture of Errors

The general pardon crowned an evening that, we are told, 'increased the Expectation of those things that were to ensue; insomuch that the common Report amongst all Strangers was so great, and the Expectation of our Proceedings so extraordinary, that it urged us to take upon us a greater State than was at the first intended' (20). On the very next 'grand night' those increased expectations were dashed when overcrowding in Gray's Inn Hall disrupted the revellers' plans, causing the delegation from the Inner Temple to leave in a huff and delaying the performance of *The Comedy of Errors*. The trial that is subsequently mounted to investigate and punish the individuals responsible for the so-called 'Night of Errors', however, instead opens up the fictional royal court to extensive criticism. While the general pardon had illuminated the problematics of lawmaking, the mock trial brings the administration of the law under scrutiny. Both episodes, however, target the potential for mechanisms of legal correction themselves to morph into instruments of disorder and exploitation, arguing implicitly through negative examples for the law's perfection and for vigilance in legal-political office. The trial not only follows the 'Night of Errors' but the actual performance of Shakespeare's *Comedy of Errors*, and the Inns revellers allude back to the play in their reconstruction and analysis of a culture of legal error.

Compared to '*Plautus* his *Menechmus*' by the narrator of *Gesta Grayorum*, *The Comedy of Errors* constitutes Shakespeare's nearest imitation of Roman New Comedy's intrigue plot.[45] Unlike its New Comedy model, however, *The Comedy of Errors* lacks an intriguer or intriguers whose scheming ignites and sustains the action of the play. Instead, characters' probable but mistaken inferences contribute to the plot's comic complications. This adaptation is central to Lorna Hutson's reading of the play and the 'association between judicial process and dramatic mimesis or dramatic illusion' that she locates in late sixteenth-century drama. Using the 'processes of suspicious imagination and detection' derived from the forensic rhetorical tradition firmly embedded in Elizabethan legal and popular culture, she argues that Shakespeare's characters go about reconstructing the most probable – the most believably realistic or mimetic – versions of events, motives and characters. The intrigue plot, that is, 'provokes the work of detection which in turn constitutes character as its effect.' Without a scheming villain, however, Shakespeare's characters' forensic efforts to evaluate evidence and to reconstruct past events and personal motives create a form of 'paranoia': the 'conspiracies and plots imagined by the "victim" . . . can be understood as the turning inward of intrigue.'[46] Put another way, characters are both constituted and deceived by their own means of establishing facts, intentions and identities. The airing of accusations and evidence that concludes the play, then, brings into question the integrity and trustworthiness of speakers as narrators and the reliability of forensic enquiry as a mode of analysis. While Hutson's argument focuses on the representation of individuals through forensic rhetoric, here I would like to examine the way in which the fictional uses of legal processes in both *The Comedy of Errors* and in the revellers' mock trial expose a general culture of error. The figure of the individual intriguer – the basis of the New Comedy plot and the focus of criminal trials – is supplanted by the problem of collective conspiracy.

The absence of an arch villain does not prevent Shakespeare's characters from channelling the violent energies generated by the plot's confusions through the judicial and forensic processes intended to discover individual culpability. Antipholus of Ephesus directs the rage sparked by his confusion and mistreatment toward a minor character who is unequivocally an unsuccessful scam artist. Dr Pinch is introduced as a conjuror and at Adriana's request he attempts to exorcise the demons of her supposedly possessed husband. Pinch may not be *the* villain masterminding the plot, but he is the pathetic scoundrel within reach. Antipholus is excited enough to accuse him in the Duke's presence, even if most of the fault seems to lie in Pinch's face. Recounting his version of the street scene in which he and Dromio were captured and bound by family and friends, Antipholus explains:

> By th'way, we met my wife, her sister, and a rabble more
> Of vile confederates. Along with them
> They brought one Pinch, a hungry lean-faced villain;
> A mere anatomy, a mountebank,
> A threadbare juggler, and a fortune-teller,
> A needy, hollow-eyed, sharp-looking wretch,
> A living dead man. This pernicious slave,
> Forsooth, took on him as a conjuror,
> And gazing in mine eyes, feeling my pulse,
> And with no face, as 'twere, outfacing me,
> Cries out I was possessed. Then all together
> They fell upon me, bound me, bore me thence . . .
>
> (5.1.235–46)

The description of 'vile confederates' widens the connotations of 'conjure' to include not only supernatural invocation, deceptive illusion and (by extension, metaphorically) stagecraft, but also 'to conspire'. Many of the medieval and early modern examples offered in the *OED* refer to rebellions, insurrections and usurpations.[47] Thus the activity of conjuring not only has parallels with dramatic mimesis, in which absent things are made present, but also with political plotting.[48] Pinch's conjuring takes place in the context of the conspiracy to capture and cure the mad Antipholus and Dromio – perhaps the only conscious act of plotting in the play. Antipholus's description of the 'threadbare juggler' reveals Pinch to be manifestly, absurdly inadequate to play the part of the masterful intriguer or plotter. The unsuccessful supernatural conjuring and the ludicrous charge against his face exonerate Pinch at the same time that they put the greater communal guilt of his 'vile confederates' into relief, who 'all together . . . fell upon me, bound me, bore me thence'.

Pinch's extraordinary role as the accused here, in comparison with his marginal role in conjuring anything, is a scenario repeated in the revellers' prosecution of a 'Sorcerer or Conjurer' charged with the 'confused

Inconvenience' of 'The Night of Errors' described above. The legal processes for identifying individual fault are, in Shakespeare's play and in
the parodic revels, harnessed and inverted to expose a general culture
of erroneous practices. What comes to light in the mock trial in Gray's
Inn Hall is an overabundance of conjuring or plotting, of conjurors and
schemers whose incompetent execution of office threatens the honour of
the royal court and the legitimacy of Purpoole's legal system. By the end
of the trial, everyone *except the defendant* is charged with misconduct in
office. 'Under Colour of these Proceedings', the narrator explains,

> were laid open to the View, all the Causes of note that were committed by our
> chiefest States-men in the Government of our principality; and every Officer
> in any great Place, that had not performed his Duty in that Service, was taxed
> hereby, from the highest to the lowest, not sparing the Guard and Porters,
> that suffered so many disordered Persons to enter in at the Court-Gates. (23)

The prisoner's defence involved a counter-accusation against his prose-
cutors that further implicated the Prince's legal servants and law enforc-
ers. The 'very Fault', the prisoner's petition boldly claims, 'was in the
Negligence of the Prince's Council, Lords and Officers of his State, that
had the Rule of the Roast, and by whose Advice the Commonwealth
was so soundly mis-governed' (24). The officers' behaviour in open
court is then transformed into supporting evidence. The prisoner's petition for justice 'was a Disclosure of all the Knavery and Juggling [that]
the Attorney and Sollicitor' used in their case against the so-called sorcerer. It compared the artifice of the revels and the play performance
with legal conjuring or technical and rhetorical sleights of hand: the
'Night of Errors' fell short of 'all this Law-stuff' of the professionals
who set out to 'blind the Eyes of his Excellency, and all the honourable Court' (23–4). Through the counter-charges, the courtroom itself
becomes the scene of new theatrical and rhetorical crimes that displace
the charges laid against the original prisoner who was, according to his
own defence, 'a poor harmless Wretch' (24). In both the prosecution
and the defence, then, 'the Prince and states-men' were 'pinched on both
sides, by both the Parties' (24). The Prince, 'not a little offended at the
great Liberty that they had taken, in censuring so far of His Highnes's
Government', released the prisoner and condemned to the Tower (i.e.
the stocks) the Attorney, the Sollicitor, the Master of the Requests, and,
on the defence's side, 'those that were aequainted with the Draught of
the Petition' (24).

The trial allowed the role-players to display their facility for legal
'Knavery and Juggling' as well as their ability to identify and reform such
corruptions in themselves and others. It failed, however, in its objective

of restoring lost honour to the revels. Instead, its illumination of a wide-spread culture of legal error shifts the focus of the proceedings from the issue of the facts of a case to the general issue of the administration of law and governance. When the revellers were finally 'wearied with mocking thus at our own Follies' through their law sports, the Prince's Council was 'reformed' and replaced by 'some graver Conceipts' (24). These new wits, presumably, took centre-stage in the orations on the art of government that were prepared by Francis Bacon, a member of Gray's Inn since 1579. The implicit question of good government that had shadowed the entire progress of the mock royal court is finally directly addressed in a device that showcased the rhetorical and political talents of the Prince's new top advisors. In the speech delivered by the fifth counsellor, moreover, Bacon succinctly articulates a vision of legal and social reform that was informed not only by his legal training but by his experience as a member of parliament. While the Prince calls for the reform of his officeholders, Bacon's fifth orator argues that reform begins with the Prince himself, who must institute policies to 'redress all' ills in the commonwealth through the operations of state and legal reform.

'Virtue and a Gracious Government'

Bacon's contribution of orations to the revels dramatised a traditional subject for, and exercise in, political debate. As the lawyer and publisher John Rastell wrote some eighty years earlier in *Le livre des assises et pleas del' corone*, a text published multiple times throughout the sixteenth and seventeenth centuries, 'wherein the Common-weal standeth, and what thing it should be, there is, and hath been ever, as well among Philosophers, Orators, Poets, as other learned men great alteration, debate and argument'. In his own version of the debate, Rastell compares the respective merits of policies to increase riches, power, honour or good laws. He defines the 'Common-weal' or the common good as 'that thing that is of it self meerly [entirely] good'. Neither 'Riches, Power, nor Honour', however, 'be very perfect good things only of themselves: because ... they cannot be attained without causing of evil things to other persons'. '[G]ood and reasonable Ordinances and Laws', on the other hand, 'lead and direct men to use good manners and conditions ... and vertuously to live among their neighbours in continual peace and tranquility; in firm concord and agreement, in an unity of will and mind; and in sincere and pure love and charity.' Rastell thus concludes that 'because Laws of themselves be good, and so great good cometh by them: The common-weal by all reason must rather stand in augmenting and preferring of Laws.' This perspective naturally augments, too, the prestige of legal authorities, parliamentarians and magistrates: 'so they that exercise and busie themselves in making Laws, in ordering or writing of Laws, in learning of Laws, or teaching Laws; or in just and true executing of Laws, be those persons that greatly increase and multiply the Common-weal.'[49]

Bacon's Gray's Inn device similarly makes the strongest case for the law and for legal reform as the central focus of government, but his route to this conclusion departs from tradition. He leaves Rastell's logical derivation of the law's goodness behind. Instead, the law's supremacy is arrived at through a form of induction and a process of elimination. Two characteristic features of Bacon's later thinking about scientific method can be found here in embryo in this early rhetorical exercise.[50] The entire debate is framed as a response to the Prince's enquiry into the best direction for the state. Inviting his new Privy Counselors to speak, he explains

> we mean not to do as many Princes use, which conclude of their Ends out of their own Honours[51] and take Counsel only of the Means (abusing, for the most part, the Wisdom of their Counsellors) [to] set them the right way to the wrong place. But We, desirous to leave as little to Chance or Humour as may be, do now give you liberty and warrant to set before Us, to what Port, as it were, the Ship of Our Government should be bounden. (32)[52]

Deliberately setting himself apart from ethically and intellectually shallow rulers, the Prince announces a sincere intent to be informed and to generate new insight through the exercise. He is not, he says, asking for advice on 'any particular Action of Our State, but in general, of the Scope and End whereunto you think it most for our Honour and the Happiness of Our State that Our Government [should] be rightly bent and directed' (32). The speeches are arranged to represent a process of elimination as each orator criticises and displaces the last. As we saw earlier in reference to the statute form, elimination or exclusion was an important part of Bacon's method. In his *Reading on the Statute of Uses*, Bacon begins by 'considering, first, what [a use] is not; and then what it is; for it is the nature of all human science and knowledge to proceed most safely by negative and exclusion, to what is affirmative and inclusive.'[53] Here in the Christmas revels, the six speeches that follow the Prince's invitation defend '*the Exercise of War*', '*the Study of Philosophy*', '*Eternizement and Fame by Buildings and Foundations*', '*Absoluteness of State and Treasure*', '*Virtue and a gracious Government*', and finally '*Pastimes and Sports*'. The policies advocated by the first four speakers are subordinated to or completely discounted by what are presented as the distinctly virtuous priorities of the fifth, while all serious plans for the state are brushed aside in response to the sixth speaker's petition for dancing, which indeed follows the orations.

The fifth counsellor's speech on good government is a sustained plea for the amendment of royal servants and for the reform and intensification of the existing machinery of the law and the state: this is 'the making of golden times' and the 'only [fit] and worthy ends of your Grace's virtuous reign' (39). The Prince is to start by considering the condition of the country: 'assure your self of an inward Peace, that the Storms without do not disturb any of your Repairers of State within' (39). The counsellor then instructs the Prince to examine the politic operations of the statesmen and courtiers closest to him:

> Beginning with your Seat of State, take order that the Fault of your Greatness [great ones] do not rebound upon yourself; have care that your Intelligence, which is the Light of your State, do not go out or burn dim or obscure; advance Men of Virtue and not of Mercenary Minds; repress all Faction, be it either malign or violent. (39)

Once he has confirmed the integrity and prudence of those servants who present the most direct threat to sovereign and state, and examined the effectiveness of the intelligence system, the Prince is then to extend his gaze further, toward the law and order of the realm. Much of the advice of this oration overlaps with the parliamentary speeches examined in the Introduction, and it is arranged in the same order. The prince must first perfect the laws and then scrutinise the execution of justice:

> Then look into the State of your Laws and Justice of your Land; purge out multiplicity of Laws, clear the incertainty of them, repeal those that are snaring, and prize [press] the execution of those that are wholesome and necessary; define the Jurisdiction of your Courts, reprize [repress] all suits and Vexations, all causeless Delays and fraudulent Shifts and Devices, and reform all such Abuses of Right and Justice; assist the Ministers thereof, punish severely all Extortions and Exactions of Officers, all Corruptions in Trials and Sentences of Judgment. (39–40)

Whereas the third counsellor advises the creation of 'new Institutions of Orders, Ordinances and Societies' (36) that could result in 'Innovation and Alteration' and a 'very turbulent and unsettled' reign (37), and whereas the fourth counsellor had advised the Prince to 'conquer here at home . . . the great Reverence and Formalities given to your Laws and Customs, in derogation of your absolute Prerogatives' (38), the fifth counsellor argues instead for a comprehensive reform of the law that would then be 'press[ed]' into just execution. This policy alone will make 'a good and virtuous Prince' (39). As James Spedding explains, the fifth counsellor's speech consists of 'an enumeration of those very reforms in state and government which throughout his life [Bacon] was most anxious to see realized'.[54] The thoughts on legal reform that Bacon would begin to articulate in works and speeches from the 1590s he would expand on throughout the rest of his career.

In Rastell's argument, the 'good and reasonable Ordinances and Laws' that 'lead and direct men to use good manners and conditions' are compared to 'the bridle and spur [that] directeth and constraineth the Horse swiftly and well to perform his journey'. Laws put constraints on nature that enable man to live socially, 'in continual peace and tranquility ... which thing duely to perform is not so given to mankind immediately and only by nature, as it is given to all other creatures'.[55] In *Measure for Measure*, the Duke of Vienna's use of the same horse metaphor implicates the coercive or oppressive work of the law in controlling man's unruly nature, a sense that is downplayed in Rastell's depiction of social 'peace and tranquility': 'strict statutes and most biting laws' are 'The needful bits and curbs to headstrong jades' (1.3.19–20). In either example, however, the 'bridle and spur' suggest intermittent measures, responses taken once the horse has strayed; they are not permanent blinkers that act continually and preventatively. In addition to the direction and coercion provided by the law, 'continual peace and tranquility' also require the subject's ongoing cooperation which had to be self-motivated. Bacon, the parliamentarian, understood social harmony or order as a practice enabled by social, economic, and political conditions that produced such a subject. 'Yet when you have done all this', the fifth counsellor continues, after describing the extensive work of systemic legal reform, 'think not that the Bridle and Spur will make the Horse to go alone without Time and Custom' (40). Time and custom are the conditions for creating habitual behaviour; they are essential to effective self-discipline and the production of virtuous conduct.

In his essay 'Of custom and Education', Bacon explains that deeds are the result of the way men have been accustomed to acting; men's thoughts and speeches are only an imperfect guide to what they will actually do. Custom 'is the principal Magistrate of mans life' because it is an internalised one. It is, moreover, 'most perfect when it beginneth in young yeeres This wee call *Education*: which is nothing but an early custome'.[56] While the law may provide direction and correction, the subject still requires a self-regulating habit of mind that, the fifth counsellor from the Gray's Inn device explains, is encouraged by good education and the social and economic conditions and institutions traditionally supported by acts of parliament:

Trust not to your laws for correcting the times, but give all strength to good education ... Then when you have confirmed the noble and vital parts of your realm of state, proceed to take care of the blood and flesh and good habit of the body. Remedy all decays of population, make provision for the poor, remove all stops in traffic ... redress all. (40)

Bacon would repeatedly discuss schemes to improve the state's surveillance system through the efforts of legal-political officers (from informers to Assize judges), but here in the fifth oration he admits law and order's dependence on a willing subject, coaxed into royal and government support through policies that addressed broadly held, inclusive notions of the common good.[57] The fifth counsellor's analysis of the ills of the commonwealth comes to a screeching halt after the excited imperative, 'redress all': 'But whither do I run, exceeding the bounds of that perhaps I am now demanded?' The speaker recalls his place in the Presence and returns to a more restrained and epideictic mode before his argument for government action reignites the revellers' culture of error once again. The speaker, in other words, dramatises rhetorical self-restraint that mimics the kind of self-regulating subject, officer, and counsellor that the state requires.

Lawyers' Labour's Lost and Won

The third counsellor in the Gray's Inn orations advises the Prince's 'Eternizement and Fame by Buildings and Foundations'. Bacon raises and rejects this argument a second time in the later tract, 'An Offer to King James of A Digest to be Made of the Laws of England'. In so doing, he collapses the distinction made above between the socio-political contribution of legal reform and the education in virtuous action:

Surely the better works of perpetuity in Princes are those, that wash the inside of the cup; such as are foundations of colleges and lectures for learning and education of youth; likewise foundations and institutions of orders and fraternities, for nobleness, enterprise, and obedience, and the like. But yet these also are but like plantations of orchards and gardens, in plots and spots of ground here and there; they do not till over the whole kingdom, and make it fruitful, as doth the establishing of good laws and ordinances; which makes a whole nation to be as a well-ordered college or foundation.[58]

Or a well-ordered Inn of Court. Paul Raffield describes the Inns as 'self-governing legal communit[ies] [that] gave physical expression to a Utopian ideal: an autonomous state governed by the equitable principles of common law ideology'.[59] The analogy between college and kingdom was literalised and dramatised during their holiday revels, the grand productions in which a mock king and his royal court were established and all offices of state were played by law students and other Inn members. Through the revels and other exercises, generations of Englishmen were trained in the regulatory, reforming operations and instruments of governance. Members developed an internal magistrate that was externalised through their revels, exhibited to the legal-political elite. If the primary function of the state was social, political and legal repair work, epitomised by Bacon's directive to 'redress all', then the revellers' ability to overcome disorders in their entertainments illustrated their ability to be effective legal officers and statesmen. Their performance of critique and self-correction demonstrated the skills in perfecting the system and the independence and judgement required for the effective execution of office.

Performed before 'a most honourable Presence of Great and Noble Personages' including 'the Right Honourable the Lord Keeper', Francis Bacon's eloquent orations contributed to an evening that finally restored credit to the Gray's Inn revellers. As the narrator relates:

> The Performance of which Nights work being very carefully and orderly handled, did so delight and please the Nobles, and the other Auditory, that thereby *Grays-Inn* did not only recover their lost Credit, and quite take away all the Disgrace that the former Night of Errors had incurred; but got instead thereof, so great Honour and Applause, as either the good Reports of our honourable Friends that were present could yield, or we our selves desire. (42)

The narrator charts the reception of the revellers' devices – estimations of credit won and lost – throughout the *Gesta Grayorum*. We have already seen how the first grand night that presented the mock parliament 'increased the Expectation of those things that were to ensue', such that the revellers were encouraged 'to take upon us a greater State than was at the first intended' (20). This becomes a fault that is exposed through the mock trial. The prisoner is accused of, among other things, having 'caused the Stage to be built, and Scaffolds to be reared to the top of the House, to increase Expectation' (23). While Bacon's orations help restore and augment the honour of Gray's Inn after the 'mischanceful accident' of the Night of Errors that 'was a great Discouragement and Disparagement to our whole State' (22), it is the explanation offered before the concluding masque presented at Queen Elizabeth's court that suggests a calculated shift in the participants' approach to their entertainments: 'the things that were then performed before Her Majesty, were rather to discharge our own Promise, than to satisfie the Expectation of others' (57). Having regained their honour the revellers now play it safe by checking their theatrical and political ambitions and concentrating instead on the execution of duty:

In that regard, the Plot of those Sports were but small; the rather, that Tediousness might be avoided, and confused Disorder, a thing which might easily happen in a multitude of Actions; the Sports therefore consisted of a Mask, and some Speeches, that were as Introductions to it. (57)

The extended pattern of performance error and correction over the course of the Christmas revels culminates in this final expression of theatrical and political decorum. From the narrator's perspective, the perfect, uneventful execution of the masque functions as evidence of the reformation of the state of Purpoole.

Notes

1. J. H. Baker, *The Third University of England: the Inns of Court and the Common Law Tradition* (London: Selden Society, 1990).
2. On the conditions of the Inns' most remarkable literary periods, of which the end of the sixteenth century is certainly one, see Jessica Winston, *Lawyers at Play: Literature, Law, and Politics at the Early Modern Inns of Court, 1558–1581* (Oxford: Oxford University Press, 2016).
3. Arthur Marotti, *John Donne, Coterie Poet* (Madison: University of Wisconsin Press, 1986), pp. 25–43.
4. Marotti, *John Donne*, p. 32.
5. Paul Raffield, *Images and Cultures of Law in Early Modern England: Justice and Political Power, 1558–1660* (Cambridge: Cambridge University Press, 2004), pp. 111, 123, 105, 92, 120–1. For a complementary account that examines the political use of Inns revels at the beginning of Elizabeth's reign to debate matters including the Queen's marriage and the succession question, see Marie Axton, *The Queen's Two Bodies: Drama and the Elizabethan Succession* (London: Royal Historical Society, 1977).
6. Michelle O'Callaghan, *The English Wits: Literature and Sociability in Early Modern England* (Cambridge: Cambridge University Press, 2007), pp. 23–7.
7. Natalie Zemon Davis, 'The Reasons of Misrule: Youth Groups and Charivaris in Sixteenth-Century France', *Past and Present* 50 (1971), p. 41.
8. Francis Bacon, *The Elements of the Common Lawes of England* (London, 1630), sig. A4^r. Henceforth this work is cited as *Maximes*.
9. Francis Bacon, *The Letters and Life of Francis Bacon*, ed. James Spedding, vol. 3 (London, 1868), pp. 19, 336.
10. Francis Bacon, 'Of Judicature', in *The Essaies of Sr Francis Bacon Knight, the Kings Solliciter Generall* (London, 1612), pp. 213–14. Hereafter, this edition is cited as *Essays 1612*.
11. Francis Bacon, 'A Proposition to His Majesty by Sir Francis Bacon ... Touching the Compiling and Amendment of the Laws of England', in *The Works of Francis Bacon*, ed. James Spedding, Robert Leslie Ellis and Douglas Denon Heath, vol. 13 (London, 1872), p. 65.
12. Edward Coke, *The Selected Writings of Sir Edward Coke*, ed. Steve Sheppard, vol. 1 (Indianapolis: Liberty Fund, 2003), p. 97.

13. Julian Martin, *Francis Bacon, the State, and the Reform of Natural Philosophy* (Cambridge: Cambridge University Press, 1992), p. 107; Barbara Shapiro, 'Codification of the Laws in Seventeenth Century England', *Wisconsin Law Review* 2 (1974), p. 437.

14. William Shakespeare, *Measure for Measure*, in *The Norton Shakespeare*, ed. Stephen Greenblatt, Walter Cohen, Suzanne Gossett, Jean E. Howard, Katherine Eisaman Maus and Gordon McMullan, 3rd edn (New York: W. W. Norton, 2016), 2.2.94, 1.3.19–21. All future Shakespeare quotations are from this edition and hereafter cited parenthetically by act, scene and line numbers.

15. John Donne, 'Satyre II', in *The Complete Poems of John Donne*, ed. Robin Robbins (Harlow: Longman, 2008), ll. 21–2, 79. All further quotations from Donne's satires are from this edition and hereafter cited parenthetically by line number.

16. On the traditions of 'free' speech and criticism within the Inns of court and within parliament, see Marotti, *John Donne*, pp. 33–4.

17. See Marotti, *John Donne*, pp. 25–43, esp. p. 40; Wilfred Prest, *The Inns of Court under Elizabeth I and the Early Stuarts, 1590–1640* (London: Longman, 1972), pp. 40–6; and Ronald J. Corthell, '"Coscus onely breed my just offence": A Note on Donne's "Satire II" and the Inns of Court', *John Donne Journal* 6.1 (1987), pp. 25–31.

18. 'ransom, n.', *OED Online* (Oxford University Press, September 2016).

19. On *The Comedy of Errors* in connection to the revels or to the Inns of Court, see Janet Clare, *Shakespeare's Stage Traffic: Imitation, Borrowing and Competition in Renaissance Theatre* (Cambridge: Cambridge University Press, 2014), pp. 86–113; Bradin Cormack, 'Locating *The Comedy of Errors*: Revels Jurisdiction at the Inns of Court' (pp. 264–85) and Lorna Hutson 'The Evidential Plot: Shakespeare and Gascoigne at Gray's Inn' (pp. 245–63), in Jayne Archer, Elizabeth Goldring and Sarah Knight (eds), *The Intellectual and Cultural World of the Early Modern Inns of Court* (Manchester: Manchester University Press, 2013); Lorna Hutson, *The Invention of Suspicion: Law and Mimesis in Shakespeare and Renaissance Drama* (Oxford: Oxford University Press, 2007), especially chapter 4; Margaret Knapp and Michal Kobialka, 'Shakespeare and the Prince of Purpoole: The 1594 Production of *The Comedy of Errors* at Gray's Inn Hall', *Theatre History Studies* 4 (1984), pp. 71–81; Barbara Kreps, 'Playing the Law for Lawyers: Witnessing, Evidence and the Law of Contract in *The Comedy of Errors*', *Shakespeare Survey* 63 (2010), pp. 262–71; Douglas Lanier, '"Stigmatical in Making": The Material Character of *The Comedy of Errors*', *English Literary Renaissance* 23 (1993), pp. 81–112; Elizabeth Rivlin, 'Theatrical Literacy in *The Comedy of Errors* and the *Gesta Grayorum*', *Critical Survey* 14.1 (2002), pp. 64–78; and Andrew Zurcher, 'Consideration, Contract and the End of *The Comedy of Errors*', in Paul Raffield and Gary Watt (eds), *Shakespeare and the Law* (Oxford: Hart, 2008), pp. 19–37.

20. Zurcher, 'Consideration', p. 33.

21. *Gesta Grayorum: or, The History of the High and Mighty Prince, Henry Prince of Purpoole . . . Who Reigned and Died, A.D. 1594* (London, 1688), p. 14. This text is cited parenthetically hereafter.

22. Zurcher reads error during the revels as strategic and only as a pretence. No

parliament was ever *really* intended; the 'Night of Errors' was more or less planned. On theatrical confusion, see also William N. West, '"But this will be a mere confusion": Real and Represented Confusions on the Elizabethan Stage', *Theatre Journal* 60 (2008), pp. 217–33. On the script and the rhetoric of interruptions and Inns of Court revels, see Ann Hurley, 'Interruption: The Transformation of a Critical Feature of Ritual from Revel to Lyric in John Donne's Inns of Court Poetry of the 1590s', in Douglas F. Rutledge (ed.), *Ceremony and Text in the Renaissance* (Cranbury, NJ: Associated University Presses, 1996), pp. 103–21.

23. David Dean, *Law-Making and Society in Late Elizabethan England: The Parliament of England, 1584–1601* (Cambridge: Cambridge University Press, 1996), p. 55. See also K. J. Kesselring, *Mercy and Authority in the Tudor State* (Cambridge: Cambridge University Press, 2003), pp. 56–73. In *A Treatise Concerning Statutes, or Acts of Parliament: and The Exposition Thereof* (London, 1677), Christopher Hatton distinguishes between those statutes whose benefits 'seem to proceed from subjects only to the Prince, as those of . . . Subsidies, and some other of like nature', and those whose benefits 'seem to proceed from the Prince only, as Pardons and Priviledges, Confirmations of Customes, and such like' (pp. 3–4).

24. Alexander Luders et al. (eds), *Statutes of the Realm*, vol. 4 (London, 1810–28), p. 883. Hereafter this text is cited by *SR* followed by the volume and page number.

25. T. E. Hartley (ed.), *Proceedings in the Parliaments of Elizabeth*, vol. 2 (Wilmington, DE: M. Glazier, 1981–95), p. 27. Hereafter this text is cited parenthetically by *PPE* followed by the volume and page number.

26. Seth Lerer, 'An Art of the Emetic: Thomas Wilson and the Rhetoric of Parliament', *Studies in Philology* 98.2 (2001), p. 173. Francis Bacon was adamant about the self-defeating work of legal verbosity:

> The loquacity and prolixity used in the drawing up of laws I do not approve. For it does not at all secure its intention and purpose; but rather the reverse. For while it tries to enumerate and express every particular case in apposite and appropriate words, expecting greater certainty thereby; it does in fact raise a number of questions about words; so that, by reason of the noise and strife of words, the interpretation which proceeds according to the meaning of the law (which is juster and sounder kind of interpretation) is rendered more difficult.

(Quoted in Donald Veall, *The Popular Movement for Law Reform, 1640–1660* (Oxford: Clarendon Press, 1970), p. 64.)

27. Philip J. Finkelpearl, *John Marston of the Middle Temple: An Elizabethan Dramatist in His Social Setting* (Cambridge, MA: Harvard University Press, 1969), p. 42.

28. Dean, *Law-Making and Society*, pp. 34–5; See also the later Elizabethan acts of general pardon in *SR* 4.758–62, 834–9, 883–8, 952–7, 1010–14.

29. Kesselring, *Mercy and Authority*, pp. 62, 63.

30. Dean, *Law-Making and Society*, p. 61.

31. See Kesselring, *Mercy and Authority*, pp. 72–3.

32. Francis Bacon, *Reading on the Statute of Uses*, in *The Works of Francis Bacon*, ed. James Spedding, Robert Leslie Ellis and Douglas Denon

Heath, vol. 7 (London: 1879), p. 417. According to Daniel R. Coquillette, Bacon's *Reading on the Statute of Uses* 'was the closest thing to a modern theory of statutory interpretation until Jeremy Bentham's *A General View of a Complete Code of Laws, Pannomial Fragments, and The Promulgation of Laws*, two centuries later' (*Francis Bacon* (Stanford: Stanford University Press, 1992), p. 59). This particular passage, however, echoes Sir Thomas Egerton's earlier treatise, *A Discourse upon the Exposicion [and] Understandinge of Statutes*, ed. Samuel E. Thorne (San Marino: Huntington Library, 1942). See also Chapter 3 below.

33. Bacon, *Reading*, pp. 417–18.
34. *Maximes*, sig. B4^v.
35. Francis Bacon, *The Advancement of Learning*, in *Francis Bacon: A Critical Edition of the Major Works*, ed. Brian Vickers (Oxford: Oxford University Press, 1996), p. 221.
36. Coquillette, *Francis Bacon*, p. 41. On the relationship between Bacon's legal practice, statecraft and natural philosophy, see Coquillette, *Francis Bacon*, and Martin, *Francis Bacon*. For a contrasting interpretation, see the work of Markku Peltonen, who argues that the various projects that captured Bacon's attention cannot be synthesised, as recent studies have sought to do: 'Politics and Science: Francis Bacon and the True Greatness of States', *Historical Journal* 35.2 (1992), pp. 279–305.
37. Lerer, 'An Art of the Emetic', p. 173.
38. Kesselring, *Mercy and Authority*, pp. 60, 61.
39. Kesselring, *Mercy and Authority*, p. 67.
40. Francis Bacon, *Of Tribute; or, Giving That Which Is Due*, in *Francis Bacon: A Critical Edition of the Major Works*, ed. Brian Vickers (Oxford: Oxford University Press, 1996), p. 40.
41. *Maximes*, sig. A4^r.
42. Dean, *Law-Making and Society*, p. 56.
43. O'Callaghan, *The English Wits*, p. 24
44. Steve Hindle, *The State and Social Change in Early Modern England, c.1550–1640* (Basingstoke: Palgrave Macmillan, 2000), p. 5.
45. On the sources and analogues of *The Comedy of Errors*, see David Bevington, '*The Comedy of Errors* in the Context of the Late 1580s and Early 1590s', in Robert S. Miola (ed.), *The Comedy of Errors: Critical Essays* (New York: Garland, 1997), pp. 335–53; and Charles Whitworth, 'Introduction', in William Shakespeare, *The Comedy of Errors*, ed. Charles Whitworth (Oxford: Oxford University Press, 2002), pp. 17–42.
46. Hutson, *The Invention of Suspicion*, pp. 165, 157, 155.
47. 'conjure, v.', *OED Online* (Oxford University Press, September 2016).
48. See Stephen Greenblatt, *Hamlet in Purgatory* (Princeton: Princeton University Press, 2001), p. 3.
49. John Rastell, 'Prologus', in *Le livre des assises et pleas del' corone moves [et] dependants devant les justices sibien en lour circuits come aylours, en temps du roy Edward le Tiers* (London, 1679). The first edition of this text appeared under the Latin title, *Tabula libri assisaru[m] [et] pl[ac]itorum corone* (1514).
50. 'Early' is a relative term: Bacon was in his thirties when he wrote this device.

51. 'Humours' according to Vickers' edition of the device in *Francis Bacon: A Critical Edition of the Major Works* (see p. 52).
52. Bacon would repeat part of this sentiment in 'Of Empire', in *Essays 1612*: 'For it is the Solecism of power, to thinke to command the ende, and yet not to endure the meane' (p. 55).
53. Bacon, *Reading*, p. 398.
54. Francis Bacon, *The Works of Francis Bacon*, ed. James Spedding, Robert Leslie Ellis and Douglas Denon Heath, vol. 8 (London, 1862), p. 342.
55. Rastell, 'Prologus'.
56. Bacon, 'Of custom and Education', in *Essays 1612*, pp. 157–60.
57. Nicholas Bacon would comment in a speech from Elizabeth's second parliament, 'yt is infallible that a thinge don unconstrayned ys much better then when they be constrayned thereunto' (*PPE* 1: 111). Voluntary service is examined in the next chapter on John Donne's 'Satyre V'.
58. Francis Bacon, 'An Offer to King James of a Digest to be Made of the Laws of England', in *The Works of Francis Bacon*, ed. James Spedding, vol. 4 (London: 1826), p. 376.
59. Raffield, *Images and Cultures of Law in Early Modern England*, p. 1.

Chapter 3

Legal Excess in John Donne's 'Satyre V'

John Donne spent five years as a member of Lincoln's Inn before entering the service of Sir Thomas Egerton, the last Lord Keeper under Elizabeth and the first Lord Chancellor under James.[1] Despite his connection with these legal environments, few studies have been devoted to the poet and the law, and even fewer to his fifth and final satire on legal reform.[2] Critical tradition has largely followed Wesley Milgate's lead in dismissing 'Satyre V' as 'the weakest' in the series, as it has 'the air of a rather hastily-put-together occasional piece'.[3] The occasional nature of the poem, however, should attract rather than repel contemporary critical interest. Composed while Donne was a legal secretary for Egerton in the late 1590s, 'Satyre V' reverberates with the complex legal, political, and literary cultures that circulated through the halls and chambers of York House, the Lord Keeper's residence. The poem not only directly addresses Egerton, but its focus on legal abuse and 'how law regulates itself' is an appeal to the sensibility of this particular Lord Keeper who was well-known for his judicial integrity and commitment to legal reform when he first came to office.[4] In an early seventeenth-century manuscript entitled 'Memorialles for Judicature', Egerton outlines four major areas of the law in need of reform: 'the mischievous growth of litigation in society, the increased costs of the courts, the excessive fees of serjeants and attorneys, and the proliferation of dishonest and inexpert men in the law profession'.[5] All of these developments in late Elizabethan and early Jacobean legal culture are at least glanced at in Donne's final satire.[6] Both M. Thomas Hester and Annabel Patterson place 'Satyre V' in the tradition of advice literature and argue that Donne equates his role as satirist with his role as legal advisor or counsellor.[7] While he praises Egerton, however, Donne does not directly advise him in the poem. Nor historically was Donne a legal *counsellor* to the Lord Keeper: Egerton had far more learned and experienced men at his disposal for that service, including Francis Bacon and William Lambarde.

'Employed as one of the Lord Keeper's three working secretaries', Louis A. Knafla explains, Donne's 'duties would have included scheduling, meeting and greeting guests, legal research and drafting memoranda for the wide range of the Lord Keeper's public, rather than private, businesses'.[8] While the details of his specific contribution to York House remain largely obscure, I argue that Donne compensates for his uncertain status as a new gentleman attendant by constructing a relationship with his patron through 'Satyre V', which analyses the organisation of the justice system – including the potential for abuse and reform – that necessitates Donne's service to Egerton, and Egerton's to the crown and the commonwealth.

'Satyre V' puts many demands on the reader, who must be able and willing to recall and interrelate multiple poetic, intellectual, ethical and legal discourses and practices. The following close reading considers the court of Chancery, statutory interpretation techniques, the structure of legal and political representation, and secretarial service, all of which mediated Donne's relationship with Egerton – presumably the intended first reader – and all of which drew extensively upon Donne's 'humane learning and languages'.[9] In the process of unpacking the argument of 'Satyre V', I discover a consistent, even obsessive or excessive, interest in excess. The satirist's critique of the legal system is expressed through the imagery of physical excess and through an analogical style that generates intellectual extensions and excesses. In the Inns Christmas revels and the general pardon statute that were examined in the previous chapter, rhetorical excess appears both accidental and strategic, a form of error as well as a function of genre. In Donne's satire, excess likewise emerges not only as a sign and effect of the abuses of the justice system, but as central to both poetic and official responses to the law's inherent imperfections. While the primary focus of 'Satyre V' is the behaviour of suitors and officers that has destabilised the justice system, the poem also evokes the legitimate additions, supplements, or extensions that were largely the result of what Mark Fortier calls the 'culture of equity' that was responsible for signature developments in early modern legal history.[10] As Lord Keeper and then Chancellor, Egerton presided over Chancery, the principal 'court of equity' that supplemented the common law when no remedy existed or when judgement at common law produced more injustice than justice. Equity also made its way *into* the common law, however, through statute interpretation, the principles and practices of which had also developed over the course of the sixteenth century. It was as a student and practitioner of the common law that Egerton first began thinking and writing about equity.

Not surprisingly given the satiric mode or form, the speaker's style hovers ambivalently between the worlds of positive and negative excesses. Is he part of the solution or part of the systemic problem? While equity required the intellectual extension of the law to address novel cases, the poem further evokes legal and political representation as a form of excess through which legal officers throughout the country and members of parliament figuratively closed the physical distance between subject and sovereign and thereby enabled the effective dissemination of justice. What comes to differentiate the speaker from the targets of his satire is the relationship between secretary and superior. Donne resorts to the courteous terms of early modern employee–employer relations that would have been familiar to readers of texts like Angel Day's letter-writing manual, *The English Secretary*. In 'Satyre V', Donne's relation-ship with Egerton, and Egerton's with the Queen, is founded on the servant's voluntary obedience. Reworking and fusing the discourse on service and Aristotle's discussion of justice in *The Nicomachean Ethics*, the satirist ultimately presents perfect justice as the virtuous, voluntary execution of service to another. The legal secretary thus becomes the model of the just legal-political intermediary who contrasts with the extremes of corrupt officeholders and suitors. Through this model of the legal secretary, a uniquely ethical version of the Donnean speaker's 'in-between' posture emerges.

Extreme Justice

'Satyre V' begins by invoking a principle of satiric decorum derived from Castiglione: 'He which did lay / Rules to make courtiers ... Frees from the stings of jests all who in extreme / Are wretched or wicked.'[11] These types, we are told, will be the speaker's 'theame', even though they are not a source of 'jests' (ll. 5–9). While the opening allusion to Castiglione seems to suggest that 'Satyre V' will pick up where 'Satyre IV' left off, it is instead a point of departure. The speaker soon shifts his attention from the royal court to the law courts: his 'theme' turns out to be, more specifically, 'off'cers' rage' and 'suitors' misery' (l. 8). Their 'extreme' circumstances stem from their own corrupt participation in the justice system. By drawing our attention to their extreme wretchedness and wickedness, Donne activates the Aristotelian conceptions of virtue and justice that were widely disseminated in early modern England. *The Nicomachean Ethics* was a core part of the university curriculum, while Aristotle's ideas about virtue and justice were disseminated at the grammar-school level through texts such as Cicero's *De officiis*.[12] In the *Ethics*, 'moderation, the pursuit of the mean, [is] equated generally with virtue and specifically with justice'.[13] The virtuous mean is defined as that which is free of excesses and deficiencies. The mean of 'just action' is further defined as the 'intermediate between acting unjustly and being unjustly treated'.[14] In 'Satyre V', Donne represents these two extremes of injustice as 'off'cers' rage' and 'suitors' misery', or as officers' abuse of authority and legal technicalities and suitors' financially ruinous exploitation of legal processes. In order to represent the destabilising influence of their machinations on the entire justice system, however, Donne couches his description of these two extremes within Plato's doctrine of likeness that emphasises the interconnection of all things.

In his discussion of Donne's paradoxical 'desperate coward' in 'Satyre III', Joshua Scodel explains that men exhibiting extreme defects or excesses on the Aristotelian scale could appear or be very similar. 'Although Aristotle contrasts rashness and cowardice as excess and defect on either side of courage', he writes, 'his detailed analysis of the rash man breaks down the distinction between these extremes by arguing that rash men are generally "rash cowards" . . . The rash man "pretends to courage which he does not possess".'[15] In 'Satyre V', the distinction between the extremes of officer and suitor likewise breaks down as Donne illuminates their correspondence within the legal system and their mutual culpability in the system's corruption. To do so, he appeals to another classical tradition. The doctrine of likeness is asserted as the premise for his analysis:

> . . . If all things be in all –
> As I think, since all, which were, are, and shall
> Be, be made of the same elements:
> Each thing each thing implies or represents . . .

(ll. 9–12)

As Hester observes, the argument derives from Plato's *Timaeus* and the works of Paracelsus.[16] Plato's *Timaeus* is the starting point for both Leonard Barkan and David George Hale's classic studies on the body politic analogy.[17] In this dialogue, Plato insists that the universe 'by unquestionable necessity . . . is an image of something'.[18] It is 'a copy in the transitory world of "becoming" of a divine original which exists in the world of "being"'. This 'doctrine of likeness', Barkan writes, 'gives rise to the notion of an infinite regress of likenesses beginning with man and proceeding all the way to the eternal principle'.[19] Similitude is thereby joined with the idea of correspondence in a vision of a universal hierarchy. In the early modern era, 'men idealised a divinely ordained system' in which, Kevin Sharpe explains, 'from the highest sphere of the planets, through the arrangements of societies, the composition of the individual and the hierarchy of beasts, a naturally appointed order was replicated.' The result was the politicisation of all aspects of life and the naturalisation of political identities, relationships and institutions: 'The language of treatises on the body, on the family, on riding, on music, on the government of cattle, was highly political because each of these analogues (and others) corresponded in some way to the commonweal, as it related to them.' Though this system was 'never descriptive of the world', it 'nevertheless presented a powerful normative depiction of it'.[20]

Within this interconnected universal hierarchy, Donne depicts the officer and suitor working in tandem to produce systemic injustice. Through methods that ultimately backfire, the legal representative exploits authority and technicalities while the litigant exploits legal process in the ruthless pursuit of their own interests. If 'Each thing each thing implies or represents',

> Then man is a world, in which officers
> Are the vast, ravishing seas, and suitors
> Springs (now full, now shallow, now dry), which to
> That which drowns them, run.
>
> (ll. 13–16)

In striving to obtain more than their legal right or in asserting rights regardless of the damage and cost to others (where the 'equitable man', according to Aristotle, often settles for less than his rights allow), greedy suitors employ legal representatives in groundless, false, or malicious suits.[21] Lawyers, in turn, exploit suitor greed, charging exorbitant fees and engaging in duplicitous practices. In 'Satyre II', the speaker claims that the lawyer Coscus, 'when he sells or changes lands, he impairs / His writings, and (unwatched) leaves out "*ses heires*"' (ll. 97–8). The result of such practices can be seen in 'Satyre V,' in which the speaker chastises a suitor for doffing his hat to 'yon off'cer', who has 'Got those goods for which erst men bared [i.e. doffed their hats] to thee' (ll. 79–80). Grasping at what is not properly his own through legal gambles, the suitor loses what he has to legal fraud and fees. For his unscrupulous efforts, he is left with mountains of useless yet expensive documents: 'and for all hast paper / Enough to clothe all th'Great Carracks' Pepper' (ll. 84–5).[22] The roles of officer and suitor are not only interconnected through the relationship between victimiser and victim; their situations are also parallel. Neither the officer nor the suitor's possessions are secure, since their practices contribute to an economy of 'controverted lands' that 'Scape ... the strivers' hands' (ll. 41–2). Legal representative and litigant alike compromise the integrity of the entire legal system. While the speaker of 'Satyre II' fears the redistribution of land and wealth through the

professional machinations of lawyers like Coscus, 'Satyre V' is a lam-
entation not for that new order, but rather for the ultimate instability
of *any* order in which legal certainty has disappeared.[23] By beginning
his argument with reference to the doctrine of likeness, Donne posits a
continuum between individual offence and systemic failure. The officer's
unethical legal practice and the suitor's exploitation of legal process thus
threaten the law's perfection or its ability to generate justice.

In his depiction of the suitor's shortsighted complicity in his own
ruin, the speaker also provides a novel response to two related questions
posed in Aristotle's discussion of justice in *The Nicomachean Ethics*:
'Can a man be voluntarily treated unjustly?' and 'Can a man treat
himself unjustly?' The philosopher's test case for this second question
is suicide. To commit an unjust act one must act 'voluntarily', but 'no
one is voluntarily treated unjustly'.[24] Hence, a man cannot voluntarily
treat himself unjustly: 'no one can commit adultery with his own wife
or housebreaking on his own house.' An unjust action must perforce
'always involve more than one person'. Suicide is illegal, therefore, and
'a certain loss of civil rights attaches to the man who destroys himself,
on the ground that he is treating the state unjustly'.[25] The man who stabs
himself performs a voluntary unjust action against the state by violating 'the right rule of life' with his own body. In 'Satyre V', however,
the suitor is presented as an Aristotelian or ethical paradox: he 'treat[s]
himself unjustly' by being 'voluntarily treated unjustly' by legal officers
and practitioners. Donne's use of direct address emphasises the suitor's
role in his own destruction:

> [Officers] are the mills which grind you, yet you are
> The wind which drives them; and a wasteful war
> Is fought against you, and you fight it; they
> Adulterate law, and you prepare their way
> Like wittals: th'issue your owne ruine is.

(ll. 23–7)

While a man cannot commit adultery with his own spouse, he can
'prepare [the] way' for another. A wittol is 'a man who is aware of and
complaisant about the infidelity of his wife'.[26] The suitor is compared to
a wittol who, unlike the cuckold, is voluntarily treated unjustly. While
Aristotle condemns 'acting unjustly' more than 'being unjustly treated',
he nevertheless cautions that 'there is nothing to prevent [the latter]
being incidentally a greater evil'.[27] In the course of his satire, Donne
represents 'suitors' misery' or 'being unjustly treated' as worse than
'off'cers' rage' for the very reason that suitors willingly bring it upon
themselves. They are worse than 'worms' meat' since they are willingly

eaten by those 'whose selves worms shall eate' (ll. 21–2). Far from offering sympathy, the speaker presents the suitor's condition as a form of self-victimisation. Both suitor and officer, however, perform unjust actions against the legal system that finally precipitate harm to themselves. Their greedy exploitation and manipulation of legal resources disable the force and certainty of the law and they thereby enable their own unjust treatment. To perform acts of vicious self-interest that harm the state and the self is an especially perverse kind of suicide.

Aristotle's definitions of justice as a mean and injustice as an extreme worked their way into English legal thought and arguments through a commonplace that derived from Cicero's *De officiis*: *summum jus, summa injuria* was regularly translated into English as, 'extreme justice is extreme injustice' or 'extreme injury'. 'Extreme justice' occurred when strict adherence to the letter of the law resulted in a disproportionate response to the circumstances of a particular case. Echoing Aristotle as well as earlier sixteenth-century treatises on equity, Egerton would explain in a seventeenth-century case that 'Mens Actions are so divers and infinite, That it is impossible to make any general Law which may aptly meet with every particular Act, and not fail in some Circumstances.'[28] The inherent imperfection of the law's generality necessitated an equitable approach to the anomalous case. In early modern England, equity provided the rationale for several courts, most importantly the Chancery. Egerton was Master of the Rolls in Chancery from 1594 to 1603, and presided over the court as Lord Keeper and then Chancellor from 1596 to 1617. The court's purpose, he explained, was 'to soften and mollifie the Extremity of the Law, which is called *Summum Jus*'.[29] It offered relief when rigorous common law procedure would produce judgements that unfairly benefited one litigant or harmed another. As William Jones writes, Chancery's jurisdiction 'proceeded from a basic understanding that legal rights were a liberty that must not be misused to take advantage of another person'.[30] As we saw in the last chapter, the general pardon improved the common good by disabling the ensnaring statutes that could be exploited to the harm of the Queen's subjects. Chancery, by contrast, extended the reach of the law to embrace individual, exceptional cases in order to remedy abuses of legal right.

The exemplary Chancery case, according to J. H. Baker, was that of the debtor who failed to have his sealed bond cancelled once payment was made: '[t]he [common] law regarded the bond as incontrovertible evidence of the debt, and so payment was no defense. Here the debtor suffered the obvious hardship of being driven to pay a second time; but the mischief was a result of his own foolishness, and the law did not bend to assist fools.'[31] The Lord Keeper or Chancellor, however, could freely evaluate any relevant evidence and circumstances surrounding a case in order to hinder those who would exploit a legal advantage for unfair profit or injury. He could proceed in this way without compromising the certainty and force of the law because his decrees only bound the parties involved; that is, his decisions could not be used as precedents that made or unmade common law. The case of the debtor who fails to cancel his bond is discussed in Christopher St German's *Doctor and Student*, the most influential sixteenth-century work on equity's relation to law, and in the anonymous *Replication of Sergeant at the Laws of England*, the first published response to St German's text.[32] Most significantly for my purposes here is the fact that this type of Chancery case closely resembles the premise of Juvenal's 'Satire 13', which served as the model for Donne's 'Satyre V'. In the Roman satire, the speaker addresses a Calvinus who has lost a lawsuit and is 'blazing, with [his] guts in a ferment, because a friend won't give back the money . . . entrusted to him'. Calvinus's grief is excessive and inappropriate not only because the sum lost is inconsequential, but also because his 'experience is something we see happen all too often'. Perjury is so widespread that it's hardly surprising the friend would 'keep the money [he's] denied receiving' in court.[33] Juvenal's speaker calls for some perspective: 'If in the whole world there's no crime you can point to as loathsome as this, I'll shut up . . . But if you see all the courts busy with similar complaints . . . do you, you precious creature, think that you should be reckoned as extraordinary?' Even though the justice system has failed, the speaker goes on to argue, the conscience of these offenders punishes them with a 'guilty awareness of their terrible deeds [that] keeps them paralysed and thrashes them with its silent whip'. Forced to 'carry in [his] breast [his] own hostile witness, night and day', the perjurer loses even when he wrongly gains through the law.[34]

In Donne's satire, too, what should be an exceptional case of injustice enabled by court practice has likewise become the norm. Suitors' misery is not only the typical outcome of the frequent recourse to law, as in Juvenal's satire, but it is also a function of judges' and officers' practices that have regularised the exploitation of suitors. Donne does not, however, credit suitors or officers with the same self-punishing interior life that we find in Juvenal. Instead, conscience is externalised in the form of the Lord Keeper, whose 'righteousnes [the queen] loves' (l. 31). Until the common lawyer Sir Thomas More held the office, the Chancellor had traditionally been a prelate who was said to judge according to his 'conscience' and to be responsible for correcting the conscience of litigants. The term drew attention to the role of personal integrity and refined judgement within the Chancellor's deliberative practice, in which he 'was to tease out the merits of a case on the facts ... rather than to apply legal rules'.[35] While the judge's and the court's association with conscience shifted in this period of legal history, the terminology persisted. Egerton could still write in the seventeenth century that, 'when a Judgement is obtained by Oppression, Wrong and a hard Conscience, the Chancellor will frustrate and set it aside ... for the hard Conscience of the Party'.[36] The Lord Keeper or Chancellor also acted as the 'conscience' of the judicial system, having 'a (claimed) supervisory jurisdiction over the "undue practices" of other courts and over the legal profession itself'.[37] According to Donne's poem, by rising to the highest legal office, 'righteous' Egerton was 'authorised [to] now beginne' (ll. 33–4) reforming systemic injustice.

Over the course of the sixteenth century and into the seventeenth, the relationship between the common law and the Chancery was not only reimagined theoretically but also tested in practice. Thanks especially to the influential writings of St German in the 1520s and 1530s, the Chancellor's 'conscience', as a source of legal judgement, was displaced by the impersonal Aristotelian principle of equity that equated justice with the original lawmakers' intentions, which were further equated, by the end of the 1500s, with the common good. The alignment of Chancery with theories of equity brought the court into competition and conflict with the common law, whose authorities and apologists had carved out a role for equity within the practice of statute interpretation. As Mark Fortier writes, 'Is equity, as the correction of the letter of the law by the intent of the law, in the law or outside it?'[38] Who had jurisdictional pre-eminence, Chancery or the common law courts? St German's writings fuelled a debate that would flare up through the end of the sixteenth century and quite spectacularly in the first two decades of the seventeenth. The above quotations from Egerton are drawn from the report of the Earl of Oxford's Chancery case of 1615. While the case concerned Magdalene College's challenge to the Earl of Oxford's title to land that had been previously sold by the college, it became the focus of a jurisdictional dispute that pitted Egerton, now Lord Ellesmere and Chancellor, against Edward Coke, Chief Justice of the King's Bench. 'The essence of Coke's complaint', Gary Watt explains, 'was that the Chancellor's practice of granting injunctions in Chancery to prevent the enforcement of common law judgements was in breach of statutes designed to prevent appeals from the common law courts.'[39] Egerton countered that common law 'Judgment is no Let to examine [a case] in Equity' since it is not 'the Truth of the Judgment' that is in doubt, but rather its justice.[40] The jurisdictional conflict was brought to James and resolved the following year. Deciding in favour of Chancery, 'the king thereby established the rule which maintains equity's pre-eminent status to the present day: where equity and law conflict, equity shall prevail.'[41] As Fortier points out, however, the case was hardly the end of tensions between the Chancery and the common law judiciary. And the success of equity, as a legal principle, did not guarantee the future of the court of Chancery, which took part, instead, in 'the devolution of equity from a jurisprudential ideal to a powerful institution to an official bureaucracy'.[42]

As the Lord Keeper's legal secretary in the 1590s, Donne was an eye-witness to a later stage of 'one of the central developments in jurisprudence and of the legal system in early modern England'.[43] Part of that experience is presented in 'Satyre V', through which satire's relationship to law is recalibrated. As Gregory Kneidel explains, when critics consider the relationship between early modern satire and law, they 'fixate on notorious instances when satire runs afoul of the law, when, that is, it is deemed libelous and thus found to be *illegal*'.[44] He has in mind the infamous 'Bishops' Ban' of 1599, a sweeping act of censorship prohibiting the publication of satires, epigrams, histories and plays.[45] The historical prompt for the ban is still debated, along with its fallout, but it unmetaphored the classical trope in which satirists expressed fears of being judged libellous. Donne, however, establishes a productive role for satiric critique from within the law. The poet's 'great innovation was to present his satires as an extension of this institutionalized or *official* equity', writes Kneidel; 'it is formal verse satire that Donne reinvents or reimagines as a poetic form most suited to Egerton's official jurisprudential agenda.'[46] If the generic reform project of the satirist is allied to the historical legal project of equity, however, equity was not – in the poem or historically – the exclusive jurisdiction of the court of Chancery. As a common law student and practitioner, Egerton composed a treatise on the principles of statute interpretation, which were also deeply informed by Aristotelian equity. Through statute interpretation, and as Chancellor Ellesmere's comments in the Earl of Oxford's Case demonstrate, Chancery and common law could also be imagined as linked by a shared pursuit: 'the [common law] Judges themselves do play the Chancellor's Parts, upon Statutes, making Construction of them according to Equity, varying from the Rules and grounds of Law, and enlarging them, *pro bono publico*, against the Letter and Intent of the Makers'.[47] Equitable judgement is evoked in Donne's poem not only through allusions to the Chancery's judge and jurisdiction, but through a mode of analysis that is self-consciously analogical and, I argue, deliberately evocative of the principles and practices of statute interpretation.

Analogical Justice

In order to illuminate the form and scope of the legal reform needed, the speaker of 'Satyre V' transforms analogies that traditionally emphasised national and political cohesion to express instead the extreme corruption that has overwhelmed the justice system. These analogies – the stuff of poetry as well as legal and political rhetoric – provided a set of concrete images and a ready vocabulary for the representation of order and disorder. The speaker innovates on the conventions repeatedly, extending the imagery to illuminate the ways in which the structure and the operations of the justice system itself could become vehicles for injustice.[48] He portrays the unscrupulous officers and suitors who abuse the law's intentions as the excremental extremities of the law. At the same time, the speaker's extension of conventional political analogies mimics the equitable method of statute interpretation that provided another means within common law to counteract injustices generated by the law's overly general character. Like the Inns revellers' parody of statutory rhetoric, the satiric speaker's analogical style demonstrates a thorough knowledge of the practices for exploiting *and* correcting the legal-political system's imperfections. In 'Satyre V', illicit extensions and excesses are analysed through, and in uncomfortably close proximity to, accepted forms of legal-political extension and excess. This close proximity between legitimate and illegitimate practices puts both the reader and speaker on alert for slippage from the one to the other. The fine distinction between legitimate and illegitimate practices necessitates and generates the self-consciousness of the legal reformer who must be able to check the conduct of others as well as himself. Like the Gray's Inn Christmas revellers, Donne fashions his own legal-political maturity as a sophisticated ability to identify and correct disorder within the law.

In his final satire, Donne transforms the body politic analogy that conventionally defended social and political relationships and institutions by naturalising them. According to classical, medieval and early modern tradition, officers, magistrates, counsellors and judges corresponded to various body parts (most frequently the eyes, ears, hands, heart, or stomach) based on their function within the system or their proximity to the prince (the head). Labourers, meanwhile, who supported the country with the most physical effort, were compared to the feet.[49] Within Elizabethan parliamentary speeches, disorder in the commonweal was frequently compared to the disorder or malfunctioning of the body. In the parliament of 1601, Sir George More, Donne's future father-in-law, would use the body politic analogy to argue that members infringed upon the prerogative by proposing a bill against monopolies granted by royal patent:

> There be Three Persons; Her *Majesty*, the *Patentee*, and the *Subject*: Her *Majesty* the Head, the *Patentee* the Hand, and the *Subject* the Foot. Now, here is our Case; the *Head* gives Power to the *Hand*, the *Hand* Oppresseth the *Foot*, the *Foot* Riseth against the *Head*.[50]

More imagines disorder and injustice in terms of dysfunctional bodily members who trespass upon the proper operations of other parts. In Donne's satire, by contrast, the structure and source of disorder and injustice within the legal system is reimagined as the result of bodily excess. After his depiction of a corrupt 'pursuivant' who deliberately misidentifies and confiscates ('mis-take[s]') items supposedly related to Catholic practice, the speaker compares the officer who abuses his authority for personal gain to the law's excremental nails:

> Oh, ne'r may
> Faire law's white, reverend name be strumpeted,
> To warrant thefts . . .
> She is all fair, but yet hath foul, long nails,
> With which she scratcheth suitors; in bodies
> Of men, so in law, nails are th'extremities,
> So off'cers stretch to more than law can do,
> As our nails reach what no else part comes to.
>
> (ll. 68–78)

Here Donne joins two groups traditionally identified with the hands of the body politic: officers and thieves. In the intricate version of the analogy found in John of Salisbury's twelfth-century *Policraticus*, Leonard Barkan explains, officials and soldiers are compared to hands because these subjects put into action the instructions received from the head (the prince), the heart (the senate) or the tongue (the judges and governors). At the same time, however, Salisbury goes on to compare dishonest magistrates with thieves, who were likewise notorious for their handiwork.[51] Donne's speaker characteristically stretches or extends the analogy and the traditional associations to focus on the excremental nails instead of the hands, the fingers' ends turned into dangerous outgrowths. Officers' abuse of legal authority is represented as the excremental byproduct of the body's extremities. The satirist thereby presents corrupt officers as a form of 'extreme justice' through the body politic imagery.

Donne similarly transforms 'the fable of the belly', an anecdote that was developed from the body politic analogy to demonstrate the interdependence of political estates through comparison with the vital collaboration among all parts of the body. The earliest account of the fable of the belly appears in the second book of Livy's *History of Rome*, translated into English by Philemon Holland in 1600. In an episode that ultimately explains how the 'Tribunes of the common people [were] first created', Menenius Agrippa appeases a rebellious gathering with a parable that compares the body's belly to Rome's senators and the other organs and members to the commons. Disgruntled with the amount of labour they appeared to perform in comparison with the belly, who 'did nothing else but enjoy the delightsome pleasures brought unto her', the other body parts decide to starve her: 'they mutined & conspired altogether in this wise, That neither the hands should reach & convey food into the mouth, nor the mouth receive it as it came, neyet the teeth grind & chew the same.' The result was that 'the whole bodie . . . pined, wasted, & fel into an extreme consumption', since it was the belly's job to feed the rest of the body 'as it received food it selfe'.[52] In Nicholas Cusanus's *De Concordantia Catholica*, the fable was reframed to compare the process of lawmaking to eating, 'including biting, tasting, chewing, and digesting'. As Barkan points out, this text 'stop[s] short of the final stages of the process beyond the stomach'.[53] Donne's speaker, however, follows the digestive analogy to its natural conclusion: 'the world [is] a man', he argues, 'in which officers / Are the devouring stomach, and suitors / Th'excrement which they void' (ll.17–19). Instead of mutually sustaining each other as collaborative members within the legal system, officers exploit suitors until they are worthless.

While the fable of the belly constitutes one anatomical development of the state–body analogy, another tradition portrays the commonwealth or the legal-political system as diseased and only to be cured through social, political, or legal reform. In Samuel Daniel's poem 'To Sir Thomas Egerton', for instance, the speaker explains in quite commonplace terms, 'whenas Justice shal be ill dispos'd / It sickens the whole body of the State'.[54] In a more vivid example from the 1601 parliament, Donne's friend, Richard Martyn, portrayed monopolists as a direct attack on the health of the country:

> The Principal Commodities both of my Town and Country, are ingrossed into the Hands of these Blood-Suckers of the Common-Wealth.
> If a Body, Mr. *Speaker*, being Let Blood, be left still Languishing without any Remedy, How can the Good Estate of that Body long remain?[55]

The speaker of 'Satyre V' skips right over the poetic and rhetorical potential of the diseased body to intimate the justice system's decomposition, taking the analogy as far as it can possibly go. 'All men are dust', we are told. Suitors, however, are 'worse than dust, or worms'

meat, / For [officers] do eat you now whose selves worms shall eat'
(ll. 19–22).

Donne repeatedly extends conventional legal-political tropes to satiri-
cally represent abuses of the law's intentions as unjust extremes. As a
result, the speaker's own analogical reasoning and extensions become
the focus of this satire as much as the offences of greedy officers and
suitors. At the turn of the seventeenth century, analogy was defined as
the '[p]roportion, agreement, or likenesse of one thing to another'.[56]
The early moderns inherited and developed an analogical mentality that
elided similitude, correspondence, harmony and justice.[57] An analogy
was an apt comparison, a balanced equation, a harmonious agreement
between two terms. The comparison's success was the result of an
equilibrium produced in the absence of deficiencies or excesses in either
term. Analogy, on the microscopic level of language, thus mirrored
Aristotle's definition of the virtuous mean and justice. In contrast with
analogy's assertion of the 'similitude' and 'correspondence' between
two terms, metaphor was defined as 'the putting over of a word from
his proper and naturall signification, to a forraine or unproper signification'.[58] Metaphor was thus on a continuum with the metaphysical
conceit in which, as Samuel Jonson wrote in the later eighteenth century,
'[t]he most heterogeneous ideas are yoked by violence together'.[59] While
Donne would become the most famous exponent of the metaphysical style, his fifth satire is saturated with the analogical reasoning that
informed the principles, organisation and operations of justice, and that
structured the relationships between subjects, legal-political representatives and the sovereign.

To understand Donne's stylistic choices in 'Satyre V', it is necessary
to understand the centrality of analogical reasoning within statute
interpretation and the centrality of statute interpretation within legal
education and practice. As a student at Lincoln's Inn, Donne would
have attended the formal lecture series on statutes delivered by 'readers'
during the Lent and summer vacations, when the courts at Westminster
were in recess. One of only two formal learning exercises at the Inns,
the readings 'initiated the student in the intricacies of legal analysis
and debate'.[60] At the same time, these lectures heralded the reader's
advancement in the profession. The barrister who was elected to reader
was chosen in recognition of his acumen and experience, which would
be on display throughout his lecture series. During this time, he was
also afforded a special status in the Inn community: '[t]hese *Readers*',
writes William Dugdale, 'do enjoy divers priviledges above the rest of
the Society'.[61] After he fulfilled all the traditional responsibilities of a
reader, a barrister became a senior member of his Inn, taking a role in

its governance. The occasion was celebrated by an excessively sumptuous yet tiresomely formal feast.[62] Along with the disputation or pleading techniques that were displayed in moots, therefore, statute interpretation skills were recognised as a constitutive aspect and as a demonstration of legal authority.

It was only in the sixteenth century, however, that practitioners began to employ and articulate standard principles of statute interpretation, after 'the great outburst of legislation that marks the reign of Henry VIII had been concluded'. Samuel E. Thorne explains:

> It was only then . . . that judges first became conscious that in restricting the words of an act, in the interests of justice, or in extending them to include equally deserving but unmentioned cases, they were performing something more than an incidental, routine function of judicial administration . . . [T]he increased necessity for reconciling the words of acts of Parliament and the simple administration of justice between party and party that faced the judges of the later period sets their practice off sharply from that which had preceded it.[63]

The earliest treatise we have on statute interpretation has been attributed to Thomas Egerton. Two copies of *A Discourse upon the Exposicion [and] Understandinge of Statutes*, written in Egerton's hand, one in English and one in law French, exist in two commonplace books dating from the 1550s to the 1570s. In *A Discourse*, the practices and arguments of Inns readers are regularly invoked. More importantly, however, Egerton's treatise lays out rules for the equitable interpretation of statutes, practices that enabled the extension of the law's sense, spirit, or reason through the identification of likeness or similitude.[64] I argue that the satirist employed a self-conscious analogical style in 'Satyre V' that evoked statute interpretation practices and principles in order to appropriate authority for his writing and to appeal to his new employer. As a legal secretary to the Lord Keeper, Donne would have had access to Egerton's collection of legal resources (by then of more use to the secretary-student than his superior) and would have known of Egerton's own interest in the topic of interpretation. As an Inns student, Donne would have associated statute interpretation skills with legal and Inns clout. Finally, methods of statute interpretation may have also been of interest to Donne in preparation for his own election to the House of Commons in the last Elizabethan parliament.

In *A Discourse*, Egerton explains that statutes are construed equitably when their 'sence & meanynge' are applied beyond the words of the text to cover novel, unanticipated cases.[65] Statutes 'taken by equytie' may be so extended because of 'reasonableness': 'you muste not take everye thinge by equytie, as thynges farre unlyke, but such things as are in the lyke reason, for the reason of the lawe is the soule & pythe of the lawe, yea, the verie lawe itselfe.' From this principle arises the legal rule that 'those that are in lyke myschiefe are in lyke lawe'. The law's reason, however, is construed according to the intentions of the lawmakers – the principle derived from Aristotle's discussion of equity in *The Nicomachean Ethics*. The lawmakers' intentions can be gathered from their own voices in parliament, from the statute's previous application or, most safely and easily, from 'the wordes of the statute either goynge before or folowinge'. These words should be read as if they automatically included a provision for analogous cases, 'as yf those wordes *et similibus* be in':

> thys openethe a gappe to all equytye, shewethe that theire myndes were that it shulde extende to lyke cases . . . And this is a sure rule, as may be, to knowe . . . where they shalbe taken by equytye . . . it availethe to the understandinge of every rule that is geven upon statutes.

In the medieval period, judges decided cases using 'lequity de lestatute', which, as Thorne explains, 'reflects nothing more than the familiar medieval definition of equity, and rests wholly upon the maxim *de similibus idem est iudicium*': there is like judgement about like things.[66] Egerton's version of statute interpretation blends medieval practice with Aristotelian legal equity that deferred to the authority of the lawmakers: the learned judge identifies analogous cases that are implicated in the more general discourse of the offence and the law found within the preambles of statutes that represent lawmakers' intentions. In practice, however, judges were free to extend, restrict, or ignore altogether the direct wording of statutes. The *over*extension of the law through interpretative practices shifted away from a process of analogic comparison toward the metaphoric, in which the differences between two terms are more pronounced than their similarities. Like other illicit extensions, these 'strained inferences', as Francis Bacon called them, threatened the internal coherence, certainty and force of the law. Those opposed to equitable interventions in the law stressed the potential for equity to turn into 'the arbitrary exercise of an individual judge's conscience'.[67]

In 'Satyre V', Donne employs analogical reasoning to analyse the sources of unjust excesses or extreme justice, identifying the individuals and operations of the legal system in need of reform. Donne's analogical style, more than his direct praise of the Lord Keeper, refracts the strategies, reasoning and processes of legal equity that Egerton was engaged in and thought about from the beginning of his long career. At the same time, however, the satiric speaker's innovative developments of traditional analogies also convey an identical potential for unjust, arbitrary judicial *over*extension, for excessive analogical reasoning that mars rather than mends the law. How fair, for example, is the speaker's characterisation of all suitors and officers as corrupt and the extension of his criticism to the entire system? At what point does analogical satirical 'railing' become another overly general (and thus imperfect, inadequate) law? Donne's motive for writing (it is a tribute to his patron) also renders his use of analogical extension and reasoning an instrument of personal gain. He risks being identified with his targets, those who bend legal resources out of shape for profit. While identifying the system's weaknesses, therefore, Donne's style invites suspicion of the speaker. The reader's literary scrutiny is thereby engaged in the same surveillance of excesses that the Lord Keeper and the legal reformer were expected to perform. The solution to the speaker's predicament will take us through a consideration of the structure of legal and political representation before we arrive at the structure of early modern secretarial service. In 'Satyre V', excesses are also revealed to be the result of the network of representatives who were in charge of governance across the country. Like the excesses or extensions already discussed, those within the system of legal and political representation could both enable and disable the workings of justice.[68]

Justice Returns

While Donne's education in statute-interpretation practices began at Lincoln's Inn, his later employment also introduced him to the parliamentary business of statute-writing and legislative reform. During his service in the Lord Keeper's household, the last two Elizabethan parliaments were called. As a secretary, Donne surely at least heard about Egerton's parliamentary work in 1597, while he had a more involved role in the parliament of 1601 as an MP for Brackley, a seat over which Egerton effectively had control.[69] In opening and closing speeches, the Lord Keeper coached MPs on their duty in terms reminiscent of the Nicholas Bacon speeches examined in the Introduction to this book. During his opening speech in the session of 1597, for example, Egerton recommended law reform rather than lawmaking because

> the number of the Laws already made are very great, some also of them being obsolete and worn out of use; others idle and vain, serving to no purpose; some again overheavy and too severe for the offence; others too loose and slack for the faults they are to punish; and many of them so full of difficulties to be understood, that they cause many controversies and much trouble amongst the Subjects.

His opening speech in 1601 reiterates the same message: 'His advice was, that Laws in force might be revised and explained, and no new Lawes made'. Egerton goes on to explain the work of legal reform and of parliamentarians through the analogy of the garden-state, as a process of 'pruning' the 'superfluities':

> You are to enter into a due consideration of the said Laws; and where you finde superfluity, to prune and cut off; where defect, to supply; and w[h]ere ambiguity, to explain; that they be not burthensome, but profitable to the Common-wealth: Which [is] a service of importance, and very needful to be required.[70]

The gardening analogy represents the parliamentary perfection of the law as a matter of routine maintenance that entails the searching and expunging of exceptions, excesses, and other defects within the law. In 'Satyre V', Donne likewise applies a horticultural trope to the activity of legal reform in his direct address to the Lord Keeper: 'You sir ... now begin / To know and weed out this enormous sin' (ll. 31–4). The verb 'to know' complicates the gardening trope by evoking the practices that precede and enable parliamentary weeding. It evokes the entire network of legal and political representatives in charge of collecting and circulating the information that eventually leads to legislative reform, an administrative network that Egerton was now effectively in charge of supervising and reforming.

If weeding is predicated on knowing, knowing is enabled by yet another recognisable form of excess, the proliferation of representatives or officers. The link between the circulation of information by representatives and effective governance can be illuminated by a return to the body politic analogy. As we have seen, the trope represented the commonwealth and its legal-political system as a unified entity, one that included all subjects and institutions as parts that coordinated within a natural, hierarchical order. Political representatives in parliament, however, were also commonly imagined as *surplus* bodily members and sense organs that established a monstrous body politic to surpass the normal human capacity for perception and for obtaining information. In *The Order and Usage of Keeping of The Parlements in England*, John Hooker explains the structure and advantages of the parliamentary system in these terms:

> And albeit the King or prince be neuer so wise, learned and expert: yet is it impossible for any one to be exact and perfit in all things, but a Senate of wise, grave, learned and expert men, beeing assembled in councel to gither: they are as it were one body, having many eyes to se, many feet to go, and many hands to labour withall, and so sircum spect they are for the government of

the commonwelth: that they se all things, nothing is hid or secret, nothing is straunge or new, nothing is to great or weightie to them ... they wilbe wel advised, and measure all things, with good reason, circumspection and policie.[71]

This figurative account of parliamentary representation stresses the productive role of excess in political process: it maximises the system's capacity for surveillance, identification and weeding or reforming of the commonwealth.

Henry Peacham's *Minerva Britanna* visually and poetically elaborates on the labour of early modern legal and political eyes and ears. Instead of parliament, however, the body-politic and garden-state analogies converge in the office and figure of the magistrate or judge. The emblem on 'Ragione di stato' ('Reason of State') is accompanied by verses that explain, he 'Who sits at sterne of Common wealth, and state' must 'Be serv'd with eies, and listening eares of those, / Who from all partes can give intelligence'.[72] It depicts a figure dressed in a robe covered with eyes and ears, who sweeps a wand, decapitating a cluster of poppies (see Fig. 3.1):

That wand is signe of high Authoritie,
The Poppie heads, that wisdome would betime,
Cut of ranke weedes, by might, or pollicie,
As mought molest, or over-proudly clime.

The robe is more familiar to modern critics from the 'Rainbow Portrait' of Elizabeth I, in which the Tudor monarch is dressed like the fairy queen and dons a remarkable gown that is covered in eyes, ears, and mouth-like folds. But Peacham's emblem is dedicated to Julius Caesar, a judge of several courts in his long career, a member of parliament in the later Elizabethan period and in most of James's reign, and appointed by Egerton to the position of Master of the Rolls in Chancery in 1614. The emblem book thus asks us to rethink our understanding of this iconography and the responsibility for weeding as a part of a magisterial and not just (or even primarily) a monarchal tradition. It illuminates the logic underlying Egerton's parliamentary remarks as well as Donne's characterisation of the Lord Keeper as authorised to both 'know and weed out this enormous sin' (ll. 31–4).

If it is the Lord Keeper's job to see that information is effectively obtained and transformed into administrative and legislative reform, knowledge serves a different function in relation to the queen. Her knowledge or ignorance is the result of the numerous intermediaries who come between – either joining or severing – the queen and her subjects. The queen's knowledge/ignorance is thus indicative of whether or not the network of legal and political representatives is functioning as a

Ragioné di Stato.   **22**

To the right Honourable Sir IVLIVS CAESAR, *Knight.*

WHO sits at sterne of Common wealth, and state
Of's chardge and office heere may take a view,
And see what daungers howerly must amate,
His ATLAS-burden, and what cares accrew
   At once, so that he had * enough to beare,
   Though HERCVLES, or BRIAREVS he were.

He must be strongly arm'd against his foes
Without, within, with hidden Patience :
Be seru'd with * eies, and listening eares of those,
Who from all partes can giue intelligence
   To gall his foe, or timely to prevent
   At home his malice, and intendiment.

That wand is signe of high Authoritie,
* The Poppie heads, that wisdome would betime,
* Cut of ranke weedes, by might, or pollicie,
As mought molest, or over-proudly clime :
   The Lion learnes, no thought to harbour base,
   The Booke, how lawes must giue his proiectes place.

E 3.   *His*

* Princeps sua
scientia non po-
test cuncta com-
plecti. Tacitus
Annal : 3. Nec
vn'us mentem
molis tantæ essa
capacem. An-
nal : 1.

* πολλοί βασι-
λέως ὀφθαλμοί
κ, πολλα ὦτα.
Xenophon. in
Pædia. Cyri.

* Rex velut deli-
berabundus in
hortum ædinæ
transit &c.
Livi : lib : primo
Decad : 1.

* Ne patiatur he-
bescere aciem
suæ authoritatis,
Tacitus
Annal : 2.

Figure 3.1 'Ragione di stato', from Henry Peacham, *Minerva Britanna; or, A Garden of Heroical Deuises, Furnished, and Adorned with Emblemes and Impresa's of Sundry Natures* (London, 1612), p. 22. Reproduced with permission from the Huntington Library, San Marino, California.

productive or obstructive excess within the commonwealth. Reporting on a meeting with the queen to discuss the issue of monopolies during the parliament of 1601, the Speaker of the House protested on her behalf 'that if the least of Her Subjects were Grieved, and Her self not

Touched, She appealed to the Throne of Almighty God; how careful She hath been, and will be to defend Her People from all Oppression.'[73] The queen's sympathy is here activated by an intimate knowledge of 'the least of Her Subjects' that must in reality be obtained through the interventions of others. Through these intermediaries, her subjects' complaints reach her and the grief she feels in turn establishes an uninterrupted continuum between the queen and her people: being touched sympathetically becomes a fiction of being in touch personally, of presence. The distance and absence presupposed by legal-political representation dissolves as the knowledge revealed through this system becomes evidence of the perfect connection between monarch and subject. According to this logic, the body politic is capable of absorbing its excess legal-political eyes and ears, not to mention the commonwealth's subjects, into a unified, harmonious whole. Enwrapped in the folds of the queen's mystical body, this monstrous version of the legal-political system satisfies 'the need to reconcile the desire for physical or ideological unity with the obvious diversity of man and of society'.[74]

In Donne's satire, the queen's level of awareness is likewise an index of the system's operational justice. While generally referring back to the injustices perpetrated by officers and suitors, the immediate antecedent of 'this enormous sinne' (in 'You sir . . . now begin / To know and weed out this enormous sin') is a comparison of the queen's ignorance of legal corruption and abuse to the unconscious destruction of the River Thames:

> Greatest and fairest Empress, know you this?
> Alas, no more than Thames' calm head doth know
> Whose meads her arms drown, or whose corn o'erflow.
>
> (ll. 28–30)

Even though she lacks malicious intent and does not voluntarily treat her people unjustly, the Queen's Thames-like ignorance perpetrates the same kind (but not magnitude) of destructiveness as the 'great seas' of judicial corruption:

> If law be the judge's heart, and he
> Have no heart to resist letter or fee,
> Where wilt thou appeal? Pow'r of the courts below
> Flow from the first, main head, and these can throw
> Thee, if they suck thee in, to misery,
> To fetters, halters. But if th'injury
> Steel thee to dare complain? Alas, thou go'st
> Against the stream when upwards, when th'art most
> Heavy and most faint; and in those labours they,
> 'Gainst whom thou should'st complain, will in thy way

Become great seas, o'er which, when thou shalt be
Forc'd to make golden bridges, thou shalt see
That all thy gold was drowned in them before . . .

(ll. 43–55)

The river analogy was initially introduced in 'Satyre III' to describe the circulation of legal-political power. In 'Satyre V' the excess officers who are supposed to facilitate the circulation of information and justice have instead overwhelmed the system with corruption. This flood of corruption impairs the flow of information to the Queen and of justice to the subject. Lynne Magnusson observes that the poem's address to the queen 'replicates the strategy of Robert Southwell's *An Humble Supplication to Her Majestie*, playing the dangerous game of postulating the Queen's non-complicity based on her ignorance in areas where she should be knowledgeable'.[75] The *Supplication* was written in response to a proclamation of 1591 that linked Catholicism with treason and established commissions to investigate and regulate Catholic activities. In the opening passages, Southwell explains to the queen that 'the due respect that every one carrieth to your gratious person, acquiteth you in their knowledge, from any meaning to have falsehood masked under the veile of your Majestie'. The unjust proclamation, therefore, must be the work of 'the Magistrates of the wole realme', who are thereby transformed into what Magnusson calls 'the loathed figure of the treacherous intermediary in state oppression' that she identifies in many of Donne's works, especially the *Elegies* and *Satyres*.[76]

The solution to the treacherous intermediary is the loyal intermediary, Egerton, whose rise in the state is figured in 'Satyre V' as closing the distance between the virgin goddess of justice and the earth. The speaker asserts that England of the 1590s has outdone the Iron Age, the last of the four ages described in Book I of Ovid's *Metamorphoses*, when Astraea fled from the world:

O Age of rusty Iron! Some better wit
Call it some worse name, if aught equal it:
The Iron Age that was when justice was sold; now,
Injustice is sold dearer far . . .

(ll. 35–8)

While Astraea deserted the world once justice was sold, Donne claims that in England now 'Injustice is sold dearer far'. Through reformulations of her myth in classical, medieval and renaissance writings, Astraea developed imperial and religious associations that were easily grafted onto the iconography of the English virgin queen.[77] John Davies, for example, another member of the Egerton circle, a poet as well as a legal theorist and member of parliament, composed a collection of acrostic poems entitled *Hymnes of Astraea* that reveal the true object of their praise through the first letters of every line of the sixteen-line poems: 'ELISABETHA REGINA'.[78] In these courtly verses, judgement and justice are united within the figure of the queen/goddess who demonstrates decorum in all ways. In Donne's satire, the queen/goddess connection enables him to maintain the myth of the queen's perfection while leaving room for injustice that abounds in her absence. Scholarship has overlooked the legal dimension of Elizabeth's Astraea guise: when Astraea returns to earth a new golden age descends that is predicated on the reform of law and order. The myth was evoked in the English parliament to praise the queen for her commitment to legal reform. In his closing oration for the 1597 session, for example, the Speaker of the House explained that, 'we be ... bound to your Majesty for reducing [i.e. restoring] again the golden world of Saturn' by accepting their legislation.[79] In 'Satyre V', Astraea's return to earth and the new golden age of legal reform are signalled by the queen's election of Thomas Egerton to the office of Lord Keeper. In the words of Virgil's fourth eclogue, Egerton is the leader of 'a new generation ... from heaven on high' that descends to earth when the virgin goddess returns.[80] In his epigram 'To Thomas, Lord Chancellor', Ben Jonson would also praise Egerton for his integrity and commitment to reform by evoking the Astraea myth. Composed in James's reign, however, the epigram presents the queen's absence as a function of her death: 'The virgin, long since fled from earth, I see, / T'our times returned, hath made her heaven in thee.'[81] In 'Satyre V', Egerton's 'righteousness' has inspired the queen to 'authoriz[e]' him as Lord Keeper 'To know and weed out' the 'treacherous intermediar[ies]' whose interference precipitates the queen's ignorance and the system's injustice.

The Legal Secretary

The question that remains is, finally, what kind of intermediary is Donne? 'All critics', writes Ronald Corthell, 'mark the movement of the satirist from a marginal position in "Satyre IV" to a place inside the circuit of power in "Satyre V".'[82] Marotti reads the direct address to the Queen and her chief legal minister in this poem as 'a way of establishing the speaker's (and author's) own position of authority and security, a gesture, on Donne's part, of separating himself from the abject misery of both courtly and judicial suitorship'.[83] In order to extricate himself from the 'abject misery' and corruption of officer and suitor, however, the speaker must do more than identify with his superiors. At the same time that he asserts his new insider status, he must also differentiate himself and the Lord Keeper from those who threaten the integrity of office-holding itself. Further complicating the speaker's position is his satiric style that also risks becoming another source of unchecked excess. Within his direct address to Egerton, therefore, the speaker buttresses his legal-political and ethical status by evoking the affective relationship between secretary and superior. While little is known of Donne and Egerton's personal relationship, secretaries were part of the ubiquitous early modern culture of service, the ideology of which was elaborated in numerous works by the end of the sixteenth century.[84] In *The English Secretary*, Angel Day models an ideal version of the rapport between a secretary and his lord in which mutual good will testifies to the integrity of each party. The proficient secretary, he explains, is rewarded with friendship, an alternative, affective exchange system that transcends the socio-economic distinctions between, and desires of, master and servant. When the secretary displays a 'zeale to well-doing [that is] voluntarily embraced' rather than 'urged or constrained by soveraigne command', this 'leaveth the reputation and estimate of our Secretory to be received as a friend'. While 'there can be no friend where an inequalitie remayneth' or '[t]wixt the party commanded and him that commandeth', friendship is nevertheless possible because the conditions of this master–secretary relationship transform over time:

> [E]ach vertue [of the secretary], kindled by the others [the master's] Grace, maketh at last a conjunction, which by the multitude of favours rising from the one, and a thankefull compensation alwayes procured in the other, groweth in the end to a sympathie inseparable, and thereby all intendment concludeth a most perfect uniting.[85]

In Izaak Walton's *Life of Dr. John Donne*, the same ideal elision of secretary and friend is repeated in his description of the Lord Keeper's treatment of Donne:

> Nor did his Lordship in this time of Master Donne's attendance upon him, account him to be so much his servant, as to forget he was his friend; and, to testify it, did always use him with much courtesy, appointing him a place at his own table, to which he esteemed his company and discourse to be a great ornament.
> [Donne] continued that employment for the space of five years, being daily useful, and not mercenary to his friend.[86]

Egerton, according to Walton, treated Donne like a 'friend' and Donne, in return, was not 'mercenary'. Donne himself asserts a similar picture of his non-mercenary character in a letter to Egerton that employs a much plainer style: 'I was four years your Lordship's secretary, not dishonest nor greedy.'[87]

In the direct address to Egerton in 'Satyre V', Day's alternative exchange system of 'friendly fidelitie' is introduced to differentiate the micro-network of Queen, Lord Keeper and legal secretary from the corrupt legal economy of officers and suitors depicted throughout the rest of the poem:

> You sir, whose righteousness she loves, whom I,
> By having leave to serve, am most richly
> For service paid, authorized, now begin
> To know and weed out this enormous sin.
>
> (ll. 31–4)

Instead of giving her 'soveraigne command', the Queen 'authorize[s]' or empowers the Lord Keeper 'To know and weed out'. This wording opens a space for the voluntary 'zeale to well-doing' of her chief legal minister through which his 'righteousness' can be externalised in the form of legal reform. The syntax of this passage positions the speaker between Egerton and the righteous work of reform, or between the main subject and verb, grammatically dramatising Donne's function as a legal-political representative or intermediary. But the self-serving potential of the intermediary is here controlled by the master–secretary dynamic. Like Egerton, Donne is not the subject of a 'soveraigne command' but instead is given 'leave to serve'. In return, the speaker claims he is paid in the currency of service itself, not rewarded directly with material wealth and, therefore, not tempted by it: 'I / By having leave to serve, am most richly / For service paid'. If initially Donne 'manages to suggest that everything corrupt is interconnected' through the doctrine of likeness, in this passage the closed circuitry of service prevents the possibility of destructive excesses that are generated by self-serving exploitations of the system.[88] Service to another creates more opportunities to serve, an ethical surplus. In reality, of course, the secretary received financial and social-political compensation for his efforts. But the servant who is self-serving through service to another or to the state is still juxtaposed to the self-serving officer and suitor who are ultimately self-harming through their harm to others and the state. Donne fuses the secretary–superior exchange system with the Aristotelian ethical system to carve out a space for the honest legal-political representative. When the secretary or servant's 'zeale to well-doing [that is] voluntarily embraced' is found within the legal-political system – when a *secretary* is *legal* – the result is voluntary just action, or perfect justice as presented in *The Nicomachean Ethics*. Aristotle explains that within justice every other virtue is comprehended because 'it is the actual exercise of complete virtue . . . towards [our] neighbour'.[89] By evoking his service as a legal secretary in 'Satyre V', Donne fashions or positions himself as the virtuous legal-political intermediary – the actual embodiment of a mean – who is engaged in voluntary just action to others.

In 'Satyre V', the figure of the legal secretary ultimately offers a new version of the often noted 'betwixt and between' character of Donne's poetry and personae. According to Anna K. Nardo, liminality is a function of Donne's self-confessed obsession with verbal play: 'play is always in-between – the precise location his poetic speakers and his preaching persona need to occupy.'[90] Ronald Corthell argues that this characteristic 'in-betweenness' draws attention to 'the processual aspect of the subject's relation to culture', its unfixed, developing nature. 'Donne creates satire whose truth . . . "is not an essence but a practice".'[91] Joshua Scodel contends that Donne's in-betweeness is a means of rejecting 'many of his contemporaries' use of the [Aristotelian] mean to justify prevailing religious and sociopolitical formations', and that 'he instead adapts the mean to enlarge the sphere of individual freedom'. In 'Satyre III', for example, 'Donne spurns the English church's self-description as the *via media* and advocates a mean of skeptical inquiry between rash acceptance and rejection of any of the rival Christian denominations.'[92] Similarly, in the verse epistle to Henry Wotton, 'Sir, more then kisses, letters mingle Soules', Donne rejects the tradition that presented the city as an ethical midpoint between the extremes of the royal court and country life, and instead he advocates being 'thine owne home, and in thyself dwell' (l. 47). To escape the limitations of any place and social rank, however, one must stay on the move, 'as / Fishes glide, leaving no print where they pass' (ll. 55–6). 'By its self-declared middleness', explains Scodel, 'the Wotton epistle both asserts and enacts the ultimate value of being in transit, neither here nor there.'[93]

In his reading of 'Satyre V', Gregory Kneidel argues that Donne's analysis of legal bureaucracy is located between an administrative tradition with sacred roots and the future of the legal system that the poet 'could not quite yet confidently think of, as [Georg Adam] Struve does over a century later, as rational, formal, centralized, and secular', a transition that overlaps with another from the tradition of 'personal service to a manorial lord to civil service of (what would become) the modern state'.[94] While the poem may refract macro historic forces of modernisation, the style and content were consciously inspired by Donne's immediate legal-political moment. Multiple legal and political processes of extension have surfaced over the course of this chapter in relation to 'Satyre V', and what these ultimately illuminate is the position of the insider satirist who has developed a relationship to in-betweenness that reverses what we have come to expect from Donne. The insider satirist is a legal secretary, a legal-political intermediary, a part of the network of extra eyes and ears that is supposed to close the gap between subject and justice, or subject and sovereign, or client and patron. Rather than distancing the speaker from 'prevailing religious and sociopolitical formations' and 'enlarg[ing] the sphere of individual freedom', the insider satirist's in-betweenness is a function of his new proximity and enlarged responsibilities to others as well as to prevailing social, legal and political forms. Through their analyses of the imperfections of contemporary law and legal culture, Donne and the Gray's Inn Christmas revellers arrive at the legal officer as the structural key to justice. His integrity and competency are hugely consequential. In the following section, the question of the magistrate's character takes centre stage in Shakespeare's *Measure for Measure* and *The Winter's Tale*.

Notes

1. The shift in title, from Lord Keeper to Lord Chancellor, signals a shift in the status, not the function, of the officeholder who presided over the court of Chancery. While Nicholas Bacon would remain a Lord Keeper under Elizabeth, both Egerton and Francis Bacon were made Barons and Chancellors under James. I refer to Thomas Egerton as Egerton and as Lord Keeper through most of this chapter because that was his name and title under Elizabeth and when he employed Donne, but most of the legal historical writings on the Chancery refer to the Chancellor as that court's presiding judge.

2. See R. C. Bald, *John Donne: A Life* (Oxford: Clarendon Press, 1970); Geoffrey Bullough, 'Donne, The Man of Law', in Peter Amadeus Fiore (ed.), *Just So Much Honor: Essays Commemorating the Four-Hundredth Anniversary of the Birth of John Donne* (University Park: Pennsylvania State University Press, 1972), pp. 57–94; Ronald J. Corthell, '"Coscus only breeds my just offence": A Note on Donne's "Satire II" and the Inns of Court', *John Donne Journal* 6.1 (1987), pp. 25–31; Gregory Kneidel, *John Donne & Early Modern Legal Culture: The End of Equity in the Satyres* (Pittsburgh: Duquesne University Press, 2016), 'Coscus, Queen Elizabeth, and the Law in John Donne's "Satyre II"', *Renaissance Quarterly* 61 (2008), pp. 92–121, and 'Donne's Satyre I and the Closure of the Law', *Renaissance and Reformation/Renaissance et Réforme* 28.4 (2004), pp. 83–103; Louis A. Knafla, 'Mr. Secretary Donne: The Years with Sir Thomas Egerton', in David Colclough (ed.), *John Donne's Professional Lives* (Cambridge: D. S. Brewer, 2003), pp. 37–73; Arthur Marotti, *John Donne, Coterie Poet* (Madison: University of Wisconsin Press, 1986); and Jeremy Maule, 'Donne and the Words of the Law', in David Colclough

(ed.), *John Donne's Professional Lives* (Cambridge: D. S. Brewer, 2003), pp. 19–36. Steven W. May's 'Donne and Egerton: The Court and Courtship' is strangely silent on the law and the legal satire that is addressed to the Lord Keeper (in Jeanne Shami, Dennis Flynn and M. Thomas Hester (ed.), *The Oxford Handbook of John Donne* (Oxford: Oxford University Press, 2011), pp. 447–59). Instead, May's piece focuses on the distinction between the royal court and the law courts. This focus seems to have been inspired by critics like Dennis Flynn, whose article on 'Satyre V' fails to delineate the two spheres and instead reads the poem as a critique of the factional politics of the late Elizabethan royal court ('Donne's Most Daring *Satyre*: "richly For services paid, authoriz'd"', *John Donne Journal* 20 (2001), pp. 107–20). For Flynn, the 'suitors' addressed throughout the poem are exclusively imagined as 'the Essexians' (p. 118) instead of the more generic legal suitors, as I take Donne to mean. May's piece does usefully emphasise the scant historical evidence relating to Donne's specific contributions as a 'gentleman attendant' for Egerton, and Flynn's piece usefully disabuses critics of inflated notions of Donne's qualifications for any significant office. These insights implicitly inform the content of this chapter which instead examines Donne's appeal to Lord Egerton through literary conventions, philosophy and legal and political practice and thought.

3. John Donne, *The Satires, Epigrams, and Verse Letters*, ed. Wesley Milgate (Oxford: Oxford University Press, 1967), p. 165.

4. Kneidel, *John Donne & Early Modern Legal Culture*, p. 167.

5. Louis A. Knafla (ed.), *Law and Politics in Jacobean England: The Tracts of Lord Chancellor Ellesmere* (Cambridge: Cambridge University Press, 1977), p. 108. For an extensive account of Egerton's work to reform legal administration and especially the system of fees in the court of Chancery, see W. J. Jones, *The Elizabethan Court of Chancery* (Oxford: Clarendon Press, 1967). Jones describes Egerton as 'the wayward hero' of his book (p. 16).

6. Herbert J. C. Grierson first linked 'Satyre V' to Egerton's plans for 'the reform of some of the abuses connected with the Clerkship of the Star Chamber' (John Donne, *Poems*, ed. Herbert J. C. Grierson, vol. 2 (Oxford: Oxford University Press, 1912), p. 126). Kneidel further links the imagery of the mill that grinds suitors to dust in the poem to the controversy over fees taken by the Star Chamber clerk, William Mill, in the 1590s (*John Donne & Early Modern Legal Culture*, pp. 156–7).

7. M. Thomas Hester, *Kinde Pitty and Brave Scorn: John Donne's Satyres* (Durham, NC: Duke University Press, 1982); Annabel Patterson, 'Satirical Writing: Donne in Shadows', in Achsah Guibbory (ed.), *The Cambridge Companion to John Donne* (Cambridge: Cambridge University Press, 2006), pp. 117–31.

8. Knafla, 'Mr. Secretary Donne', p. 44.

9. John Donne, *John Donne: Selected Letters*, ed. P. M. Oliver (New York: Routledge, 2002), p. 36.

10. Mark Fortier, *The Culture of Equity in Early Modern England* (London: Routledge, 2005).

11. John Donne, 'Satire V', in *The Complete Poems of John Donne*, ed. Robin Robbins (Harlow: Longman, 2008), pp. 416–22, ll. 2–6. All references to

Donne poems are from this edition and hereafter cited parenthetically by line numbers. Unfortunately, *The Variorum Edition of the Poetry of John Donne, Volume 3: The Satyres* is not yet in print.

12. Joshua Scodel, *Excess and the Mean in Early Modern English Literature* (Princeton: Princeton University Press, 2002), p. 2.
13. Kevin Sharpe, *Remapping Early Modern England: The Culture of Seventeenth-Century Politics* (Cambridge: Cambridge University Press, 2000), p. 52.
14. Aristotle, *The Nicomachean Ethics*, trans. David Ross, J. L. Ackrill and J. O. Urmson (Oxford: Oxford University Press, 1998), p. 121.
15. Scodel, *Excess and the Mean*, pp. 23–4.
16. Hester, *Kinde Pitty and Brave Scorn*, p. 109.
17. Leonard Barkan, *Nature's Work of Art: The Human Body as Image of the World* (New Haven: Yale University Press, 1975), pp. 9–14; David George Hale, *The Body Politic: A Political Metaphor in Renaissance English Literature* (The Hague: Mouton, 1971), p. 23.
18. Plato, *Timaeus*, Donald J. Zeyl (trans.), in Plato, *Plato: Complete Works*, ed. John M. Cooper (Indianapolis: Hackett, 1997), p. 1235.
19. Barkan, *Nature's Work of Art*, pp. 9–10.
20. Sharpe, *Remapping Early Modern England*, pp. 43–4.
21. Aristotle, *Ethics*, p. 134.
22. In both 'Satyre II' and 'Satyre V', Donne alludes to the excessive length of legal documents through which legal practitioners increased the fees charged to suitors. In 'Satyre II', the lawyer Coscus

> In parchment then, large as his fields, he draws
> Assurances, big as glossed civil laws,
> So huge that men (in our time's forwardness)
> Are Fathers of the Church for writing less. (ll. 87–90)

The results are seen in 'Satyre V', in which the litigant is left with nothing but papers for all his time spent in frivolous suits.

23. On this aspect of 'Satyre II', see Kneidel, 'Coscus, Queen Elizabeth, and Law', and Ronald Corthell, *Ideology and Desire in Renaissance Poetry: The Subject of Donne* (Detroit: Wayne State University Press, 1997), pp. 34–5.
24. Aristotle, *Ethics*, pp. 129, 134.
25. Aristotle, *Ethics*, pp. 134–5.
26. 'wittol, n.', *OED Online* (Oxford University Press, September 2016).
27. Aristotle, *Ethics*, p. 135.
28. 'The Earl of Oxford's Case in Chancery', in *The Third Part of Reports of Cases, Taken and Adjudged in the Court of Chancery, in the Reigns of King Charles II. King William, and Queen Anne,* vol. 3 (London, 1716), p. 6. See also Christopher Saint German, *Here after foloweth a Dialoge in Englisshe bytwyxte a Doctour of Dyvynyte and a Student in the Lawes of Englande* (London, 1531), sig. D2ᵛ.
29. 'Earl of Oxford's Case', p. 7.
30. Jones, *The Elizabethan Court of Chancery*, p. 424. On the court of Chancery and equity in Early Modern England, see also J. H. Baker, *An Introduction to English Legal History*, 4th edn (Oxford: Oxford University

Press, 2007), pp. 97–116; Knafla, *Law and Politics*; and Mark Fortier, *The Culture of Equity*, and 'Equity and Ideas: Coke, Ellesmere, and James I', *Renaissance Quarterly* 51.4 (1998), pp. 1255–81. In connection to officers' and suitors' extreme condition in 'Satyre V', Kneidel recalls 'the start of Satyre 2 where Donne reimagines the satirist as a sort of chancellor, equitably exempting those who are "wretched or wicked" "in extreame" from the otherwise normal functioning of the law' (*John Donne & Early Modern Legal Culture*, p. 161).

31. J. H. Baker, *An Introduction*, 2nd edn (London: Butterworths, 1979), pp. 87–8.
32. Fortier, *The Culture of Equity*, pp. 63–4.
33. Juvenal, 'Satire 13', in Juvenal, *Juvenal and Persius*, ed. and trans. Susanna Morton Braund, Loeb Classical Library 91 (Cambridge, MA: Harvard University Press, 2004), pp. 435, 443.
34. Juvenal, 'Satire 13', pp. 445, 450–1.
35. Baker, *An Introduction*, 4th edn, p. 106.
36. 'The Earl of Oxford's Case', p. 10.
37. Kneidel, *John Donne & Early Modern Legal Culture*, p. 18.
38. Fortier, *The Culture of Equity*, p. 71.
39. Gary Watt, 'Earl of Oxford's Case (1615)', in Peter Cane and Joanne Conaghan (eds), *The New Oxford Companion to Law*, online edn (Oxford University Press, 2009). See Fortier's discussion of 'The Earl of Oxford's Case' in *The Culture of Equity*, pp. 76–81.
40. 'The Earl of Oxford's Case', p. 7.
41. Watt, 'Earl of Oxford's Case'. See also Knafla, *Law and Politics*, pp. 155–81.
42. Kneidel, *John Donne & Early Modern Legal Culture*, p. 20.
43. Fortier, *The Culture of Equity*, pp. 60, 59.
44. Kneidel, *John Donne & Early Modern Legal Culture*, p. 5.
45. See William R. Jones, 'The Bishops' Ban of 1599 and the Ideology of English Satire', *Literature Compass* 7.5 (2010), pp. 332–46.
46. Kneidel, *John Donne & Early Modern Legal Culture*, pp. 18, 5. Hester provides an alternative religious account of satire's relationship to reform within Donne's poem. As a satiric legal advisor, it is the speaker's job to counsel the Lord Keeper on how to be a Christian satirist in order for the Lord Keeper in turn 'to force the suitor to realize the same kind of ethical education'. Hester concludes that, '[t]he figure of Egerton . . . provides the satirist with the capacity to *realize* on a national scale, to actualize in the fallen world, that reform that has been central to all his poems' (*Kinde Pitty and Brave Scorn*, pp. 102–4).
47. 'Earl of Oxford's Case', p. 12.
48. Donne's stylistic extensions go even further than my account suggests. For example, John T. Shawcross observes that '[t]here is a higher percentage of hypermetric lines in Satire 5 than in the others' ('All Attest His Writs Canonical', in Peter Amadeus Fiore (ed.), *Just So Much Honor: Essays Commemorating the Four-Hundredth Anniversary of the Birth of John Donne* (University Park: Pennsylvania State University Press, 1972), p. 264).
49. Barkan, *Nature's Work of Art*, p. 72.
50. Heywood Townshend, *Historical Collections: or, An Exact Account of*

the Proceedings of the Four Last Parliaments of Q. Elizabeth of Famous Memory. Wherein is Contained the Compleat Journals Both of the Lords [and] Commons, Taken from the Original Records of Their Houses (London, 1680), p. 234.

51. Barkan, *Nature's Work of Art*, pp. 72, 86. Kneidel discusses Horace's use of fingernails as a metaphor for the craft of poetry, arguing that 'Donne exactly reverses the original Horatian connotation of polished finality since the nails signify the incompleteness of legal judgment and the absence of organizational control' (*John Donne & Early Modern Legal Culture*, p. 162).

52. Livy, *The Romane Historie Written by T. Livivs of Padua ... Translated out of Latine into English, by Philemon Holland* (London, 1600), p. 65. See also Hale, *The Body Politic*, p. 26.

53. Barkan, *Nature's Work of Art*, p. 74.

54. Samuel Daniel, 'To Sir Thomas Egerton', in Samuel Daniel, *Poems and 'A Defence of Ryme'*, ed. Arthur C. Sprague (Cambridge, MA: Harvard University Press, 1930), p. 105.

55. Townshend, *Historical Collections*, p. 234. Commenting on his contribution to the next session, Tom Cain describes Richard Martyn's parliamentary rhetoric as 'closely allied to satire in its ironic venom: wit and eloquence are deployed with the deeply serious aim of either securing liberty, or ... to show that it was not given up easily' ('Donne and the Prince D'Amour', *John Donne Journal* 14 (1995), p. 99).

56. John Bullokar, *An English Expositor: Teaching the Interpretation of the hardest words used in our Language* (London, 1616), sig. B7^r.

57. Sharpe, *Remapping Early Modern England*, pp. 51–2.

58. Robert Cawdrey, *A Table Alphabeticall, conteyning and teaching the true writing, and understanding of hard usuall English wordes, borrowed from the Hebrew, Greeke, Latine, or French* (London, 1604), sig. F5^v–F6^r.

59. Samuel Johnson, *Lives of the English Poets*, vol. 1 (Oxford: Oxford University Press, 1906), pp. 14–15.

60. Baker, *An Introduction*, 2nd edn, p. 139.

61. William Dugdale, *Origines Juridiciales; or, Historical Memorials of the English Laws, Courts of Justice, Forms of Tryal, Punishment in Cases Criminal, Law-Writers, Law-Books, Grants and Settlements of Estates, Degre of Serjeant, Inns of Court and Chancery*, 3rd edn (London, 1680), p. 209.

62. On Inns of Court readers and readings, see J. H. Baker's *An Introduction* and *Readers and Readings in the Inns of Court and Chancery* (London: Selden Society, 2000). On their feasts, see A. Wigfall Green, *The Inns of Court and Early English Drama* (New York: Benjamin Blom, 1965). For a detailed early modern account of all the traditional responsibilities of a reader, see Dugdale, *Origines Juridiciales*, pp. 194–5, 203–10.

63. Samuel E. Thorne, 'Introduction', in Thomas Egerton, *A Discourse upon the Exposicion [and] Understandinge of Statutes; with Sir Thomas Egerton's Additions*, ed. Samuel E. Thorne (San Marino: Huntington Library, 1942), p. 3.

64. In addition to Thorne's thorough introduction to *A Discourse*, see also Louis A. Knafla's comments on Egerton's interest in statute interpreta-

tion in the context of late sixteenth-century England in *Law and Politics*, pp. 46–8.

65. Egerton, *A Discourse*, p. 140. In his later speech, *Touching the Post-Nati*, Egerton writes that 'words are taken and construed sometimes by Extension . . . sometimes by equity out of the reach of the wordes' (quoted in Knafla, *Law and Politics*, p. 224).

66. Egerton, *A Discourse*, pp. 147, 153–4, 45.

67. Lorna Hutson, 'Not the King's Two Bodies: Reading the "Body Politic" in Shakespeare's *Henry IV*, Parts 1 and 2', in Victoria Kahn and Lorna Hutson (eds), *Rhetoric and Law in Early Modern Europe* (New Haven: Yale University Press, 2001), p. 171.

68. Kneidel describes 'the principal-agent problem' in political science terms, that is 'endemic to any geographically dispersed administrative program' (*John Donne & Modern England Legal Culture*, p. 145).

69. See I. A. Shapiro, 'John Donne and Parliament', *Times Literary Supplement* (10 March 1932), p. 172.

70. Townshend, *Historical Collections*, pp. 80, 130. Nicholas Bacon also used the gardening analogy to describe the work needed to be done by magistrates in charge of executing justice at the local level:

> Weare yt not a meer maddnes . . . for one to provide faire and handsome tooles to pruine and reforme his orchard or garden and lay them upp without use? And what a thing else is yt to make wholesome and provident lawes to guide our goeing in the common wealth and to pruine and reforme our manners and then to close those lawes in faire bookes or rowles and to lay them upp safe without seeing them executed? (*PPE* 1: 190–1)

71. John Hooker, *The Order and Usage of Keeping of a Parlement in England, and The Description of Tholde and Ancient Cittie of Fxcester* [*sic*] (London, 1575), pp. 2–3.

72. Henry Peacham, *Minerva Britanna; or, A Garden of Heroical Devises, Furnished, and Adorned with Emblemes and Impresa's of Sundry Natures* (London, 1612), p. 22. See Fig. 3.1.

73. Townshend, *Historical Collections*, p. 248.

74. Barkan, *Nature's Work of Art*, p. 89.

75. Lynne Magnusson, 'Danger and Discourse', in Jeanne Shami, Dennis Flynn and M. Thomas Hester (eds), *The Oxford Handbook of John Donne* (Oxford: Oxford University Press, 2011), p. 751. See also R. C. Bald's introduction to Robert Southwell, *An Humble Supplication to Her Maiestie*, ed. R. C. Bald (Cambridge: Cambridge University Press, 1953), and Corthall's discussion of the *Supplication* in *Ideology and Desire*, pp. 42–3.

76. Robert Southwell, *An Humble Supplication to Her Majestie* (London, 1595), sig. A3; Magnusson, 'Danger and Discourse', p. 746.

77. See Frances A. Yates, *Astraea: The Imperial Theme in the Sixteenth Century* (London: Routledge & Kegan Paul, 1975). On the representation of Astraea in Spenser's *Faerie Queene*, see Chapter 1.

78. John Davies, *Hymes of Astraea, in Acrosticke Verse* (London, 1599).

79. Quoted in J. E. Neale, *Elizabeth I and Her Parliaments, 1584–1601*, vol. 2 (London: Cape, 1953–7), p. 366.

80. Virgil, 'Eclogue IV', in *Eclogues, Georgics, Aeneid: Books 1–6*, trans.

H. R. Fairclough, Loeb Classical Library 63 (Cambridge, MA: Harvard University Press, 1999), p. 49.

81. Ben Jonson, *The Complete Poems*, ed. George Parfitt (London: Penguin Books, 1996), p. 58.

82. Corthell, *Ideology and Desire*, p. 51.

83. Marotti, *John Donne*, p. 117.

84. David Schalkwyk, *Shakespeare, Love and Service* (Cambridge: Cambridge University Press, 2008). On the Protestant construction of the master-servant relationship as rooted in love and voluntary obedience, see Schalkwyk's opening chapter, pp. 16–56.

85. Angel Day, *The English Secretary, or Methode of Writing of Epistles and Letters: With a Declaration of Such Tropes, Figures, and Schemes, as either Usually or for Ornament Sake Are Therin Required* (London, 1599), pp. 111, 113, 114. Piers Brown examines secretarial service from the perspective of humanist reading practices within the satiric *Courtier's Library*, a fictional catalogue of learned books that Donne composed between 1603 and 1611 ('"*Hac ex consilio meo via progredieris*": Courtly Reading and Secretarial Mediation in Donne's *The Courtier's Library*', *Renaissance Quarterly* 61.3 (2008), pp. 833–66). Brown does not consider the publications on secretarial service in the period, nor 'Satyre V'.

86. Isaak Walton, *The Lives of Dr. John Donne, Sir Henry Wotton, Richard Hooker, George Herbert, and Dr. Robert Sanderson* (Boston: 1860), pp. 578.

87. John Donne, *Selected Letters*, p. 14. While voluntary well-doing disguised the servant's economic desire, the superior's courtesy could just as easily substitute for more substantial compensation and is the subject of Donne's mockery in 'Elegy VI' or 'Love's Recusant':

> Oh let me not serve so as those men serve
> Whom honour's smokes at once fatten and starve,
> Poorely enriched with great men's words or looks . . .
> (ll. 1–3)

On the blending of political and private service in Donne's poetry, see Aschsah Guibbory, '"Oh, let me not serve so": The Politics of Love in Donne's *Elegies*', *English Literary History* 57 (1990), pp. 811–33.

88. Patterson, 'Satirical Writing', p. 121.

89. Aristotle, *Ethics*, p. 108.

90. Anna K. Nardo, 'John Donne at Play in Between', in Claude Summers and Ted Larry Pebworth (eds), *The Eagle and the Dove: Reassessing John Donne* (Columbia: University of Missouri Press, 1986), p. 157.

91. Corthell, *Ideology and Desire*, pp. 46, 54.

92. Scodel, *Excess and the Mean*, p. 21. Similarly, Corthell reads the truth-seeker of 'Satyre III' as 'the dynamic mountain climber who takes his stand "in strange way", occupying a no-man's land where conventional social relations seemed suspended' (*Ideology and Desire*, p. 46).

93. Scodel, *Excess and the Mean*, pp. 39, 44.

94. Kneidel, *John Donne & Early Modern Legal Culture*, p. 164.

Part II

Execution

Chapter 4

The Assize Circuitry of *Measure for Measure*

[C]ourt motions are up and down, ours circular; theirs like squibs cannot stay at the highest nor return to the place which they rose from, but vanish and wear out in the way; ours like mill-wheels, busy without changing place; they have peremptory fortunes, we vicissitudes.[1]

This is why the saying of Bias is thought to be true, that 'rule will show a man'; for a ruler is necessarily in relation to other men, and a member of a society.[2]

I know there be many good [justices], and I wish their number were increased; but who be they? even the poorer and meanest Justices, by one of which more good cometh to the Commonwealth, than by a hundred of greater condition and degree.[3]

And this you shall finde, that even as a King, (let him be never so godly, wise, righteous, and just) yet if the subalterne Magistrates doe not their parts under him, the Kingdome must needes suffer: So let the Judges bee never so carefull and industrious, if the Justices of Peace under them, put not to their helping hands, in vain is all your labour: For they are the King's eyes and eares in the countrey.[4]

We have already heard the central government's pessimistic perspective on local justice as it was communicated in Nicholas Bacon's parliamentary speeches. In his closing oration, the Lord Keeper addressed the country's provincial magistrates, admonishing them to put into practice the statutes that were especially prioritised by central policy. He warned of the dangers of bad justices who failed to enforce the law, and especially of negligent and corrupt officeholders who posed the most insidious threat to order by inviting the contempt of all authority. Beyond parliamentary chastisement, however, what could actually be done 'to remove from the bench those that are drones and not bees'?[5] At the turn of the seventeenth century, the court of Assize was responsible for overseeing and reforming the execution of local justice and governance throughout the country. The court was an itinerant tribunal that convened twice a year, generating a cyclical representation of central authority in which judges from the Westminster courts brought legal expertise, the voice of the sovereign and the Privy Council, and imposing ceremonial grandeur to their sessions in the English counties. Through its operations, the national policies of the Privy Council were disseminated and corrupt or incompetent local officers were identified and reformed (corrected, fined, shamed or removed from office). The court thus exemplified, in Steve Hindle's words, the 'interdependence of the legal and administrative arms of state [and] the centrality of judicial machinery to the execution of public policy'.[6] The Assizes, I argue, supply a historical analogue through which the representation and reformation of legal administration in *Measure for Measure* can be newly analysed. This chapter reads Shakespeare's problem play alongside the history and structure of the Assizes, including the socio-political tensions it was designed to mitigate and those it inadvertently instigated in its direction and reform of local justice. The Assizes were a regular and dynamic feature of English life that provided an accessible context through which audiences might construe the legal plot and ethics of the play.

The first scene of *Measure for Measure*, in which the Duke departs abruptly and leaves the governing of Vienna in the hands of his substitute Angelo, bears the mark of the Assizes' abrupt dissolution and withdrawal from county life after their sessions had concluded. Likewise, the last scenes of the play, which chart the Duke's return to Vienna and resumption of power, parallel the court's grand return to the counties.[7] From the very beginning, Vienna is infused with an English legal tradition that capitalised on socially destabilising absences and representations that eventually enabled the performance of social reconstruction. Imagining the play as framed by the cyclical structure of the Assizes, moreover, generates new insight into the nature of its supposed irresolution, the conclusion's indeterminacies for which the play is most famous. As Conal Condren explains, the play's 'striking openness is widely accepted, but often as a challenge'.[8] I argue that the play's conclusion is a final statement on the multiple models of reform presented by officers throughout the play. I examine the final trial scene in reference to the Assize trial's functions of exposing local officers and promoting ongoing local surveillance. The effects of the Assize trial, through which private knowledge was transformed into public fact, are diffused throughout Viennese culture generally via the final marriages that subject characters to accountability and potential exposure on a daily basis.

The main action of the play takes place between the two Assize-like coordinates of the Duke's departure and return. The plot develops in the absence of the Duke, or during the invisible part of the court's cycle in which local officers were disconnected from central oversight and support. This situation was a source of anxiety for both central and local authorities alike: the Privy Council had to rely on reports or rumour about order in the counties, while local officers faced pressure from the community when the implementation of central policy and national law jarred with the interests of local magnates or local custom. In *Measure for Measure*, Angelo and Escalus, acting like justices of the peace (JPs) for their county, attempt to put the Duke's commission into execution, to put legal-political policy into local practice. The problematics of legal administration that subsequently develop are secretly monitored by the Duke. The Assize system was organised to bring the efficacy and ethics of local officers to the notice of higher authorities. In *Measure for Measure*, this is achieved through the Duke's disguised presence in Vienna, which enables him to expose Angelo and promote the Provost in the concluding trial. While the local execution and administration of the law was continually and cynically suspected by central authorities, Shakespeare's play ultimately derives a pattern for justice from the local Provost, who executes his function by safeguarding the integrity of the law *and* the life of the individual. He provides an example of legal-political prudence that contrasts especially with Angelo's judicial style and limitations. The Provost's judgement, refined through knowledge and experience of the community, is the mirror for the Duke's execution of justice and the rearrangement of relationships in the final scene. The Duke has been the focal point for numerous critical discussions of Shakespeare and James I. Instead of comparing the Duke to the English and Scottish King's political theology, legal ideology or early reign, I argue alternatively that, like an Assize judge, Vincentio takes the pulse of a city and discovers, along with corruption, an exemplary exponent of local law enforcement.[9] This chapter is divided into discussions of the function and form of the court of Assize that then inform a close reading of the structure and office-holders of *Measure for Measure*.

The Assize Judges and the Reformation of Local Justice

The need to reform local officers and governance was an ongoing concern for major Elizabethan statesmen.[10] In the early years of the Queen's reign, Nicholas Bacon had proposed a commission of 'certaine experte and proved persons ... to trye out and examine by all meanes and wayes the offences of all such as have not seene to the due execucion of lawes' by means of a 'visitacion' every two or three years throughout the realm.[11] By the end of Elizabeth's reign, this job had been meted out to the judges of Assize in addition to their regular legal work. Twice a year, judges from the central courts at Westminster were selected to preside over cases in the six circuits into which England was divided for that purpose. This system of delivering justice to local communities eliminated the inconveniences that would have attended the transportation of litigants, suspects, witnesses, and jury members to Westminster. For the two to three days that the sessions lasted, the court tried both criminal cases and civil suits.[12] Despite their extensive jurisdiction and the remarkable time constraints for clearing dockets, the Assize judges had in addition broad-ranging duties in government administration and oversight. These duties were outlined in charges delivered by the Lord Keeper or the sovereign in Star Chamber to judges going out on circuit and to JPs residing within the vicinity of London.[13] These speeches emphasised government policies for dissemination in the countryside and pressured judges to carefully scrutinise and report on local justice.[14] As J. S. Cockburn explains, Tudor and Stuart domestic policy required 'reliable media for conveying to provincial agencies the content and implications of relevant legislation and for ensuring that the programmes therein expressed were fully and persistently implemented'. For the period that he studies (1558 to 1714), Cockburn claims that 'there can be little doubt that this function was most regularly and successfully discharged by the judges of Assize'.[15]

In a letter of advice to James's favourite, the Duke of Buckingham, Francis Bacon explained the importance of choosing 'the learnedest of the profession ... the prudentest and discreetest' men to be judges, 'because so great a part of the Civil Government lies upon their charge'.[16] This was most obviously and publicly the case with Assize judges, 'the visitors for tooe times in the yeare, not for Justice alone, but for the peaceable gouernement of the Cuntrye, put in greate truste by his Majestie'.[17] Time and again in Star Chamber charges, the Lord Keeper or sovereign emphasised the importance of the Assize judges' attention to the administration of the counties. In his 1601 charge, Thomas Egerton goes so far as to present the legal work of the court as secondary to the work of governing. Her Majesty, he explained, 'hath chosen you to be Justices [of Assize] for your wisdom and integrity ... not onely to try a *Nisi prius* [a civil suit], or decide some petty Cause, but with special care and diligent observance, to look into the disorders of your Circuits.' The Queen thus 'would have you spend more time in understanding the faults and grievances in every of your Circuits'.[18] In his 1616 oration, James reiterated publicly his 'ordinary charge' that 'I use to deliver to the Judges before my Councell, when they goe their

Circuits': 'Remember that when you goe your Circuits, you goe not onely to punish and prevent offences, but you are to take care for the good government in generall of the parts where you travell, as well as to doe Justice in particular betwixt party and party, in causes criminall and civill.'[19] 'The diligence of magistrates and other local officials', writes Cockburn, 'together with a careful manipulation of the religious climate form the core of most [. . .] circuit charges'.[20] Within these late Elizabethan and Jacobean speeches the instructions are already conventional, suggesting that the Assize judge's administrative responsibilities to monitor and reform local justice had become entrenched functions of the office and important mechanisms for social maintenance.

The judges executed these responsibilities by facilitating a temporary, nationwide information highway along which the Privy Council's programme for the country was disseminated and court officials gathered intelligence on various aspects and activities of local community life.[21] In charges to grand juries at the beginning of their sessions, the judges presented national policy updates to a public audience and reminded local officeholders of their obligations. While the impanelled men were directly addressed, it was made clear that judges' speeches were intended to be heard by a much wider audience. Before the Norwich Assizes of August 1606, for instance, Edward Coke explained, 'though my speech shall principally be directed to you of the Jury which are sworn, yet . . . I hope that all my words shall extend unto the general good of all these here present; unto whom they are spoken.'[22] Addressing the jury at the York Lent Assizes of 1620, 'selected out of all freeholders of this shyre to beare a princypall part in the publick service', Serjeant John Davis explained that 'when I speake to yow I conceave that I speake to the whole countye . . . for yow represent the whole bodye of this whole countye'.[23] At the same time that they were responsible for disseminating vital public information through these speeches, Assize judges were also expected to perform local intelligence-gathering. In his 1617 Star Chamber charge, Francis Bacon reminded the judges

> that besides your ordinary administration of justice, you do carry the two glasses or mirrors of the state; for it is your duty, in these your visitations, to represent to the people the graces and care of the king; and again, upon your return, to present to the king the distastes and griefs of the people.[24]

The Lord Keeper or sovereign regularly reminded Assize judges of their duty to provide their first-hand report of conditions on the circuits. As the 'best intelligencers of the true state of the Kingdom', Bacon argued that Assize judges were 'the surest means to prevent or remove all growing mischiefs within the body of the Realm'.[25]

The Lord Keeper, Elizabeth and James repeatedly stressed that Assize judges were to gather information and report on JPs in particular. The JPs were 'the Kings eyes and eares in the countrey'. If they did not exercise 'their helping hands' the kingdom 'must needes suffer'. Since Assize judges were responsible for recommending local gentry for the Commission of the Peace, they were also made responsible for culling bad justices from the list. James's comments in his 1616 charge explain the process:

> The Chancellour under me, makes Justices, and puts them out; but neither I, nor he can tell what they are: Therefore wee must bee informed by you Judges, who can onely tell, who doe well, and who doe ill; without which, how can the good be cherished and maintained, and the rest put out?[26]

In the 1595 charge, the Queen complained through the Lord Keeper and the Treasurer that 'the number of Justices of the peace are growne allmoste infinite, to the hinderaunce of Justice', 'that there are more Justicers then Justice' and that

> she would not have any to be in Commission of the Peace to serve her ... that are unlearned & negligente in there places, & that the Justices of Assise showld looke narrowly unto this, & they to remoove those that in discrecyon they thoughte not meete for the place.

The following year the charge was more precise: 'the Justices of Assise [are] to looke very strictly to all these articles [of the JPs' responsibilities], & to be instructed who hathe bene forwarde in the reforminge hereof, & by particular instance what & how it is done ... & to punishe where it is not done.' In successive speeches through the end of the sixteenth century, the Queen charged Assize judges 'especially to regard the negligence of some Justices of the Peace, and the forwardness of others, and to punish the one and to recompense the other, and to make report of this to her Majesty'. They were 'to remove from the bench those that are drones and not bees, with disgrace and punishment; and the diligent and industrious to notify to the Queen to encourage them'.[27] In a plainer style, James was equally insistent that the judges take account of the JPs: 'You have charges to give to Justices of peace, that they doe their dueties when you are absent, aswell as present: Take an accompt of them, and report their service to me at your returne.'[28]

A good Assize judge had to be independent in his investigation of the quality of JPs and the state of local justice. He was cautioned to rely on his own observation of local gentry and officeholders rather than on the advice or word of others. In his 1608 charge, Egerton addressed the issue of JP selection by explaining that 'he [the Chancellor] puts in few into Commission but upon Commendacyon from the lordes or Judges, whoe showlde Certifye upon knowledge, & not informacyon'.[29] In discussing the judge's responsibility for general intelligence-gathering, Francis Bacon would similarly distinguish between first-hand 'knowledge' and unreliable local 'informacyon'. The king, he explains, 'ought to be informed of any thing amiss in the state of his countries from the observations and relations of the judges, that indeed know the pulse of the country, rather than from discourse'.[30] The problem with relying on 'information' or 'discourse' from the local community was the biased nature of its source. 'Justice of the Peace' was a coveted title that enabled gentry or magnates to wield social, political and even economic influence. Many vied for the position without having any intention of conscientiously fulfilling its mundane and potentially quite burdensome duties.[31] Because of personal affinities and self-interest local recommendations for the office could not be taken at face value, and Assize judges were criticised for crediting them.[32] Instead, the reports and recommendations of the judges, as well as their work on the bench, were supposed to reflect an unbiased observation of county life and local justice.[33] At one and the same time, then, they were responsible for injecting neutrality into legal proceedings and the arbitration of local affairs *and* gaining an intimate understanding of the local context to report back to the heads of state.

The Assize judge was thus a prominent legal-political representative of central government who was officially responsible for monitoring and reforming the execution of local justice and who presided over a court with an expansive jurisdiction. While Egerton may have subordinated the hearing of 'petty Causes' to the largely out-of-court work of administrative review, the judges' supervision of local society was possible in part because their trials drew the attention of the community. The theatrics of the Assize sessions as well as the court's efficient (and therefore economic) process were strong attractions.[34] The stateliness of the judges' entrances into towns, the extensive display of both royal authority and the upper echelons of local society, the judges' grand jury charges and the trial of officers and others all produced a powerful spectacle for public consumption. As Cynthia Herrup writes, 'No other local courts (aside from the special jurisdiction of the Cinque ports) could invoke capital punishment; no other tribunals handled cases so cheaply, conveniently or quickly; no other forums were so communal in their involvement of local residents and in their determination to make decisions a public spectacle.'[35] The same coupling of local surveillance and legal spectacle that was orchestrated by the Assize judge is easily observed in Shakespeare's *Measure for Measure*, in which Duke

Vincentio secretly surveys the operations of the Viennese justice system and then exposes its corrupt elements in trial. Before moving on to a detailed reading of the play, however, the next section outlines more closely the features of the historical spectacle and the impact of the itinerant court on local life and officeholders.

The Cycle and Spectacle of the Assizes

The cycle of the Assizes can be divided into four stages that each had a shaping influence on community life: the judges' formal entrance into counties, accompanied by all the pomp that the local elite could muster; the process of the trials themselves; the judges' abrupt departure; and the invisible part of the cycle in which local magistrates struggled to fill the legal-political vacuum left in the sessions' wake. The first two stages drew a crowd and involved many local participants. A large part of the Assizes' effectiveness as a vehicle for legal reform was due to the spectacle of its procession and trials that attracted both the interest and awe of the region. This cycle generated and reflected an expansive early modern conception of justice in practice that embraced formal legal procedure as well as the public exposure and shaming of offenders and officers. While this expansive definition of justice increased the number of forms that punishment and reparation could take, it also put many more demands on the magistrate than the mere execution of the letter of the law. The difficulties of local governance, of successfully putting law and policy into local practice, thus also surface in any account of the Assizes. The ethics and operations of local justice that are depicted below will ultimately help us reimagine the ethical import of the actions of legal representatives in Shakespeare's fictional Vienna. Most importantly, they provide a vivid contrast with the administration of the deputy Angelo, who reductively equates justice with the letter of the law.

The formal Star Chamber charge discussed above was followed by ceremonial grandeur as the judges were welcomed into the counties where their temporary seats of justice were established. As Cockburn writes, 'there is much to suggest that for rural society and average litigant alike Assizes assumed the awful remoteness of a divine visitation'.[36] The anonymous late seventeenth-century manual, *The Office of the Clerk of Assize*, describes the extensive formalities of the judges' welcome:

> When the Judges set forth for that County, the Sheriff sends his Bailiff to the edge of the County, to bring them the best way to that place where the Assize for that County is to be held; and before they come thither, the Sheriff

attended with his Under-Sheriff, and Bailiffs, with their white Staves and his Livery-men with their Holdberds in their hands, and accompanied with the chief of the Gentry of the County do wait upon the Judges at the usual place, and conduct them from thence to their Lodgings at the Town where the Assizes be appointed to be held.

When the Judges have reposed themselves at their Lodgings; and the Gentry have paid their respects to them, and they have put on their Robes; then the Sheriff covered, with this white Staff in his hand, attended by his Under-Sheriff bare-headed, and his Bailiffs, uncovered, with their white Staves in their hands, and his Livery-men, uncovered, with their Holdberds in their hands, two by two on foot, wait on the Judges from their Lodgings to Church, where the Minister of the Parish reads Prayers, and the Sheriff's Chaplain gives them a Sermon; and when that is done, the Sheriff waits on them in the same manner from Church to the usual place appointed for holding the Assizes, or General Gaol-delivery for that County.[37]

This extended, grand procession, involving many of the county's elite, was a biannual event through most of the early modern period and into the nineteenth century.[38]

The Assize sermon, briefly mentioned in the quotation above, has attracted an increasing amount of attention from historians in recent years. In a survey of 200 examples, Barbara Shapiro explains that the occasion of these sermons 'naturally generated expressions of uneasiness about the administration of justice' and that 'advice and criticism' were 'typical features'.[39] In 'A Sword of Maintenance', a sermon preached 'before the Right Worshipfull the Judges of Assise, and gentlemen, assembled at Hertford, the 13 of July 1599 for the execution of Justice', William Westerman begins with the biblical passage, 'Hate the evill, and love the good, and establish Judgement in the gate.' By 'Judgement in the gate' we are to understand that '*Judgement is a common good*', and that it should therefore 'be practised in a publike place of free resort, *In the gate*'. He explains that 'Judges & Rulers sate openly in a common place to heare and determine all matters' so that 'justice might gloriously shine ... to the chearing up of all faithfull hearts, and open shame and ignoraminie of evil workes.' All people were thereby provided 'free accesse [to justice] without danger or disturbance by any locall priviledges'. The preacher emphasises that this public justice must also be performed regularly: 'It is not onelye some single action which the Lorde urgeth, but a continuall exercise and practise of Judgement. It is not enough to doe some things justlie, at some times, and upon some occasions.' The magistrate therefore requires 'a readie hand to practice: not resting in contemplation, but proceeding to such action as the place and vocation of every man exhorteth him unto for the maintenance of judgement at the gate'.[40] Westerman's interpretation of the Biblical text is infused with the structure and strategies of the Assize trials. It reiterates themes that appear in the Star Chamber charges as well as the Assize judges' charges to grand juries that are discussed below.

Importantly, as Shapiro explains, the discourse in these sermons on 'the divine authority and obligations of those that exercised governmental offices' was applied to 'judges and magistrates as well as kings'. She reports that many of the preachers 'referred to all these offices interchangeably, sometimes in the same sentence. Magistrates had their authority from God and were called Gods; magistrates and judges were God's deputies in the dispensation of justice. Several sermons referred to kings and magistrates as God's vicegerents.'[41] Far from voicing a strident common-law ideology, then, when Edward Coke claimed in his 1606 Norfolk Assize speech 'that kings, rulers, judges and magistrates are "Gods on earth"', he was instead merely '[e]choing such sermons'.[42] The godlike responsibility for justice linked the monarch to the magistracy rather than distinguishing him or her from it. Shapiro's evidence from the Assize sermons invites a re-evaluation of the tradition of *Measure for Measure* criticism that reads the Duke as a figure for King James, and that focuses on the unique representational and ideological questions that arise from the monarch's singularity within the legal-political hierarchy. The comparison that I develop below, between the Duke and the Assize judge, is the result instead of attending to the more inclusive connotations of the language and representations of magistracy that implicate all the play's officers in the problems of legal office and reform. The outcome is an admittedly more modest claim about Vincentio's reformation of local justice rather than his 'refound[ing] of the state'.[43]

Once in court and before the local assembly, the Assize judges delivered the charge to the grand jury that 'echoed and embellished' the Lord Keeper's Star Chamber address.[44] With the backing of their superior authority and learning, the judges encouraged juries to bring the clandestine offences of local officeholders to light despite personal associations or fears of reprisal.[45] In his Norwich speech, Coke appealed to the members of the grand jury to present those men who have abused their position. He 'point[ed] out ... some severall officers, whose actions not beeing sufficiently looked into, many abuses are committed, which passe unpunished.' These officers included 'Excheaters', the 'Clarke of the Market', the 'Purueyor' and the 'Salt-peter man'. No officer was too lowly for the court's notice: '[a]ny such fellow, if you can meete withall, let his misdemenor be presented, that he may be taught better to understand his office: For by their abuse the countrey is oftentimes troubled.' These minor officers were known for swindling money and resources out of the public through the misrepresentation of the rights conveyed in their quite limited commissions. Offending officeholders were to be made a particular example at the Assizes where they could be accused and tried under the auspices of central authority and where local society could witness it all:

> You of the Jurie therefore for the good of your selves and yours, carefully looke to the proceedings [of officers] and such abuse as you shall find therein, let it be presented. And such as shall bee found offendors, they shall know, that we have lawes to punish them. For proofe whereof, I would you could find out some, of whom there might be made an example.[46]

The Assizes were an especially apt venue for public shaming since they put on display neighbours before neighbours, subordinates before superiors, and superiors before subordinates. Anthony Fletcher recounts the case of Henry Winston, who was prosecuted in the court of Star Chamber in 1602 by a fellow JP and faced punishment at his home Assizes. Charged with beating a bailiff for arresting one of his servants and alleged to have shown unwarranted mercy to offenders who were also his dependents, Winston 'pleaded with Sir Robert Cecil for remittance of the punishment of public confession of his offence at Gloucester Assizes. "I desire rather to remain in prison", he wrote, "than to receive open disgrace in my country".'[47] In many cases, concerning officers or other kinds of offenders, the 'open disgrace' of formal accusation was punishment enough. As Bernard William McLane explains, '[l]ocal opinion may have held that the process of being publicly prosecuted was an unambiguous means of putting certain individuals on notice that they had seriously, but not fatally, violated accepted standards of conduct and should mend their ways.'[48] Assize justice was thus a function of public enquiry, accusation and exposure as much as, or more than, conviction (which might or might not occur, which might or might not involve punishment proportionate to the offence).

The judges' charges to grand juries focused not only on the presentment of men with local power, but also on the communal process by which their offences were brought to light. While the Star Chamber charges outlined the Assize judge's responsibility for local surveillance, John Davis explained to the assembly at the York Assizes that the judge's 'private knowledg' could only be brought to light and acted upon through the 'publick inquisicyon and presentment' of the grand jury and the 'tryall' of the petty jury. He compares this process of the 'publick justice of England' to God's own execution of justice against Sodom and Gomorrah:

> wee that are judges cannot proceed agaynst offenders without the service and ministrye of yow that are jurors, without your inquisicyon and presentment

noe malefactor can be brought to his aunswer. And herein the publick justice of England doth observe the lyke course as the divine justice did in proceeding agaynst those sinfull cyttyes, for though there sinns were crying sinnes and most notoryous to the worlde, and most perfectlye knowne to God himselfe ... yet was the Divine Majesty please to make an enquirye thereof before he would give anye judgment agaynst them ... Not that God was ignorant of theyre most secret offences, but for that it was his most dyvine pleasure to give an example or precident to the judges of the earth how they should proceede in causes brought before them, not grounding theyre judgements upon their own private knowledg but upon solemne and publick inquisicyon and tryall.[49]

In the Assizes, the concentration was overwhelmingly on the process of bringing offences to light – through judicial and community effort. Judicial knowledge had to be coupled with a public display that legitimised the legal process and shamed offenders (suspected or convicted).[50] In his grand jury charge, Davis emphasised the shared responsibility of bringing offences to light as well as the shared benefit. Public justice is in the service of the public good: entire cities are scourged in his Biblical example. By bringing to light the offences of officeholders in particular, the entire common weal benefits.

The spectacle of the Assizes came to a conclusion with the judges' hasty retreat after only two to three days in the county. Their exit presented a stark contrast with the ceremonial grandeur of their entrance. '[T]he fact that the judges arrived, presided, and then immediately departed lent an air of mystery and finality to the Assizes', writes Herrup. The court temporarily constrained tensions between neighbours and between local and central interests within highly formal public ceremony and legal process before disappearing into 'airy nothing'. '[Francis] Bacon's description of the circuits as "rivers in Paradise" is particularly apt', Herrup continues: '[l]ike rivers they visited many areas, but also like rivers they ran through the kingdom, permanently impermanent, leaving a silt of orders and commands and moving on before the deposit had fully settled.' The legal-political vacuum they left in their wake had to be filled by the efforts of (hopefully) conscientious and competent JPs. With neither the expertise nor the authority of the Westminster judges, the local JPs were responsible for seeing that the legal-political policies introduced during the Assizes reverberated effectively throughout the community. 'The Assizes were like any other grand visitation; their authority was momentous and their grandeur was awesome, but their real power rested ultimately on far less eminent officials than the judges.'[51]

The Assize judges' local legal authority was effectively terminated at the end of their sessions. The JPs, on the other hand, were magistrates all year round, with significant duties outside their own court, the Quarter sessions. They were responsible for arbitrating among neighbours and factions, forestalling suits or cases at law, investigating crime, and preventing unlawful assemblies and riots whenever possible. As Sharpe explains, a JP could 'bind over the unruly to be of good behaviour; he was to stop affrays . . . and enquire into apprenticeship disputes and differences between master and servant; he could also take steps to suppress vagabonds, rogues, nightwalkers, nocturnal hunters in masks, and players of unlawful games.'[52] While the Assizes were responsible for the oversight of JPs, the JPs were responsible for the oversight of the county itself on a day-to-day basis. While he was humbly 'to inform and to listen' during the Assizes, 'for most of the year and in most of the county, the [JP] could claim to be the key to justice – he arbitrated, licensed, bonded, tried, and punished'. '[A]ccessible' and 'highly visible', the good JP cultivated an extensive knowledge of local activities and people that helped him keep tabs on the region. Yet his intimate involvement in and knowledge of the community meant that he was, as the central government feared, far from neutral on the topics of local politics and economic interests. 'The Privy Council', writes Herrup, 'doubted the ability of local justices to reach dispassionate, rational decisions.'[53] The Assize judges were supposed to counterbalance the influence of self-interest in local justice.

Central authorities were obsessively concerned with the quality of the justices of the peace; however, the rigorous pursuit of statutory offences by an energetic and vigilant JP could do more to disrupt social harmony than to consolidate it. Keith Wrightson explains, 'the very process of definition and statutory regulation which was involved in the legislative initiative might ultimately threaten to create new problems of order and obedience at the point at which precise national legislation came into contact with less defined local custom.'[54] Intended to reform and maintain local order and justice and to preserve its consonance with the expectations of central government, the Assizes' instructions to JPs could also foment disorder and alienate locals (including magistrates) unprepared, unable or unwilling to conform to the directives. In Francis Bacon's words, 'it is not possible to find a remedy for any mischief in the commonwealth, but it will beget some new mischief.'[55] In the case of the statute form that Bacon was analysing, provisos mitigated the potential harm of new legislation. In the case of the execution of local justice, a great deal of legal-political and interpersonal savvy was needed to effectively perform the uncomfortable task of imposing national policy and standards upon local behaviour. In *Measure for Measure*, Angelo's attention to nothing but the execution of the strict letter of the law should by now appear to be an entirely inadequate understanding of his responsibilities as a magistrate.

The major features of the Assize system – the stages of its cyclical structure, the aspects of legal spectacle, the alternating surveillance and exposure of local officeholders, the expectation that justice and legal process transformed private into public knowledge, the tensions between central and local authorities, between Assize judges and JPs, and between the rule of law and its execution – all inform the plot and the characterisation of legal officers in *Measure for Measure*. The play begins where the Assizes ended, with the evacuation of central authority and the creation of a legal-political vacuum that must be filled by subordinate officeholders, guided by rhetorical reminders of their duties and commissioned with new policies for local implementation. What opens in the opening scene is the local officer's dilemma over the proper way of executing his duties or enforcing policy and law, a problem that unavoidably engages individual judgement. The relationship between the law and its execution is thus also the measure of a legal officer. The following close reading examines Shakespeare's magistrates' various approaches to the administration of the law against the historical operations and expectations of the Assizes and local justice. In the analyses below, I distinguish between Angelo, Escalus, the Provost, and the Duke, based on the form and extent of each officer's intervention in local justice. I argue that Shakespeare evokes the ideal of the proactive JP (discussed in the Lord Keeper's parliamentary orations, Star Chamber and grand jury charges, and Assize sermons) against which we can judge the ethics and efficacy of his officers. While Angelo represents a passive judicial philosophy, Escalus's judicial efforts illustrate both the necessity and difficulty of actively bringing offences to light. The Provost and the Duke, meanwhile, exemplify a proactive justice that balances the letter of the law against social realities, preserving the certainty and force of the law as well as human life. Instead of relying on the unreliable reformative power of punishment or mercy, they employ a particularised knowledge of local circumstances to forcibly redirect offenders' energies into lawful activities and lifestyles.

From Commission to Execution: The Opening of *Measure for Measure*

Debora Shuger writes that '[t]he political theme dominates from the outset' of *Measure for Measure*, 'its importance signalled by the opening line of the Duke's first speech: "Of government the properties to unfold"'. From the first line, she situates the play within the political world of the new Stuart court, describing the tragicomedy as 'a sustained meditation on … the political moment of James's accession'.[56] Many critics have read the play this way: the Duke of Vienna is a figure for James and therefore the play is heavily invested in questions of sovereignty and political theology.[57] Yet neither James nor any English sovereign had much to do directly with governing at the ground level, the level that is the overwhelming focus not only of the opening scene but of the entire play. Instead, governance was the work of local legal officers who were subjected to intermittent oversight by Assize judges. By reorganising local authority in Vienna before a hurried retreat, Duke Vincentio resembles an Assize judge, who was responsible for the revision of the Commission of the Peace and the admonishment of those in charge of local order. His verbal charges to his deputies echo those in which Assize judges instructed JPs to 'doe their dueties when [the judges] are absent'.[58] When reading his opening lines, I argue that it is more productive to consider *to whom* the Duke speaks than his own character or status. He is speaking to one of two deputies, Escalus, who will, among other things, handle an inept constable and cases of bawdry and prostitution:

> Of government the properties to unfold
> Would seem in me to affect speech and discourse,
> Since I am put to know that your own science
> Exceeds in that the lists of all advice
> My strength can give you. Then no more remains
> But that, to your sufficiency, as your worth is able,
> And let them work. The nature of our people,
> Our city's institutions, and the terms
> For common justice, you're as pregnant in
> As art and practice hath enriched any
> That we remember. There is our commission
> From which we would not have you warp.[59]

While the Duke explains that a rehearsal of the traditional 'properties' of 'government' is unnecessary, given Escalus's experience, by beginning with a rhetorically disingenuous dismissal of the formality he indicates that such comments were routine under such circumstances. What he offers is a brief, courteous lecture on the decorum or prudence that should shape judicial discretion in the administration of the law. If you read past the first line, you discover that the Duke expects his subordinate to wed personal merit or ability ('sufficiency') with his sociopolitical status ('worth'), and to combine learning (theory or 'science' and a knowledge of 'The [particular] nature of our people, / Our city's institutions, and the terms / For common justice') with practical skills and wisdom honed through experience ('art and practice'). The speech reflects the balancing act that local justices had to perform on a daily basis. It is justifiably complicated because it draws our attention to the complications of governance: this is the theme that dominates from the outset of the play.

The combination of qualities that the Duke enumerates, in fact, resembles that found within 'artificial reason', the mode of professional deliberation that was considered unique to those trained in the common law. In *The English Lawyer*, John Doddridge explains:

> the Law ... is called reason; not for that every man can comprehend the same; but it is artificiall reason; the reason of such, as by their wisedome, learning, and long experiences are skilfull in the affaires of men, and know what is fit and convenient to bee held and observed for the appeasing of controversies and debates among men, still having an eye and due regard of justice, and a consideration of the commonwealth wherein they live . . .[60]

The resemblance between the Duke's opening speech and Doddridge's treatise suggests that Escalus is being deliberately characterised in the opening scene of the play as a legal authority representing legal professionalism, and not as a weak and ineffective magistrate who is simply a foil for Angelo's legal rigour. As it emerges in the opening scene, moreover, the distinction between Escalus and Angelo maps easily onto the types of JP that were organised through the Commission of the Peace. Revised for each Assize session, the Commission included the Westminster judges' names at the top of the list of justices, giving them the status of highest local authorities while they held their sessions.[61] Country gentlemen were then named according to their social status and/or legal expertise. Some JPs were specifically included in a subcategory called the 'quorum'. In his popular manual for JPs, the *Eirenarcha*, William Lambarde explains that 'These of the *Quorum*, were ... chosen, specially for their learning in the lawes of the Realme.'[62] The quorum formed a distinct group within the Commission; its members were not necessarily the most senior magistrates. Thus two potentially competing forms of authority, local status and legal expertise, complicated the organisation and working relationships of officeholders. Through the Duke's opening speeches, the deputies are introduced as representatives of these two basic types of JP: Escalus is the more experienced and professional magistrate, while Angelo is given a higher rank. Tellingly, when asked about Angelo's ability to substitute for the Duke, Escalus refers to his fellow deputy's social status rather than legal knowledge: 'If any in Vienna be of worth / To undergo such ample grace and honour, / It is Lord Angelo' (1.1. 22–4). The historical structure of the Commission of the Peace removes some of the mystery, then, behind the Duke's explanation to Angelo that, 'Old Escalus, / Though first in question, is thy secondary' (1.1.45–6).

While the Duke's instructions to Escalus outline the complex responsibilities and decorum of local governing, his instructions to Angelo evoke a very different branch of the discourse on Justices of the Peace. To Angelo he gives a lecture on the necessity of putting virtue into action that uses the same torch metaphor for the administration of the law that appears in Elizabethan Lord Keepers' parliamentary orations: 'lawes without execucion be as a torche unlighted or body without a soule. Therfore looke well to th'executinge' (*PPE* 1:11–12). In the Duke of Vienna's words:

> . . . Thyself and thy belongings
> Are not thine own so proper as to waste
> Thyself upon thy virtues, they on thee.
> Heaven doth with us as we with torches do,
> Not light them for themselves. For if our virtues
> Did not go forth of us, 'twere all alike
> As if we had them not.

> (1.1.29–35)

This warning expresses the Aristotelian idea of justice as virtuous action toward our neighbours that was discussed in Chapter 3. In his 1616 Star Chamber charge, King James likewise explained to Assize judges and JPs, 'To bee righteous, is to a mans selfe: To bee just, is towards others.'[63] The Duke's emphasis on this principle is a response to Angelo's public reputation, the 'character in thy life / That to th'observer doth thy history / Fully unfold' (1.1.27–9). In a later scene with Friar Thomas, he describes his deputy as 'A man of stricture and firm abstinence' (1.3.12). Here in 1.1, the Duke's advice suggests that this quality of 'firm abstinence' conflicts with the duty to put virtue in action or with the extensive public immersion required of a JP. His comments refract widespread concerns over legal officers' inactivity that were voiced in Star Chamber charges, grand jury charges, Assize sermons and in the parliamentary speeches examined in the Introduction.[64] Thomas Egerton, for instance, cited 'the number of newe & younge knightes' who sought a place in the Commission of the Peace only to 'stande there lyke an Idoll to be gazed upon, & doe nothinge'.[65] James described bad justices as those who 'thinke it is enough to contemplate Justice, when as *Virtus in actione consistit*: contemplative Justice is no justice, and contemplative Justices are fit to be put out.'[66] Justices were suspected, moreover, of covering negligence with the guise of virtue: JPs 'doe dayly . . . cloke these their faultes with the title of quietnes', Nicholas Bacon complained, 'where in very deed they seeke only ease, profitt and pleasure to them selves, and that to be sustayned and borne by other men's cares and labours as drones doe among bees' (*PPE* 1: 50). The Duke's instructions to his primary deputy thus immediately remind the theatre audience of the historical criteria for evaluating the conduct of JPs. From the play's opening scene abstinence is not only potentially hypocritical (firm abstinence-*cum*-negligence), but it is also juxtaposed with a basic principle of local or community justice. Justice required local legal-political representatives to be agents or actors, not idols.

By reading the opening scene through the lens of the Assizes and the Commission of the Peace, we can see how the Duke's actions and his subordinates' reactions refract the process and the problems of early modern legal delegation and law enforcement. The Duke's rushed and unceremonious departure presents a version of the historical scene in which the Assize judges moved on from one locality to the next. His 'haste from hence is of so quick condition / That it prefers itself, and leaves unquestioned / Matters of needful value' (1.1.53–5). The result is that his brief remarks in 1.1 fall short of adequately informing and reforming the local officeholders, who are left pondering the exact nature of their responsibilities. While critics and modern audiences or readers have speculated about the Duke's mysterious motives for leaving, his substitutes find nothing about his behaviour remarkable. Instead, they ponder the correct way in which to put the verbal charges and written commissions into local practice. Escalus immediately appeals to his new superior for guidance:

> I shall desire you, sir, to give me leave
> To have free speech with you, and it concerns me
> To look into the bottom of my place.
> A power I have, but of what strength and nature
> I am not yet instructed.
>
> (1.1.76–80)

Angelo, who is to be the principal authority in Vienna in the Duke's absence, responds to his associate's request for a tête-à-tête by affirming that he is equally nonplussed: ''Tis so with me' (1.1.81). So ends the scene. Inciting more questions than answers through his instructions and departure and subsequently, in disguise, overseeing the impact of his policy change in Vienna, the Duke follows in the footsteps of the Assize judges, who likewise held the same potential to disrupt local justice and who were also responsible for monitoring and reforming officers through practices of information-gathering that would result in public exposure.

In order to secretly monitor the effects of this shake-up of local governance, the Duke adopts the disguise of a friar through which he can 'Visit both prince and people' (1.3.45).[67] At the same time that power changes hands, then, a closer scrutiny of the execution of justice is also instituted. Though his new deputy asks for 'more test made of my metal' (1.1.48) before he takes his commission, the Duke's scheme transforms the exercise of local authority into a continual test of the magistrate's character and judgement. It is a test, moreover, that is also overseen by an audience who witnesses first-hand more secret 'passes' than even the Duke himself (5.1.372). When the Duke adopts the role of spectator, the audience member or reader is pulled into a communal surveillance project and reminded of his or her responsibilities in a participatory justice system that necessitated the conscientious noting and reporting of suspicious or illicit conduct, even or especially in officers. The responsibility for the surveillance of local officeholders is shuttled between Duke and audience just as it was between Assize judge and local community during the judge's charge to the grand jury, through which the middling and upper ranks of society were reminded of their obligation to detect and present offenders.

In the opening verbal charges of 1.1 and the account of his scheme in 1.3, the Duke steers our attention toward the evaluation of his substitutes and only secondarily to the state of crime in Vienna. Victoria Hayne argues that this focus of the Duke's distinguishes his project within the dramatic tradition of disguised ruler:

> Like his precursors, the disguised Duke . . . has a political and social quest, but, unlike them, his is a very specific one: he goes into disguise not to correct social abuses himself but to 'behold [Angelo's] sway', to find out 'what our seemers be' when they have power 'to enforce or qualify the laws'.[68]

The first officeholder to be reformed in the play, however, is the Duke himself. His scheme, which requires a new level of immersion in his city, reforms his own self-confessed failures at governance. His surveillance activities thus simultaneously turn inward and outward. If Duke Vincentio has, as Escalus claims, 'contended especially to know himself' (3.1.463–4), the outcome of this contemplative activity is finally the reform of justice and the local order, marking his divergence from the contemplative and negligent justices described above. While the disguised ruler may be 'utterly unmimetic of anything outside the theater', as Hayne maintains, the Duke's hidden presence nevertheless facilitates the same difficult negotiation that was demanded of Assize judges who were supposed to gather first-hand knowledge of order in the counties while maintaining a neutrality in the reformation of local justice.[69]

Through his disguise as Friar Lodowick, he manages to comingle intimately with Viennese society while maintaining a critical, and frequently moralistic, stance on all that he observes.

Vienna's Justices

The second scene to feature Angelo and Escalus picks up right where 1.1 leaves off. Act 2 opens with the two officers debating the correct execution of the law. In the course of defending his decision to behead Claudio for fornication, Angelo describes the process of law as essentially passive, a perspective that is in direct contradiction with early modern English ideas about the JP's role as the local leader of a communal, participatory justice system. According to Angelo, instead of actively searching out offences, justices must wait until offences reveal themselves. His judicial aloofness or legal abstinence, hinted at in Act 1 and developed over Act 2, derives from an idiosyncratic philosophy through which the law seeks only what is already found:

> The jury passing on the prisoner's life
> May in the sworn twelve have a thief or two
> Guiltier than him they try. What's open made to justice,
> That justice seizes. What knows the laws
> That thieves do pass on thieves? 'Tis very pregnant,
> The jewel that we find, we stoop and take't,
> Because we see it; but what we do not see
> We tread upon, and never think of it.
>
> (2.1.19–26)

Angelo is undeniably correct that only 'What's open made to justice, / That justice seizes.' He misunderstands or ignores, however, the responsibility this creates for the magistrate to actively investigate cases within his region and to make suspicious conduct visible to the law by representing it in the terms and categories of legal offences. In Nicholas Bacon's words, the JP must 'become a diligent searcher out, follower and corrector of felons, murderers, and such like common enemyes to the common wealthe' (*PPE* 1: 50). Angelo's analogy of the found jewel suppresses not only the magistrate's work, but the network of conscientious individuals involved in the extensive effort to bring offences to light, from the beginnings of cases to their conclusions, and troublingly implies that justice instead relies on chance. That the law can only act upon what is brought within its gaze is, in fact, the greatest case that could be made for the officer's proactive efforts on the law's behalf and for the monitoring of the quality of the law's administration.

Considering Angelo's passive understanding of legal administration, it is unsurprising that we see him *do* very little, despite the Duke's admonition to put virtue into action. Instead, the deputy becomes an 'Idoll to be gazed upon', to use Egerton's words, or a 'looming presence', to use Pamela K. Jensen's.[70] Confronted with the constable Elbow and his case against Pompey (the suspected bawd) and Master Froth (the suspected john), Angelo exits the scene apparently out of boredom, leaving Escalus to sort out a convoluted hearing that 'will last out a night in Russia / When nights are longest there' (2.1.123–4). (Indeed, Angelo's departure here is much more disturbing than the Duke's initial exit that has attracted far greater critical attention.) When the Duke makes the extraordinary gesture of allowing Angelo to judge his own cause in the final scene, it is Escalus instead who takes the lead in questioning plaintiff and witnesses. Both the Duke (in disguise) and Escalus manage to visit the prison for humane reasons, while Angelo is the only character who never makes an appearance there. Both Escalus and the Provost have a wide knowledge of community members, while Angelo seems to be the only character unaware that Claudio has a sister. Angelo's virtue 'goes forth' while he personally stays behind. His strict adherence to the letter of the law – which radically reduces the amount of gray area in legal interpretation and saves the deputy the trouble of considering the particular mitigating circumstances of any case – gains him a 'name' or reputation, as Claudio complains, without the deputy ever having to steep himself in local affairs (1.2.146–60). In his vision and delegation of judicial labour, Angelo invites the kind of criticism found in Nicholas Bacon's closing remarks to parliament, in which the Lord Keeper complained of negligent justices who 'cannot endure to have their eares troubled with hearinge of controversies of their neighbours for the good appeasinge of the same'. These men are 'sustayned and borne by other men's cares and labours as drones doe among bees' (*PPE* 1: 50).

While Angelo's speech at the opening of 2.1 emphasises readily apparent, gleaming facts as the proper object of the law, the Elbow and Pompey episode that immediately follows in the same scene illustrates the great difficulty of bringing offences to light in a legally recognisable form and the degree to which justice depended not only on local officeholders' initiative but on their oversight and reformation. Through the constable's inept execution of the law, very little – nothing actionable – of Pompey's bawdry is proven, even though it is apparent from every other angle. Escalus repeatedly attempts to get Elbow to defend his accusations with concrete evidence. He enquires, 'How know you that' (2.1.63) and 'How dost thou know that, constable?' (2.1.71). But Elbow's malapropism-filled account comes short of describing a chargeable offence. When Angelo exits the scene, he leaves his secondary with the hope that 'you'll find good cause to whip them all' (2.1.126). Escalus is barred from proceeding further, however, because of the constable's incompetence. The bawd remains only suspected. 'Truly, officer', Escalus tells Elbow, 'because [Pompey] hath some offences in him that thou wouldst discover if thou couldst, let him continue in his courses till thou know'st what they are' (2.1.170–2). The deputy's decision prompts another misconstruction from the constable, who tells Pompey, 'Thou art to continue now, thou varlet, thou art to continue', as if this were a punishment (2.1.174–5). The verbal misunderstanding pointedly associates the failure of the legal process (the continuance of a flagrant offender) with the officeholder's stupidity. With a character like Elbow playing a pivotal role in bringing offences to light, the only hope for justice in Vienna is that crime will, through its continuance, accidentally manifest itself in a legally recognisable form – that it will suddenly appear like a found jewel. Although Pompey is left to his own devices by the end of this episode, the constable is not. The scene comes to a close by shifting attention from the reform of the suspect to the reform of local justice.

While the Duke takes the principle of being 'a diligent searcher out' to a comical extreme through his undercover operation, Escalus's more modest judicial methods are put on display in this hearing. In criticism, Escalus has commonly been implicated in the lax, ineffective justice that the Duke describes as characteristic of Vienna at the beginning of the play, and this episode with Elbow and Pompey would seem to be emblematic of the counterproductive overextension of mercy. As Lars Engle writes, Escalus 'finds himself condemning others to continue what they are doing'.[71] The result of this policy, Jensen explains, is that the offenders are all 'tempted by "continuance" of their freedom into committing new [sins]'.[72] This critical perspective ignores the fact that the deputy's decision is constrained by the inadequate presentation of evidence and the incompetence of the local officer. Significantly, the deputy's attention shifts quickly from Pompey and Froth to the incompetent constable. Escalus has the greatest chance of reforming local justice by replacing or reforming Elbow. He enquires into the backstory of the constable who, it turns out, has been in office for more than seven years because his neighbours have shirked the responsibility (presumably because it is more burdensome than profitable). This information inspires Escalus to begin a different kind of investigation, and he orders Elbow to bring him the names of 'some six or seven, the most sufficient of your parish' (2.1.246–7), in order, presumably, to eventually replace the constable and to admonish those community members who have sidestepped their civic responsibility. If Escalus's justice is incapable of effectively redirecting Pompey from his trade and Froth from the brothels, he nevertheless starts the process of improving the competency with which the office of constable will be executed. Through the replacement or reform of Elbow, the system has a better chance of bringing to light at law the activities of types like Pompey.

The Prince and the Provost

Through Pompey's comments, we learn that legal punishment is as ineffective in altering behaviour as Angelo believes its merciful reprieve to be. While Escalus lets Pompey off with the threat of a whipping if he is brought before the court again, the bawd responds in an aside by asserting his imperviousness to such reform: 'Whip me? No, no, let carman whip his jade; The valiant heart's not whipt out of his trade' (2.1.231–2). The case of Pompey seems to support Angelo's legal philosophy, which construes character as unalterable and which therefore legitimises the death penalty. According to the deputy, one error leads necessarily to another, and so the offender must be cut off to prevent inevitable future crimes: '[I] do him right that, answering one foul wrong, / Lives not to act another' (2.2.104–5). Instead of investigating past facts, it is the law's job to treat manifest offences as signs of more to come. The law is 'like a prophet' that

> Looks in a glass that shows what future evils
> Either new, or by remissness new-conceived
> And so in progress to be hatched and born,
> Are now to have no successive degrees,
> But ere they live to end.
>
> (2.2.95–9)

But if to err is a feature of human nature, then Angelo's strict policy must, as Pompey suggests, devastate the entire population (2.1.217–21). The more practical and humane approach of Escalus presents the correction or replacement of the officeholder as an alternative method and focus of reform. Yet even if more skilled local officers can be discovered or educated who can more successfully represent offences in legally actionable terms, offenders like Pompey will continue in their 'trade', impervious to the law's non-capital punishment and to mercy. The drawbacks of continuance and capital punishment establish the limits of formal legal process and punishment as instruments of social and individual reform. Those same limitations, however, are circumvented through the more nuanced practices of the Provost and the Duke, who safeguard the integrity (the certainty and force) of the law as well as human life. Through several substitutions these latter officers redeem individuals incapable of character reform by redirecting their energies away from illicit practices. The work of the Provost and the Duke, moreover, reflects an early modern legal mentality that preferred the reorganisation of relationships and the reallocation of resources through negotiation, arbitration, and community intervention in lieu of final decrees and punishments.[73]

By 3.1, justice in Vienna does seem to be more effectively administered. When Elbow appears again, he is more competent in his office, a change signalled by his vastly improved language use. His verbal mistakes are at an end, and instead he manages a very coherent joke in which he compares bawdry to theft. Pompey is in tow once more, but this time his crime is manifest and the culprit openly admits he's a bawd. Elbow may have been successfully re-educated and/or Pompey's continuing crimes may have become especially or accidentally visible before the law; in any case, the audience has been prepared to expect the failure of legal remedies against this particular, resolute offender. The conventional 'correction and instruction' of physical punishment and moral admonishment that the Friar-Duke initially prescribes for Pompey, however, are sidestepped entirely by the Provost who keeps the prison (3.1.286). In 4.2 the Provost offers Pompey the alternative trade of executioner's assistant. Faced with this unexpected opportunity, the first thing the bawd does is pun. He explains that he 'ha[s] been an unlawful bawd time out of mind', but that he 'will be content to be a lawful hangman' (4.2.13–14). In the bawd's speech, the sexual connotations of 'hangman' come out: Pompey has been the unlawful kind that helps johns to sexual gratification, sexually transmitted diseases and even the noose – all of which 'hang' a man. Despite the actual differences between a bawd and an executioner's assistant, the linguistic consonances established between the two shape this new opportunity into a reasonable, lateral career move. Certainly Pompey remains an assistant in both cases and deals with the same clientele. The position has all the disreputability he could wish for, with a great deal more job security. The Provost invites the executioner, Abhorson, to 'compound with [Pompey] by the year, and let him abide here with you' (4.2.19–20). While Pompey had shirked conviction and punishment for years, the Provost gets the now former bawd to agree to dwell in prison voluntarily and indefinitely in his new occupation.

When Abhorson protests that Pompey will 'discredit our mystery' (4.2.23–4), the Provost replies, 'Go to, sir, you weigh equally: a feather will turn the scale' (4.2.25–6). Neither a hangman nor a bawd was socially reputable. The all-important difference between the two trades is the legality of the one and the illegality of the other. Several characters in the play suggest that this difference could be overcome by simply rewriting the law to accommodate human desire and behaviour. Pompey himself had earlier recommended that the law change to accommodate his profession:

> ESCALUS. How would you live, Pompey? By being a bawd? What do you think of the trade, Pompey? Is it a lawful trade?
> POMPEY. If the law would allow it, sir.
>
> (2.1.204–6)

The clown's reasoning here recalls the story of the 'sanctimonious pirate', related in the course of Lucio's conversation with two nameless gentlemen at the beginning of 1.2. The 'sanctimonious pirate . . . went to sea with the Ten Commandments, but scraped one out of the table' (1.2.7–9). 'Thou shalt not steal' was 'a commandment to command the captain and all the rest from their functions' (1.2.12–13). Instead of changing the law, the Provost changes Pompey's job, and in so doing he deflects two threats to the law: first, the threat to the law's force posed by the bawd's continuance, and, second, the threat to the law's certainty posed by redefinition. He also, of course, saves the prisoner from physical punishment. The Provost's success with Pompey introduces a new option for legal practice in the play, a type of remedy that does not hinge on the effectiveness of character reform through punishment or mercy. It is a remedy that hinges not on an interpretation and application of the law, but on the Provost's extensive knowledge of the characters in his prison and of economic opportunity within the local community. If magistrates were ideally supposed to proactively search out and bring to light offences, the Provost demonstrates the equal importance of reforming the socio-economic conditions that lead to criminality as much as, or more than, character or human nature. His efforts attract the attention and admiration of the Duke who, through the bed-trick, employs a similar substitution strategy that turns a false bargain into the satisfaction of an older, honest one. Reinforcing the contiguity between the Provost's and the Duke's justice is the fact that Pompey makes his career change at the same time that the bed-trick is put into action offstage.

Together, the Provost and the Duke devise a plan to protect the integrity of the law and the lives of Vienna's citizens by switching Claudio's head for that of a dead pirate when Angelo demands the fornicator be executed. The legal advantages of this substitution come to light in the final trial that the Duke orchestrates. The head switch enables the Duke to deny mercy to his officer in a case of abused legal authority.

After Angelo is initially sentenced to death for the unjust execution of Claudio, Isabella asks the Duke to wink at the crime: 'Look, if it please you, on this man condemned / As if my brother lived' (5.1.448–9). But 'What's open made to justice, / That justice seizes', and the Duke refuses to redescribe his deputy's crime. Instead, Claudio's continuing existence is finally revealed, thus altering the facts of the case and the judgement that Angelo deserves. The Duke's knowledge and elaborate orchestration of the final trial establish a policy of proactive local justice that has been taken to a theatrical extreme. His penchant for substitution has long been a focus of criticism.[74] What has not been observed is the fact that this technique has the same effect of upholding life and the integrity of the law as the Provost's management of Pompey's career options. The Provost's legal practice, the efforts of this minor officer to negotiate the expectations of his superiors and the needs of locals, offers the promise of order in the absence of a superior or central authority and a model for the Duke's own reformed approach to governance. The extensive cynicism about local justice that is generated by the play's complications is at least partially counterbalanced by the Duke's discovery of the Provost, whose merits, along with Angelo's secret 'passes', are brought to light through the Assize-like surveillance and exposure of local officers. The Duke's Assize-like public re-entrance culminates in a hearing that is the setting for a public shaming and commendation of local officeholders.

The Duke's Return

The Duke's public re-entry into Vienna evokes the multi-step, ceremonial reappearance of the Assize judges in the English counties.[75] Commissions are sent before his arrival, instructing his substitutes to 'Give notice to such men of sort and suit / As are to meet him' and inviting his subjects to submit petitions for justice (4.4.14–15). Cockburn writes that the Assize judges 'went first to their lodgings. There they received leading members of the local gentry who probably reported briefly on the state of the county.'[76] The Duke initially gathers Valencius, Rowland, Crassus, Flavius, and Varrius where he is staying (4.5.6–10). He is thus apparently 'accompanied with the chief of the Gentry of the County', who usher him from his lodgings to the city gates.[77] There he is greeted with trumpets and by Angelo and Escalus who are stationed to publicly 'redeliver [their] authorities' (4.4.4–5). The initial gathering of local gentry (organised but not represented onstage) substantiates the Duke's claim, upon reuniting with his substitutes, that 'We have made enquiry of you' (5.1.5). The report from the leading members of the community has been unequivocally favourable, and the Duke explains that public recognition is the purpose behind his proceedings: 'we hear / Such goodness of your justice that our soul / Cannot but yield you forth to public thanks, / Forerunning more requital' (5.1.5–8). Like a conscientious Assize judge, however, the Duke has not actually relied on the 'information' or 'discourse' of others. In his greeting, he immediately and ironically begins to hint at a private knowledge that must be revealed. 'O, but your desert speaks loud', he tells Angelo, 'and I should wrong it / To lock it in the wards of covert bosom' (5.1.10–11). He explains that his public greeting will represent to the people his inward sense of Angelo's worth:

> . . . Give we our hand,
> And let the subject see, to make them know
> That outward courtesies would fain proclaim
> Favours that keep within.
>
> (5.1.14–17)

What happens in the trial is a process through which the private knowledge of the Duke, gathered and established over the course of the play, is transformed into public fact. His role as judge, as Isabella declares, is 'To make the truth appear where it seems hid' (5.1.71). Her expectations for the trial echo the grand jury charge of Serjeant John Davis, who explained that the 'publick justice of England' uses 'solemne and publick inquisiyon and tryall' to reveal 'the judges . . . own private knowledg'. The Duke's version of 'justice at the gate' accomplishes precisely this.

The truths hidden to the Viennese public, however, are well-known to the offstage audience long before the trial: we know that Angelo is innocent of a crime, that Lucio is a slanderer and that Isabella is chaste. Lorna Hutson contrasts the transparency of *Measure for Measure* to the 'evidential uncertainty' of George Whetstone's *Promos and Cassandra*. '[W]here Whetstone's Cassandra yields to the magistrate and then complains for justice to a King who must decide, *without knowing the facts*, whether or not she is telling the truth and whether or not Promos is guilty', Hutson observes, 'Shakespeare's Duke Vincentio stage-manages not only the chastity-preserving bed-trick, but the feigned evidential uncertainties of the whole trial.'[78] The result, I argue, is that Shakespeare's audience or reader is asked to concentrate instead on the nature and justice of the methods by which secret practices are brought to light. The Duke deliberately steers the on- and offstage audience's attention away from the issue of Angelo's guilt or innocence and toward the motives of the deputy's accusers. In answer to Isabella's account of Angelo's false bargain (her chaste body for her brother's freedom), the

Duke presents his deputy's innocence as unquestionable ('his integrity / Stands without blemish ...' (5.1.113–218)). Cutting short the case against Angelo, he insists repeatedly that 'This needs must be a practice' (5.1.129), and instructs his subordinates 'To find out this abuse, whence 'tis derived' (5.1.253). The Duke draws the crowd's attention directly and eventually to his own secret practices as Friar Lodowick. The dramatic climax of the trial is thus the unmasking of the Duke's secret identity as much as that of Angelo's hypocrisy.

The revelation of the Duke's surveillance of Viennese justice and society collapses the distinction that Angelo draws earlier in the play between what the law can and cannot see. Through the Duke's undercover operation and final public resumption of power, all action appears subject to the law's observation. Thus Angelo immediately confesses upon the disclosure of the Duke's false identity:

> I should be guiltier than my guiltiness
> To think I can be undiscernible
> When I perceive your Grace, like power divine,
> Hath looked upon my passes.
>
> (5.1.369–72)

The comparison between the Duke's knowledge and 'power divine' is regularly read as a revealing comment on the nature of his political and theatrical power. Instead, I argue that it's more productive to focus on the speaker here. Angelo's lines are indicative of his overly narrow perspective on magisterial duty. Embracing a philosophy and practice of legal abstinence, he cannot imagine the extensive effort exerted by the Duke and the Duke's helpers to orchestrate the trial. To the deputy, the exposure of his own offences must logically be a miracle. To the theatre audience that has witnessed the Duke's activities, the revelations of the trial are the result of a makeshift and communal attempt at the reformation of justice. If the Duke is godlike in this scene, it is precisely as a function of his execution of justice, as the language of the Assize sermons suggest. Upon the public exposure of his abuse of power, Angelo not only confesses but seeks his own death:

> No longer session hold upon my shame,
> But let my trial be mine own confession.
> Immediate sentence, then, and sequent death
> Is all the grace I beg.
>
> (5.1.373–6)

The request is consistent with the deputy's own policy and logic. He had earlier argued that, 'When I that censure him do so offend, / Let mine own judgement pattern out my death, / And nothing come in partial' (2.1.29–31). Like an extreme version of the case of Henry Winston who preferred prison to public exposure at the Assizes, Angelo may truly prefer death to a public shaming that launches a direct attack against what the deputy most prizes: his reputation for 'gravity' (2.4.9–10). In a community where justice can indeed see all, false reputation has a much greater chance of being realigned with reality.

Measure for Measure has attracted a great deal of critical attention for the supposedly unsatisfactory nature of the Duke's resolution to the problems of justice in Vienna: Angelo, Lucio, and Claudio are pardoned and married off or engaged to the women whose reputations they've harmed. This 'collapse into quick fixes by way of forced marriages ... has disappointed and puzzled commentators', writes Engle. 'Modern readers cannot imagine that this solution leads to lasting comfort.'[79] Harriet Hawkins claims that 'the kinds of solutions offered by the Duke – whether Shakespeare intended them to or not – seem hopelessly inadequate in the face of the psychological, sexual, and moral conflicts they are supposed to have resolved.'[80] The ending of the play is now more frequently admired for the complex realism of the irresolution and indeterminacy of its themes and conflicts. Yet critics have consistently failed to evaluate the Duke's public exposure of officers' practices, his general gaol delivery, and his marriage solution in relation to the models for reform offered elsewhere in the play: Angelo's capital punishment, Escalus's continuance and the Provost's and Duke's substitutions. The labour-intensive substitution practices of the Provost and the Duke are successful specifically because they compensate for imperfect characters and safeguard life and law alike. The concluding marriages are a part of this same strategy, while the new tensions created by the marriages point toward the practical necessity of the ongoing work of local governance and social vigilance.

Part of what disgruntles modern ethical-literary expectation is the fact that Angelo, Lucio, and the rest are the same characters, psychologically, at the end of the play as they are at the beginning. If the plot is sparked by the Duke's determination to reform justice in Vienna, this outcome apparently presents quite a thorough failure. But the marriage solution, which contrasts with beheadings and continuance, may be more promising than has traditionally been supposed. Through their arranged marriages, Angelo and Lucio undergo the same kind of conversion as Pompey the bawd had earlier: the specific fault of fornication is redirected toward a legitimate avenue for its expression. Marriage, moreover, binds these characters in intimate relationships through which their faults or offences are more easily subject to regular observation and exposure. Comically, these newly married or engaged men – Angelo, Lucio, and the Duke too – will soon be under the surveillance of their wives, women whom we know have the bravery to publicly expose these men. Despite Lucio's claim that 'Marrying a punk . . . is pressing to death, / Whipping, and hanging' (5.1.525–6), the Duke's solution propels the members of each couple into relationships that increase their social ties, their accountability and their visibility. Those characters who would withdraw from society – Angelo and Lucio (who would prefer death to their marriages), Isabella (who would prefer the convent), Mariana (who had been cloistered at the grange), Claudio and Julietta (who had kept their relationship a secret) and the Duke himself (who preferred 'the life removed') – are all more deeply embedded in the community at the end of the play, more fully subject to all of its constraints and opportunities. In the concluding trial, the Duke transfers the responsibility for local governance and surveillance from the judge to the locals themselves, just as the Assize judge's charges emphasised the grand jury's responsibility of the presentment of local officeholders and other offenders.

What emerges through this reading of Shakespeare's problem play is an early modern attitude toward governing that recognised the impracticality or unreliability of character reform as a legal-political objective. Instead, the reform of individuals in *Measure for Measure* comes about through substitution and redirection practices – practices ethically consistent with the kinds of interventions demanded of Assize judges and local officers within the community. Shakespeare champions a legal decorum that preserves the integrity of both law and life and that can be found in Dukes and Provosts alike. But the dissemination of this kind of justice throughout the system requires that Duke and Provost meet, an exchange facilitated historically by the structure of the Assize system and within the play by the Duke's disguise. The individual, custom-made solutions that Duke and Provost devise require ongoing 'weeding' or regular maintenance. They require that magisterial virtue be put into action regularly in order to bring offensive conduct to light. They require that responsibility for governance be shared across the community and between local and central authorities, reflecting the wide participation in early modern justice that was both encouraged and scrutinised during the Assizes.

I have already cited Victoria Hayne's account of the Duke's unique focus on legal reform within the disguised ruler genre. In *Measure for Measure*, Shakespeare couples the disguised ruler plot with that of the corrupt magistrate. This second plot type relates the story of an official who abuses his authority through the violation or attempted violation of a woman and who is then prevented from doing so or punished by a higher, central or external authority. In her treatment of continental precedents like the tale in Cinthio's *Hecatommithi*, Leah Marcus concludes that these 'have in common ... a conflict [that is] resolved through a process of bureaucratic centralization and its imperative for legal reform'. Marcus goes on to read the Duke in *Measure for Measure* as a figure who manifests James's imperialistic tendencies: the Duke's resumption of authority in the play's concluding trial scene is a 'victory of unlocalized law'.[81] Louise Halper likewise discovers 'the triumph of Tudor and Stuart centralization of the law over more local versions' within the play.[82] In fact, Shakespeare discourages just such a reading by having the Duke rely on a number of characters in order to stage-manage the outcome of the concluding trial. The final scene is a triumph of the *coordinated* efforts of local and central authorities to bring legal abuse to light. This departure from the continental model of the corrupt magistrate plot distinguishes Shakespeare's version as a refraction of a particular English legal historical moment in which the relationship between local and central justice had reached a new level of maturity through the Court of Assize's assumption of the responsibility for the surveillance and reform of local justice.

While the reform of justice in *Measure for Measure* is achieved through the same intersection of jurisdictions and the coordination of legal responsibilities that made the historical Assizes effective, in the following and final chapter I argue that justice in *The Winter's Tale* is instead restored through the more careful observance of the boundaries between legal and political power. In his later romance, Shakespeare registers the tensions in James's reign over the proper jurisdictions of the King and his common-law judges. Justice in Sicilia is disrupted for the very reason that the King does not observe the proper limits of his authority, while justice is reformed in the final scene as the King resumes his proper place within the legal-political hierarchy.

Notes

1. J[ohn] D[onne], 'News from the Very Country', in Thomas Overbury, *Characters: Together with Poems, News, Edicts, and Paradoxes Based on the Eleventh Edition of A wife Now the Widow of Sir Thomas Overbury*, ed. Donald Beecher (Ottawa: Dovehouse Editions, 2003), p. 304.
2. Aristotle, *The Nicomachean Ethics*, trans. David Ross, J. L. Ackrill and J. O. Urmson (Oxford: Oxford University Press, 1998), p. 108.
3. From Thomas Egerton's 1601 Star Chamber charge to Assize judges, printed in Heywood Townshend, *Historical Collections: or, An Exact Account of the Proceedings of the Four Last Parliaments of Q. Elizabeth of*

Famous Memory. Wherein is Contained the Compleat Journals Both of the Lords [and] Commons, Taken from the Original Records of Their Houses (London, 1680), p. 355.

4. James VI and I, *Political Writings*, ed. Johann P. Sommerville (Cambridge: Cambridge University Press, 1994), p. 220.

5. From the 1599 Star Chamber charge to Assize judges, printed in William Paley Baildon (ed.), *Les Reportes del Cases in Camera Stellata, 1593–1609, from the Original MS. of John Hawarde* (1894), p. 106.

6. Steve Hindle, *The State and Social Change in Early Modern England, c. 1550–1640* (Basingstoke: Palgrave Macmillan, 2000), p. 30.

7. If the play's inversion of the Assize sessions' structure makes the analogy sound unlikely, we need only look at a play like *Othello*, in which the general's trial in the senate happens in Act 1, while his crime takes place in Act 5.

8. Conal Condren, 'Unfolding "the Properties of Government": The Case of *Measure for Measure* and the History of Political Thought', in David Armitage, Conal Condren, and Andrew Fitzmaurice (eds), *Shakespeare and Early Modern Political Thought* (Cambridge: Cambridge University Press, 2009), p. 160.

9. For other readings of *Measure for Measure* in relation to local authorities, see Leah S. Marcus, *Puzzling Shakespeare: Local Reading and Its Discontents* (Berkeley: University of California Press, 1988); and Theodore B. Leinwand, 'Negotiation and New Historicism', *PMLA* 105.3 (1990), pp. 477–90.

10. T. E. Hartley explains that '[t]he problem of law enforcement had been a well-nigh constant preoccupation of Lords Chancellor and Keeper throughout the reign' (*Elizabeth's Parliaments: Queen, Lords, and Commons, 1559–1601* (Manchester: St. Martin's Press, 1992), p. 33). Lorna Hutson reports that 'recognition that local administration was defective and needed reform was strongly advocated by Sir Nicholas Bacon, Lord Burghley, Sir John Puckering, and Sir Thomas Egerton' (*The Invention of Suspicion: Law and Mimesis in Shakespeare and Renaissance Drama* (Oxford: Oxford University Press, 2007), p. 162).

11. T. E. Hartley (ed.), *Proceedings in the Parliaments of Elizabeth I*, 3 vols (Wilmington, DE: M. Glazier, 1981–95), 1: 82–3. Hereafter this text is cited parenthetically by *PPE*, followed by the volume and page number.

12. The Assize's jurisdiction was established by three documents: it functioned according to the commissions of oyer and terminer, of gaol (jail) delivery, and under the writ of *Nisi Prius*. Oyer and terminer empowered Assize judges to 'inquire into, hear and determine . . . all offences committed within the counties and liberties of the circuit'. Gaol delivery entailed the determination of cases involving those suspects committed to prison or bailed between Assize sessions and the Quarter sessions presided over by JPs. 'Between them', writes J. S. Cockburn, 'the commissions of oyer and terminer and gaol delivery gave the Assize judges unlimited criminal jurisdiction within their circuit' (*Calendar of Assize Records: Home Circuit Indictments, Elizabeth I and James I: Introduction* (London: Her Majesty's Stationery Office, 1985), p. 19). Through the writ of *Nisi*

Prius, civil cases begun at one of the common law courts at Westminster could be brought before and concluded by Assize judges in the country.

13. See, for instance, the 1595 Star Chamber charge that was addressed to an 'audience of such Justices as are in Towne & of other of her Judges of Circuites of Assise whome we have requyred to be here' (Baildon, *Les Reportes del Cases in Camera Stellata*, p. 20).

14. While charges were used irregularly, they were 'consistently used in periods of acute governmental anxiety, especially in the critical period 1595–1602 (when seven charges were issued)' (Hindle, *The State and Social Change*, p. 6). Cockburn explains that in 1595 the Lord Keeper's practice of delivering a public speech on the state of the commonwealth at the end of legal terms was revived after a lapse of more than twenty years: '[i]t appears to have been no accident that the practice was resumed in June 1595 as the impact of two consecutive bad seasons was beginning to make itself felt in food riots and the soaring price of corn. Significantly the Lord Keeper's address, apparently for the first time, gave greater prominence to the responsibilities of the judges of Assize, some of whom were specifically commanded to attend and hear it' (*A History of English Assizes, 1558–1714* (Cambridge: Cambridge University Press, 1972), p. 182).

15. Cockburn, *A History of English Assizes*, p. 179. On Star Chamber charges see Cockburn, *A History of English Assizes*, pp. 181–2; Hindle, *The State and Social Change*, pp. 6–7; and Louis A. Knafla, *Law and Politics in Jacobean England: The Tracts of Lord Chancellor Ellesmere* (Cambridge: Cambridge University Press, 1977), pp. 181–2.

16. Francis Bacon, 'A Letter of Advice Written by Sir Francis Bacon to the Duke of Buckingham when He Became Favourite to King James', in *The Works of Francis Bacon*, ed. James Spedding, Robert Leslie Ellis and Douglas Denon Heath, vol. 13 (London: 1872), p. 18.

17. 1608 Star Chamber charge in Baildon, *Les Reportes del Cases in Camera Stellata*, p. 368.

18. 1601 Star Chamber charge in Townshend, *Historical Collections*, pp. 355, 356.

19. James VI and I, 'Speech in Star Chamber of 20 June 1616', in *Political Writings*, p. 219.

20. Cockburn, *A History of English Assizes*, p. 58.

21. Cockburn, *A History of English Assizes*, p. 154.

22. Edward Coke, *The Lord Coke His Speech and Charge. With a Discoverie of the Abuses and Corruption of Officers* (London, 1607), sig. B1^r.

23. From the 'Preamble to the charge given to the grand jury by Serjeant Davis at York Assizes Lent 1620', transcribed by Cockburn in *A History of English Assizes*, p. 308.

24. Francis Bacon, 'The Speech which was used by the Lord Keeper of the Great Seal, in the Star-Chamber, before the Summer Circuits, the King being then in Scotland, 1617', in *The Works of Francis Bacon*, vol. 4 (London, 1826), p. 498.

25. Bacon, 'A Letter of Advice', p. 18.

26. James VI and I, *Political Writings*, pp. 220, 221.

27. Baildon, *Les Reportes del Cases in Camera Stellata*, pp. 20–1, 57–8, 101–2, 106.
28. James VI and I, *Political Writings*, p. 220.
29. Baildon, *Les Reportes del Cases in Camera Stellata*, p. 367.
30. Bacon, 'Speech . . . 1617', p. 499.
31. Cockburn, *A History of English Assizes*, p. 156. J. A. Sharpe estimates that as many as 300 statutes accumulated to specify the 'duties and powers' of the JP between the mid-fourteenth century and the late sixteenth century (*Crime in Early Modern England, 1550–1750* (London: Longman, 1984), p. 28). See also Hindle, *State and Social Change*, p. 10. In light of such numerous regulatory responsibilities, Elizabeth's representation of her justices as inept and ignorant seems unfair.
32. In the parliament of 1601, a member complained that corrupt justices owed their existence to Assize judges who, 'ignorant of local affairs', simply certified the names recommended by local JPs (Cockburn, *A History of English Assizes*, p. 159).
33. 'The Assizes ideally reduced considerations of individual demands to a minimum and dealt in the universality of legal principles' (Cynthia Herrup, *The Common Peace: Participation and the Criminal Law in Seventeenth-Century England* (Cambridge: Cambridge University Press, 1987), p. 51). On the statute forbidding judges to preside in their native county, see also Cockburn, *A History of English Assizes*, pp. 49–50.
34. On judicial complaints about the inadequacy of court premises for the size of the audience gathered, see Cockburn, *A History of English Assizes*, pp. 66–7.
35. Herrup, *The Common Peace*, p. 44. Herrup's comment was applied to the Assize and Quarter sessions.
36. Cockburn, *A History of English Assizes*, p. 3.
37. *The Office of the Clerk of Assize: Containing the Form and Method of the Proceedings at the Assizes, and General Gaol-Delivery, as Also on the Crown and Nisi Prius Side. Together with The Office of the Clerk of the Peace. Shewing the True Manner and Form of the Proceedings at the Court of General Quarter-Sessions of the Peace* (London, 1682), pp. 23–4.
38. Cockburn, *A History of English Assizes*, p. 65. This image of the ceremony and display that accompanied the Assize judges persists well into the time of Charles Dickens, who juxtaposes the appearance of a judge on circuit with a judge on vacation in *Bleak House*:

    > If the country folks of those Assize towns on [the judge's] circuit could only see him now! No full-bottomed wig, no red petticoats, no fur, no javelin-men, no white wands. Merely a close-shaved gentleman in white trousers and a white hat, with sea-bronze on the judicial countenance, and a strip of bark peeled by the solar rays from the judicial nose, who calls in at the shell-fish shop as he comes along, and drinks iced ginger-beer! (*Bleak House*, ed. Stephen Gill (Oxford: Oxford University Press, 1998), p. 278)

39. Barbara Shapiro, 'Political Theology and the Courts: A Survey of Assize Sermons *c.*1600–1688', *Law and Humanities* 2.1 (2008), pp. 27, 19. While this sermon genre was relatively stable across the early modern period, Arnold Hunt argues that, by the early seventeenth century, the focus of these

sermons 'had begun to shift from religious to social disorder' (*The Art of Hearing: English Preachers and their Audiences, 1590–1640* (Cambridge: Cambridge University Press, 2014), p. 312). See also Hugh Adlington, 'Restoration, Religion, and Law: Assize Sermons, 1660–1685', in Hugh Adlington, Peter McCullough, and Emma Rhatigan (eds), *The Oxford Handbook of the Early Modern Sermon* (Oxford: Oxford University Press, 2011), pp. 423–41.

40. William Westerman, *Two Sermons of Assise: The One Intituled; A prohibition of Revenge: The other, A Sword of Maintenance* (London, 1600), pp. 18, 31, 7.

41. Shapiro, 'Political Theology and the Courts', p. 6.

42. Shapiro, 'Political Theology and the Courts', p. 7.

43. Andrew Majeske, 'Equity's Absence: The Extremity of Claudio's Prosecution and Barnardine's Pardon in Shakespeare's *Measure for Measure*', *Law and Literature* 21.2 (2009), p. 169.

44. Hindle, *The State and Social Change*, p. 6.

45. The grand jury's oath included 'you shall present no man for envy, hatred, or malice, neither shall you leave any man unpresented for love, fear, favour, or affection, or hope of reward, but you shall present things truly as they come to your knowledge, according to the best of your understanding, so help you God' (*Clerk of Assize*, p. 31).

46. Coke, *The Lord Coke His Speech and Charge*, sig. G3^r–H2^r, H1^r, G3^v.

47. Anthony Fletcher, 'Honour, Reputation and Local Officeholding in Elizabethan and Stuart England', in Anthony Fletcher and John Stevenson (eds), *Order and Disorder in Early Modern England* (Cambridge: Cambridge University Press, 1985), p. 101.

48. Bernard William McLane, 'Juror Attitudes toward Local Disorder: The Evidence of the 1328 Trailbaston Proceedings', in J. S. Cockburn and Thomas S. Green (eds), *Twelve Good Men and True: The Criminal Trial Jury in England, 1200–1800* (Princeton: Princeton University Press, 1988), p. 61.

49. Cockburn, *A History of English Assizes*, p. 310.

50. On 'the concern at all levels of early modern government to draw a distinction between public and private knowledge', see Michael J. Braddick, 'Administrative Performance: The Representation of Political Authority in Early Modern England', in Michael J. Braddick and John Walter (eds), *Negotiating Power in Early Modern Society: Order, Hierarchy and Subordination in Britain and Ireland* (Cambridge: Cambridge University Press, 2001), p. 174; and Paul Griffiths, 'Secrecy and Authority in Late Sixteenth- and Seventeenth-Century London', *Historical Journal* 40.4 (1997): 925–51.

51. Herrup, *The Common Peace*, pp. 51, 56, 57.

52. Sharpe, *Crime in Early Modern England*, p. 28.

53. Herrup, *The Common Peace*, pp. 61, 54–5, 44.

54. Keith Wrightson, 'Two Concepts of Order: Justices, Constables and Jurymen in Seventeenth-Century England', in John Brewer and John Styles (eds), *An Ungovernable People: The English and Their Law in the Seventeenth and Eighteenth Centuries* (London: Hutchinson, 1980), p. 22.

55. Francis Bacon, *Reading on the Statute of Uses*, in *The Works of Francis*

Bacon, ed. James Spedding, Robert Leslie Ellis, and Douglas Denon Heath, vol. 7 (London: 1879), pp. 417–18.

56. Debora Kuller Shuger, *Political Theologies in Shakespeare's England: The Sacred and the State in* Measure for Measure (Basingstoke: Palgrave, 2001), p. 1. On *Measure for Measure* and political theology, see also Julia Reinhard Lupton, *Citizen-Saints: Shakespeare and Political Theology* (Chicago: University of Chicago Press, 2005).

57. Scholars have suggested that the play was written or revised for performance at Whitehall (John Wasson, '*Measure for Measure*: A Text for Court Performance?', *Shakespeare Quarterly* 21.1 (1970), pp. 17–24); that the Duke either 'mouths James's opinions' or 'apes his actions' (Jonathan Goldberg, *James I and the Politics of Literature: Jonson, Shakespeare, Donne, and Their Contemporaries* (Baltimore: Johns Hopkins University Press, 1983), p. 231); that aspects of the play echo very early events in James's English reign, including the trials related to the 'Bye' and 'Main' plots (Craig A. Bernthal, 'Staging Justice: James I and the Trial Scenes of *Measure for Measure*', *Studies in English Literature, 1500–1900* 32.2 (1992), pp. 247–69) and the King's immediate problems with the English Parliament (Leonard Tennenhouse, 'Representing Power: *Measure for Measure* in its Time', in Stephen Greenblatt (ed.), *The Power of Forms in the English Renaissance* (Norman, OK: Pilgrim Books, 1982), pp. 139–56; Louise Halper, '*Measure for Measure*: Law, Prerogative, Subversion', *Cardozo Studies in Law and Literature* 13.2 (2001), pp. 221–64); and that the ending marriages reflect the practices of Elizabeth and James in granting consent to aristocratic alliances (Tennenhouse, 'Representing Power', pp. 151–3).

58. James VI and I, *Political Writings*, p. 220.

59. William Shakespeare, *Measure for Measure*, in *The Norton Shakespeare*, ed. Stephen Greenblatt, Walter Cohen, Suzanne Gossett, Jean E. Howard, Katherine Eisaman Maus, and Gordon McMullan, 3rd edn (New York: W. W. Norton, 2016), 1.1.3–14. All future Shakespeare quotations are from this edition and hereafter cited parenthetically by act, scene and line number. For a reading of this opening scene in relation to 'imperial deputation', see Richmond Barbour, '"There is our commission": Writing and Authority in *Measure for Measure* and the London East Indian Company', *Journal of English and Germanic Philology* 99.2 (2000), pp. 193–214.

60. John Doddridge, *The English Lawyer* (London, 1631), p. 242. The development of the discourse on artificial reason, including Doddridge's definition, is discussed in chapter 2 of Glenn Burgess, *The Politics of the Ancient Constitution: An Introduction to English Political Thought, 1603–1642* (University Park: Pennsylvania State University Press, 1993), pp. 19–78.

61. Cockburn, *A History of English Assizes*, p. 61.

62. William Lambarde, *Eirenarcha; or, Of The Office of the Justices of Peace, in two Bookes* (London, 1582), pp. 55–6.

63. James VI and I, *Political Writings*, p. 204.

64. Cockburn, *A History of English Assizes*, p. 147.

65. Baildon, *Les Reportes del Cases in Camera Stellata*, p. 368.

66. James VI and I, *Political Writings*, p. 222.

67. On surveillance in *Measure for Measure*, see Jonathan Dollimore's now classic essay, 'Transgression and Surveillance in *Measure for Measure*', in Jonathan Dollimore and Alan Sinfield (eds), *Political Shakespeare: New Essays in Cultural Materialism* (Manchester: Manchester University Press, 1985), pp. 72–87.

68. Victoria Hayne, 'Performing Social Practice: The Example of *Measure for Measure*', *Shakespeare Quarterly* 44.1 (1993), pp. 23–4. For discussions of the disguised ruler genre in relation to *Measure for Measure*, see also Stephen Cohen, 'From Mistress to Master: Political Transition and Formal Conflict in *Measure for Measure*', *Criticism* 41.4 (1999): 431–64; Tennenhouse, 'Representing Power'; Kevin A. Quarmby, *The Disguised Ruler in Shakespeare and his Contemporaries* (New York: Routledge, 2016), pp. 103–38.

69. Hayne, 'Performing Social Practice', p. 23.

70. Pamela K. Jensen, 'Vienna Vice: Invisible Leadership and Deep Politics in Shakespeare's *Measure for Measure*', in John A. Murley and Sean D. Sutton (eds), *Perspectives on Politics in Shakespeare* (Lanham, MD: Lexington Books, 2006), p. 114.

71. Lars Engle, '*Measure for Measure* and Modernity: The Problem of the Sceptic's Authority', in Hugh Grady (ed.), *Shakespeare and Modernity: Early Modern to Millennium* (London: Routledge, 2000), p. 97.

72. Jenson, 'Vienna Vice', p. 114.

73. Timothy Stretton emphasises the degree to which a final decree at law was relatively rare and even systematically avoided in preference for arbitrated solutions to interpersonal conflict. 'The successful resolution of suits', he writes, 'did not always require the making of decisions or the granting of decrees ... few cases stayed the distance to a final court order' (*Women Waging Law in Elizabethan England* (Cambridge: Cambridge University Press, 1998), p. 82). See also Sharpe, *Crime in Early Modern England*, p. 65, who explains that this was equally true for civil and criminal cases; and Virginia Lee Strain, 'Preventive Justice and *Measure for Measure*', in Kevin Curran (ed.), *Shakespeare and Judgment* (Edinburgh: Edinburgh University Press, 2016), pp. 21–44.

74. On substitution in *Measure for Measure*, see Julia Briggs, 'Shakespeare's Bed-Tricks', *Essays in Criticism* 44.4 (1994), pp. 293–314; Goldberg, *James I and the Politics of Literature*; Alexander Leggatt, 'Substitution in *Measure for Measure*', *Shakespeare Quarterly*, 39.3 (1988), pp. 342–59; Nancy S. Leonard, 'Substitution in Shakespeare's Problem Comedies', *English Literary Renaissance* 9 (1979), pp. 281–301.

75. Brian Gibbons provides an alternative reading of the Duke's ceremonial re-entry in relation to James I's 1604 Royal Entry into the city of London. See '"Bid Them Bring the Trumpets to the Gate": Staging Questions for *Measure for Measure*', *Huntington Library Quarterly* 54 (1991), pp. 31–42.

76. Cockburn, *A History of English Assizes*, p. 65.

77. *Clerk of Assize*, pp. 23–4.

78. Hutson, *The Invention of Suspicion*, pp. 288–9.

79. Engle, '*Measure for Measure* and Modernity', pp. 87, 102.

80. Harriet Hawkins, '"The Devil's Party": Virtues and Vices in *Measure for*

Measure', in Harold Bloom (ed.), *Measure for Measure* (New York: Chelsea House, 1987), p. 82.

81. Marcus, *Puzzling Shakespeare*, pp. 186, 185.
82. Louise Halper, '*Measure for Measure*: Law, Prerogative, Subversion', *Cardozo Studies in Law and Literature*, 13.2 (2001), p. 22.

Chapter 5

The Winter's Tale and the Oracle of the Law

Oracles have a bad reputation in early modern literary history, as Howard Felperin has observed: 'The fondness of pagan oracles for ambiguity, obscurantism, equivocation, and general verbal trickery is commonplace in Elizabethan literature.'[1] Stephen Orgel underscores their spiritual dubiousness: the oracle in *The Winter's Tale*, he argues, 'would have been rather like the word of the ghost in *Hamlet* – something the play requires you to believe but that you knew, as a good Reformation Christian, you were supposed to reject.'[2] What critics have not noted, however, is that this perspective coexisted with another oracular tradition that functioned in the legal-political and literary contexts contemporaneous with Shakespeare's romance. The epithet 'oracle' also distinguished a legal-political type, the legal expert and wise counsellor whose authority was established through deliberative and self-fashioning practices that suggested the rhetorical mode and performance style of the oracles of antiquity. Adopting an appropriately epideictic tone, Thomas Blount honours several legal luminaries in the *Nomo-lexikon* by claiming that '[t]he first and principal' motive for writing his law dictionary was 'to erect a small Monument of that vast respect and deference, which I have for your *Lordships*, who are . . . the *Oracles* of our *Law*, and *Grand Exemplars* of *Justice*'.[3] While the judiciary cultivated its own oracular image through professional practices, this same kind of oracle was repeatedly depicted as a recognisable social type in a literary form that gained momentum in the first two decades of the seventeenth century, the 'charactery' or character essays that were compiled in miscellanies like Joseph Hall's *Characters of Vertues and Vices* and Nicholas Breton's *The Good and The Badde: or, Descriptions of the Worthies, and Unworthies of This Age*.[4] The oracle of the law, then, was a culturally widespread (professional and amateur, legal and literary) figure who exploited the mystique of the classical oracle in the exercise of his judgement and the cultivation of his authority.

This alternate tradition enables a reimagining of *The Winter's Tale*, in which Apollo's supernatural oracle evokes human judicial figures. I argue that the play thereby resonates with the explosive tensions between the judiciary and the sovereign in early seventeenth-century England. While Apollo's oracle makes a minor appearance in the form of its pronouncement that is revealed during the trial scene, its judicial presence is nevertheless extended throughout the play via its avatars, Paulina and Camillo. A number of critics have identified Paulina as 'Apollo's representative'. Through her role at the end of the trial and her orchestration of the final scene in which Hermione's statue is awakened, she becomes 'the spiritual guide for Leontes, eventually leading to his new health and that of the body politic'.[5] Her function as Apollo's representative, however, is also legal. In 5.3, Shakespeare's 'much noted – and celebrated – effort to turn Ovid's story of Pygmalion into one about the transforming powers of theatrical representation' hinges on Paulina's animating voice.[6] Her success, I argue, derives from her association with the early modern oracles of the law, through which Shakespeare further transforms the Pygmalion story into a pun on the performative power of legal language.

In contrast to the commentary available on Paulina, her counterpart Camillo (to whom she is finally linked in marriage) has received scant attention. Addressing the lacuna in a critical tradition that has largely ignored the predominance of counsel and counsellors in the play, Stuart M. Kurland has examined Camillo's role in relation to humanist advice literature and James's relationships with court favourites.[7] More recently, David Schalkwyk has presented Camillo as an instrument for Shakespeare's exploration of 'the crisis of service in the face of tyranny'.[8] I argue that Camillo's approach to counsel and service is informed by his identity as an oracle of the law. He is a judicial figure who embodies wisdom as it was represented in the charactery and legal writings of the day, and whose behaviour helps countermand the tragic missteps of King Leontes.

As we saw in the last chapter, the reform of justice in *Measure for Measure* involved the officeholder's greater immersion in local affairs through his proactive efforts to put virtue into action and to bring offences to light. By contrast, *The Winter's Tale* centres on a king who overextends his sovereign authority: Leontes's extraordinary intrusion into the legal process produces injustice. The reform of justice in *The Winter's Tale* is achieved through processes of restoration – one of the major early modern connotations of 'reform'. In the conclusion to the play, the restoration of Hermione and Perdita partially reverses the errors and tragic consequences of Leontes's past judgements. At the same time, the re-establishment of the distinct jurisdictions of king and legal oracle guarantees the future of justice in Sicilia.

Early Modern Oracles of the Law and the Oracular Method

A number of legal cases in the early seventeenth century raised questions about the royal prerogative, the scope of judges' powers and the jurisdictions of courts, including parliament. One response to the challenges faced by legal authorities involved a narrative of the common law's coherence and authority through time. The narrative that would come to be called historical jurisprudence argued that the common law had not changed since it first materialised as customary law, as the practices of the English people. Common law, it was argued, had survived multiple conquests and had remained essentially the same since Anglo-Saxon or pre-Roman times. Or, if it had changed, it was still coextensive with the spirit of the people it served, that is it had changed with the people. Or, if it was no longer coextensive with the spirit of the people – if it had deteriorated – this erroneous trajectory could and would be corrected by a process of restoration, a return to the proper course of the law through further judicial decisions and legislation.[9] This judicial narrative manufactured judicial authority in the process of representing it as historically determined, so that at the moment of its assertion it appeared to have always already existed. The narrative veiled the actuality that judicial authority – always in the process of becoming, of being freshly instantiated, as it made arguments about its own historicity – was a projection into the near and distant future through the contribution of a living judge. The individual judge accessed the largely unwritten common-law tradition of judicial decision-making (the profession's past that he claimed to represent) through 'artificial reason', the refinement of natural reason that involved 'long study and experience' with professional practices.[10] Artificial reasoning ensured that what was spoken by any one judge mirrored the collective opinion of all legal authorities. As Edward Coke put it, 'all the Judges and Justices in all the severall parts of the Realme . . . with one mouth in all mens cases pronounce one and the same sentence'.[11] When a judge delivered an opinion from the bench, then, he did not make new law or speak for himself; instead, he merely declared the law as it had been, was and would be. Authorised by this construction of the past, the judiciary's pronouncements were, in effect, self-fulfilling prophecies, the infallibility of its opinions rhetorically and logically contrived.

Historical jurisprudence was not systematically or comprehensively explicated. It developed as a patchwork in the period, an admixture of comments and claims scattered among various writings, the result of a professional mentality oriented toward practice rather than theory. Nevertheless, even its stitched narrative provides insight into a judicial method by which the judicature established its authority. The legal story I have outlined here is subtended by two strategies. The first involves a line of reasoning that relies on the temporal continuity, and thus the internal coherence, of the common-law tradition, to lend the judiciary its historical credibility and prophetic aspect. The second takes the form of a performance in which the individual judge reveals the collective understanding of that tradition that is otherwise concealed from all but the professional insider. Together, these strategies form the heart of an oracular method that shaped judicial identity, an identity that in turn suggested that of the classical oracle whose own authority was constituted by a rhetorically distinct message and a particular style of ceremonial performance.

Such a method was ascribed to the most prominent legal oracle of Shakespeare's day, Edward Coke, Solicitor General, Attorney General, Chief Justice of Common Pleas and later of King's Bench, Privy Councillor, parliamentarian, and author of the multi-volume *Reports* and *Institutes of the Laws of England*. His tomb announces, 'Here Lies Edward Coke ... Spirit, Interpreter, and Inerrant Oracle of the Laws, Discloser of its Secrets – Concealer of its Mysteries.'[12] The epitaph's phrasing directly links Coke's professional reputation to the oracular practices of revealing (or disclosing) and concealing. It is a method that conceals the terms of judicial deliberation and has therefore more often than not been viewed by legal historians (as well as early modern contemporaries) as an impediment to recovering the largely unwritten common-law tradition of judge-made law. 'It seems to have been a long time before courts were legally required to give reasons for their decisions', J. H. Baker reports. He goes on to give an instance of a case from 1594: 'after the Queen's Bench had given a judgement without reasons, [a reporter writes in law French,] "Mr Attorney presse eax pur render overtment lour opinions; mes ils huddle up the judgment et fell to other matters."'[13] Coke himself links the importance of the oracular concealment of reasoning to judicial reverence. In the course of detailing the several sources of the common law in Part Three of the *Reports*, he explains:

> [In] the judiciall records of the Kings Courts, wherein cases of importance and difficultie are upon great consultation and advisement adjudged and determined ... the reasons or causes of the Judgements are not expressed; For wise and learned men doe before they judge, labour to reach to the depth

of all the reasons of the cases in question, but in their judgements expresse not any: And in troth, if Judges should set downe the reasons and causes of their judgements within every Record . . . in mine opinion [they would] lose somewhat of their present authoritie and reverence; And this is also worthie for learned and grave men to imitate.[14]

The oracular method was meant to cultivate a faith-based reverence for judicial opinions that was surely buttressed by the gravity of legal ceremony.

The rhetoric of Shakespeare's own oracular pronouncement reflects this same emphasis on judicial reserve through a strategic revision of the source text, Robert Greene's prose romance *Pandosto. The Triumph of Time*. The inheritance from Greene's text has been largely overlooked by the few critics who seriously consider the function of Apollo's oracle. Yet the wording of the oracular pronouncement in *The Winter's Tale* replicates the wording in *Pandosto* minus the commonplaces that preface the latter text's judgement:

Suspicion is no proof; jealousy is an unequal judge; Bellario is chaste; Egistus blameless; Franion a true subject; Pandosto treacherous; his babe an innocent; and the King shall live without an heir if that which is lost be not found.[15]

The commonplaces or axioms supply external principles of evaluation, or standards of probability and proof that are superimposed upon the case at hand in order to reach a conclusion. The validity of the judgement is verifiable by reference to its premises which are themselves derived from solid proverbial wisdom: 'Suspicion is no proof; jealousy is an unequal judge'. Regardless of the oracle's supernatural powers, therefore, the deliberative process involved in its decision-making is rendered transparent to, and reproducible by, Greene's reader. In contrast, by dropping these commonplaces the reasoning behind Shakespeare's oracle becomes submerged:

Hermione is chaste, Polixenes blameless, Camillo a true subject, Leontes a jealous tyrant, his innocent babe truly begotten; and the King shall live without an heir if that which is lost be not found.[16]

In Greene's romance, the oracle's pronouncement is immediately legitimised by the commonplaces. In Shakespeare's, it adopts the judicial method of suppressing, and thus mystifying, deliberative practices. The final demonstration of the prophecy's truthfulness (its fulfilment in the rediscoveries of Hermione and Perdita) must validate the oracle's claim regarding the past facts of the Queen's case. In lieu of Greene's commonplaces, Shakespeare supplies Paulina and Camillo, his own characters who safeguard the oracle's relationship to the royal family and its relevance to the political reality by enabling the return of mother and daughter: Paulina obstructs plans to have Leontes produce a new heir and secretly harbours Hermione, and Camillo directs Perdita and Florizel to run away to Sicily. The oracle's supernatural powers of truth-finding are thus directly related to the success of the human advisors in the play, whose own powers, I will demonstrate, evoke the tradition of the legal-political oracle. Camillo illuminates the signature deliberative techniques and character traits, and Paulina the performance and performative aspects, of these historical oracles.

The Oracle of the Law in Charactery

Edward Coke made strong claims for the legal professional who was uniquely qualified through his education and experience to execute the law. Yet in the quotation above from his *Reports*, the strategy whereby judges 'labour to reach to the depth of all the reasons of the cases in question, but in their judgements expresse not any' is also said to be 'worthie for learned and grave men to imitate', implying that these oracular strategies had a range of applications beyond legal questions and contexts. His own extensive resume suggests that they were useful in the roles of the legal expert, statesman, counsellor and courtier. The oracular method, in fact, was consonant with both legal and popular notions of what constituted refined or wise judgement. These notions get taken up by character writers in the period and deployed in 'discrete essay[s] in prose about a fictive person whose presiding "virtue" or "vice" is manifest in a number of tell-tale traits and gestures'.[17] The metaphor of the ancient oracle and the contemporary reasoning and self-fashioning practices that it signified shape Joseph Hall's depiction of the 'Character of the Wise Man' in his *Characters of Vertues and Vices*:

> His free discourse runnes backe to the ages past, and recovers events out of memory, and then preventeth Tyme in flying forward to future things; and comparing one with the other, can give a verdict well-neer propheticall: wherein his conjectures are better than anothers judgements . . . He is his own lawyer, the treasury of knowledge, the oracle of counsel; blind in no man's cause, best sighted in his own.[18]

Good judgement, as it is represented here, is a matter of the mind's working upon matter from the past to project conclusions onto the future. The wise man's reasoning, which thus appears 'well-neer propheticall', is accompanied by a distinct mode of self-fashioning that Hall depicts earlier in the same sketch. He explains that the wise man

seeks his quietnesse in secrecy, and is wont both to hide himselfe in retired-
nesse, and his tongue in himself. He loves to be gessed at, not known; and
to see the world unseen; and when hee is forced into the light, shewes by his
actions that his obscuritie was neither from affectation nor weaknesse.[19]

Hall's portrayal of this character suggests that this carefully modulated
performance of concealing and revealing is what generates the wise
man's authority in the eyes of others.

In *The Good and the Badde: or, Descriptions of the Worthies,
and Unworthies of This Age*, Breton's account of 'A Worthie Privie
Counceller' puts Hall's wise man to work in numerous political functions:

A Worthy privie Counceller is the Pillar of a Realme, in whose wisdome
and care, under GOD, and the King, stands the safety of a Kingdome ...
hee is an Oracle in the Kings eare, and a Sword in the Kings hand, an even
weight in the ballance of Justice, and a light of grace in the love of truth:
he is an eye of care in the course of law, a heart of love in his service to
his Soveraigne, a mind of honour in the order of his service, and a braine
of invention for the good of the Common-wealth: his place is power-
full, while his service is faithfull, and his honour due in the desert of his
employment.[20]

Here the oracular judgement of the Privy Councillor is redeployed in
various arenas of civic life – including the law – depending on his sovereign's and the commonwealth's needs. In comparison to Hall's allegorical figure, the particularised individual surfaces in this essay through the
evocation of the business and busyness, the numerous titles and functions, of the sovereign's most valued servants.

In the satiric style associated with the collection of Thomas Overbury's
Characters, Shakespeare himself would lampoon the shallow affectation
of this character type in *The Merchant of Venice*, where Graziano cautions Antonio against the posture of a 'Sir Oracle':

There are a sort of men whose visages
Do cream and mantle like a standing pond,
And do a wilful stillness entertain
With purpose to be dressed in an opinion
Of wisdom, gravity, profound conceit –
As who should say, 'I am Sir Oracle,
And when I ope my lips let no dog bark'.
O my Antonio, I do know of these
That therefore only are reputed wise
For saying nothing, when I am very sure
If they should speak, would almost damn those ears
Which, hearing them, would call their brothers fools.

(1.1.88–99)

Here are the tell-tale gestures of the oracle minus the virtue. As easily mocked as Sir Oracle himself are those who assume that great social standing necessarily entails the possession of oracular judgement and authority. John Earle writes in his *Microcosmography* that 'A Vulgar-Spirited Man' is one '[t]hat worships men in place, and those only; and thinks all a great man speaks oracles'.[21]

In *The Winter's Tale*, Shakespeare revisits the character type to craft the morally genuine article. Camillo could as easily be a tribute to Edward Coke as to Breton's Privie Counceller or Hall's Wise Man. His multiple titles and functions in the Sicilian court reinforce his association with Apollo's oracle, the oracle of the law and the oracular character of the essays. Until he branches from the King's 'diseased opinion' (1.2.297), he is Leontes's most valued advisor:

> . . . I have trusted thee, Camillo,
> With all the nearest things to my heart, as well
> My chamber-counsels, wherein, priest-like, thou
> Hast cleansed my bosom. I from thee departed
> Thy penitent reformed.
>
> (1.2.235–9)

While judges were dubbed 'oracles of the law', there was also a long tradition of calling them 'priests'.[22] In *Foure Bookes of Offices: Enabling Privat Persons for the Speciall Service of All Good Princes and Policies*, Barnabe Barnes conflates the functions of all three: 'A judge is as it were . . . a priest of divine justice . . . so is the judge properly called th'interpreter of those lawes . . . and oracle of the Commonwealth.'[23] Here the judge's interpretative function is the central attribute that links him to priest and oracle. Camillo's power to aid the commonwealth through his own legal and political interpretative expertise, however, is circumscribed by Leontes, who reduces his servant's position to that of a personal confidante, just as he reduces all law to his own prerogative ('the ordering on't – / Is all properly ours' (2.1.170–1)).

Camillo is even more directly associated with the judicature a little later in the same scene, when Leontes suggests that his legal expertise and authority particularly qualify him to judge the King's personal situation. In his attempt to conscript his subordinate into a scheme to poison Polixenes, the King assumes that Camillo, 'whom I from meaner form / Have benched and reared to worship' may 'see / Plainly as heaven sees earth and earth sees heaven / How I am galled' (1.2.313–16). The *OED* offers 'to seat on a bench' and 'to seat oneself, or take a seat, upon a bench' as the possible senses in which to take Leontes's claim to have 'benched' Camillo. But 'to bench' is used in a more specific legal sense here and in the instances cited by the *OED*. In *King Lear*, the mad Lear holds an imaginary session and appoints Edgar, the Fool and Kent as presiding judges of his case: 'Thou, his yokefellow of equity, / Bench by his side', he tells the Fool. And in Thomas Heywood's *The Captives*, a friar is described as having 'like a surly Justyce bencht him selff'.[24] The benches in question clearly refer to seats of justice. Leontes imagines that Camillo derives a special perspective from the bench that should enable him to judge the King's most intimate affairs as clearly as he sees the most apparent physical differences (as 'Plainly as heaven sees earth and earth sees heaven').

When Leontes offers him a title too many, the role of murderer, Camillo gives us an example of the oracular reasoning that informs his actions. Like Coke's judge, Camillo 'labour[s] to reach to the depth of all the reasons of the cas[e]' in an aside where, like Hall's wise man, he 'seeks his quietnesse in secrecy'. His asides reveal the part of common-law process that is concealed from the legal record and, as we will see, that is fatally absent from Leontes's own reasoning: judicious and wise deliberation. Camillo considers his commission to poison Polixenes in terms that show him a more balanced judge of his own cause than Leontes proves to be:

What case stand I in? I must be the poisoner
Of good Polixenes, and my ground to do't
Is the obedience to a master, one
Who in rebellion with himself will have
All that are his so too. To do this deed,
Promotion follows. If I could find example
Of thousands that had struck anointed kings
And flourished after, I'd not do't. But since
Nor brass, nor stone, nor parchment bears not one,
Let villainy itself forswear't. I must
Forsake the court. To do't or no is certain
To me a break-neck. Happy star reign now.

(1.2.351–62)

Whereas Leontes projects his own perception and reasoning hegemonically onto the world, or 'impose[s] the kingdom of the mind upon his subjects' (as Jonathan Goldberg writes of James I's literary projects), Camillo here brings various perspectives to bear upon his current condition, investigates the moral and pragmatic implications of his actions, and considers relevant precedents or authorities to decide on the safest course for the future.[25] His method is as oracular as Coke and Hall could wish.

Camillo's concealed reasoning is opposed in the same scene by

Leontes' inferences about his counsellor's character and motives. The King initially assumes that Camillo has formed the same conclusion about Hermione and Polixenes' relationship. When his contrary opinion is revealed, Leontes reads it as the sign of a bad counsellor. The debate that ensues over Camillo's nature incorporates the kinds of traits that were itemised repeatedly in character essays:

> To bide upon't; thou art not honest; or,
> If thou inclin'st that way, thou art a coward,
> Which hoxes honesty behind, restraining
> From course required; or else thou must be counted
> A servant grafted in my serious trust,
> And therein negligent; or else a fool
> That seest a game played home, the rich stake drawn,
> And tak'st it all for jest.
>
> (1.2.242–9)

The fault line in Leontes's reasoning, which leads him to threaten the lives of his closest family and friends, is traceable in this account of Camillo. Disagreement with the King signals dishonesty and disloyalty in his judge or counsellor; moreover, he invests the act with retroactive significance. This one apparently dishonest act of Camillo is an indicator of how his character was already disposed. His history is rewritten to reflect perfectly the King's current perception of him. Camillo's new history then provides evidence of the current and future dishonest state of his character. This is the same kind of reasoning Hermione is subjected to. Leontes concludes that she was unfaithful to him in the conception of Perdita; therefore, according to his logic, she must always have been unfaithful. Face to face with his son Mamillius in 1.2, Leontes is not in doubt about the boy's paternity, but rather in the grip of paradoxical certainties: his son is not his son, and yet the boy looks just like him (1.2.128–35). The King's mind goes to extreme lengths to construct rigid accounts of character continuity, in effect replacing the particularised individual with a caricature or type. His mental agility is both singular and formidable, for the pattern dictates that with any new evidence or actions that he is forced to accept, he must continue rewriting, reinventing character histories, so that someone is always becoming what they have always already been and will always be. This process comes at a great cost: the King's mind is palpably shocked and permanently destabilised over the course of the play.

Leontes' reasoning presents a tyrannical form of historical jurisprudence in which the past is manufactured to reflect the present judge's opinion (in this case, to reflect the King's will). In his version of the oracular method, a strict conception of continuity is forcibly overlaid upon the world of human action and character. The result is the foreclosure of the mode of correction or reform otherwise built into legal thought in which future judicial decisions and legislation present the potential to restore or redirect the law should it veer off course. The past is so thoroughly overwritten or reconceived in Leontes's thinking that if Camillo proves to be a bad councillor now, then there has never been any good in him and thus never will be. Camillo's subsequent self-defence, however, complicates this oversimplified approach to character-reading and, at the same time, illuminates oracular reasoning at its best.

Despite the multiple roles Camillo appears to perform, Leontes would now limit him to one. The 'or', however, that characterises the King's argument above (his counsellor is *either* dishonest, a coward, negligent *or* a fool) is countered by the inclusive, conjunctive 'and' in Camillo's response:

> I may be negligent, foolish, and fearful;
> In every one of these no man is free,
> But that his negligence, his folly, fear,
> Among the infinite doings of the world,
> Sometime puts forth. In your affairs, my lord,
> If ever I were willful-negligent,
> It was my folly; if industriously
> I played the fool, it was my negligence,
> Not weighing well the end. If ever fearful
> To do a thing where I the issue doubted,
> Whereof the execution did cry out
> Against the non-performance, 'twas a fear
> Which oft infects the wisest. These, my lord,
> Are such allowed infirmities that honesty
> Is never free of.

> (1.2.250–64)

In an anonymous essay on 'What a Character Is' from the Overbury collection, the writer explains, 'To square out a character by our English level, it is a picture, real or personal, quaintly drawn in various colors, all of them heightened by one shadowing.'[26] Similarly, in Camillo's answer, individual actions are evaluated against a person's predominant trait, in this case a virtue: the questionable 'infinite doings of the world' can thus coexist with 'honesty'. His self-defence, however, brings out the contribution of time that is otherwise marginalised by the essay's picture analogy and by Leontes' character-reading. Camillo's argument is subtended by a method of oracular accommodation that emphasises both the potential for error and its correction as well as historical continuity. The 'Sometime' that puts forth 'his negligence, his folly, [and] fear', that both 'makes and unfolds error' (4.1.2) as the Chorus later says, is the same time through which honesty or dishonesty, as a trait, is revealed. The complex structure of character defended here is demonstrated much later in the play. Hermione's listless self-defence against charges of adultery enacts the futility of attempting to prove one's virtuousness ('it shall scarce boot me / To say "Not guilty"' (3.2.24–5)). Nevertheless, the constancy of counsellor and Queen is successfully established over time: Camillo's allegiance to Leontes persists even after sixteen years in another king's service, and Hermione comes back from the dead. Because Hermione's restoration is the result of theatrics and not witchcraft – because she has actually been alive all along – her aging statue represents the temporally inflected virtue of constancy that further testifies to her original and continuing innocence. It was a legal and popular commonplace that truth was the daughter of time, a conviction reflected in the full title of Greene's romance: *Pandosto, The triumph of time. Wherein is discovered by a pleasant historie, that although by the meanes of sinister fortune truth may be concealed, yet by time in spite of fortune it is most manifestly revealed.* In *The Winter's Tale*, Shakespeare asks us to imagine character truths as the product of an extended process of temporal revelation.

Apollo's Oracle of the Law

The exchange between Camillo and Leontes prefigures the King's assumption of the oracle's support and his subsequent refutation of its authority once its contrary opinion is revealed in court. Just as there is no truth in the independently minded judge or counsellor, so there is no truth in an oracle that contradicts him. While the reasoning practices of the legal-political decision-maker surface through the above argument over character, the source and scope of legal and political powers are contested in the course of Hermione's trial, convened ostensibly to determine a question of fact, her innocence or guilt of adultery and treason. In this later scene, Apollo's oracle evokes its early modern counterparts through its legal function and its challenge to the King's free reign over the state's legal process. Leontes' flawed deliberative strategies prove to be a prelude to his misappropriation of legal powers and mismanagement of legal procedure during the trial. The dramatic fallout brings to the fore the concurrent historical struggle between James and the judiciary over the sovereign's relationship to the law and the jurisdiction of courts. Obliged to resolve the onstage conflict, however, Shakespeare activates complimentary aspects of James's and Coke's ideologies that are reflected in the orchestration of a new balance – at the very least a separation – of powers at the end of the scene.

As Leontes admits, as his counsellors are aware and as Hermione herself intuits, the queen has already been convicted within Leontes's imagination or reason.[27] The King arrives at his own 'diseased opinion' (1.2.297), as Camillo calls it, long before the trial begins. We learn that he has dispatched Cleomenes and Dion to the temple in Delphos for Apollo's opinion on the case, because, 'Though [he is] satisfied and need no more / Than what [he] know[s], yet shall the oracle / Give rest to th' minds of others' (2.1.190–2). Assuming that the oracle's judgement will amplify or over-determine his own, Leontes convenes the trial, then, not to decide the fact of the case; rather, as A. E. B. Coldiron, David M. Bergeron and Daniel J. Kornstein all point out, he intends to vindicate himself.[28] In his opening remarks in court, he announces, 'Let us be cleared / Of being tyrannous since we so openly / Proceed in justice, which shall have due course' (3.2.4–6). The King directly invites the on- and offstage audience to evaluate the justice of his legal process rather than the evidence in Hermione's case; and it is legitimate process that Leontes defies most violently when he perceives Apollo's anger.[29]

In *Pandosto*, Apollo's oracle reveals that the eponymous King has falsely accused his wife of adultery and attempted regicide, whereupon Pandosto immediately cedes to the oracle's authority. Bergeron points out that the order of events shifts in Shakespeare's dramatisation of the trial scene. After the oracle's judgement is read out in court, King Leontes first questions the honesty of the speaking officer and then the honesty of the oracle itself: 'There is no truth at all i' th' Oracle', he decides, 'The sessions shall proceed: this is mere falsehood' (3.2.137–8). As Bergeron observes, 'Pandosto immediately relented; Leontes commits sacrilege and blasphemy against Apollo.'[30] The very next thing announced in court is the death of the King's son, and Leontes interprets it as immediate punishment for angering the god.[31] Lynn Enterline alone considers what Leontes believes he is being punished *for*: 'Mamillius's death . . . results from Leontes' having doubted oracular speech. Or so Leontes understands it.'[32] The King goes on to ask Apollo pardon for, 'My great profaneness 'gainst thine oracle' (3.2.150–1). This 'profaneness', I argue, is his conduct during the trial scene and *not* his earlier extraordinary and unjust treatment of Hermione, Camillo, Polixenes, Perdita and even Antigonus.

By challenging the oracle's authority, Leontes upends what is presented in the play as established legal procedure. Pre-'condemned / Upon surmises' (3.2.109–10), Hermione concludes her futile self-defence by requesting the judgement of the oracle, to which a lord with officiating powers responds: 'This your request / Is altogether just. Therefore, bring forth, / And in Apollo's name, his oracle' (3.2.114–16). Initially inscribed by Leontes as a supplement to or extension of the monarch's authority, here, at trial, the oracle is reinscribed as a customary feature of 'open' proceedings – at the very least, for a Sicilian state trial of this magnitude, it is considered 'altogether just'. By annexing legal procedure to his will, identifying justice with his own reasoning and behaviour, Leontes threatens the standard operations for the identification and correction of error in Sicily. By acting upon his own construction of the royal prerogative, the King 'cannot choose but branch' (1.1.21) from the oracle, a force that is more closely concerned with the practical execution or 'ord'ring' of the law than has yet been understood. The judicial authority of sovereign and of oracle are thus pitted against one another in a jurisdictional battle that is at once extremely topical in the early seventeenth century and understandable in terms of the available pseudo-historical narratives of the development of the political nation.

In *De Republica Anglorum*, Thomas Smith explains that, in the beginning, a kingdom was ruled by an absolute monarch, such that his subjects 'obeyed him for his great wisedome and forecast, went to him in doubtfull cases as to an oracle of God, feared his curse and malediction as proceeding of Gods own mouth'.[33] In 'the first and most natural beginning and source of cities, towns, nations, and kingdomes, and of all civil societies', judicial or oracular powers were centred within the King.[34] But far from that ancient or mythical absolutism was Henry de Bracton's England, whose King was 'under God and the Law',[35] or John Fortescue's England, whose 'kingdome politique' he championed in opposition to 'royall gouernement'.[36] James himself explained to parliament that 'all Kings that are not tyrants, or perjured, will be glad to bound themselves within the limits of their Laws ... For it is a great difference between a Kings government in a settled State, and what Kings in their original power might do in *Indiuiduo vago*'. J. P. Sommerville translates '*Indiuidiuo vago*' as 'an undefined individual; i.e. before [a King's] power had been regulated'.[37] Two different sources of authority underwrite these historical claims about the development of England. The first involves the process of substitution: the gradual transference of sovereign powers to subordinate delegates for the more efficient administration of the law and government. The second involves the 'settling' of the state, especially the gradual establishment of laws and legal-political institutions and offices that come to be legitimised by reference to their own history and practices. These two processes provided opposing claims to judicial authority in the seventeenth century, yet legal-political substitution, which naturally engages questions of representation, has received far greater literary critical attention. Jonathan Goldberg has explicated the literary and political uses of 'the voice of power', which is, 'in Foucault's definition, to speak beyond oneself, ascribing one's powers elsewhere'.[38] More recently, Holger Schott Syme has illuminated the 'logic of substitution that governed the construction of authority and authenticity in judicial and theatrical performances'.[39] Much less attention has been paid to the process of settling, although it was the basis for judicial opposition to crown interference in legal causes during James's reign.

The King's right and fitness to intervene in or personally judge legal issues came under scrutiny in a jurisdictional dispute that arose between the common-law judges and the ecclesiastical court of High Commission in the course of Fuller's Case (1607). The Archbishop of Canterbury, appealing to James to intervene, argued, much like Leontes, that 'The matter – / The loss, the gain, the ord'ring on't – / Is all properly [the King's]' (2.1.169–71) because he is the fountainhead from which all legal authority springs: 'the Judges are but delegates of the King, and . . . the King may take what causes he shall please to determine, from the determination of the Judges, and may determine them himself.'[40] The Archbishop's argument rests on the logic that delegated powers can be resumed. In response, Coke (then Chief Justice of Common Pleas) emphasised that the form in which judgement is given is in the name of the King's courts: the judges do not speak for the King or for themselves. More radically (and to James, infuriatingly), he further argued that the King was not qualified for the job. He goes on in his report of this case in *Prohibition del Roy* to portray the judiciary as possessing much more than delegated monarchal authority:

> [T]he King said, that he thought the Law was founded upon reason, and that he and others had reason, as well as the Judges [to determine the law]: To which it was answered by me, that true it was, that God had endowed his Majesty with excellent Science, and great endowments of nature; but his Majesty was not learned in the Laws of his Realm of England, and causes which concern the life, or inheritance, or goods, or fortunes of his Subjects; they are not to be decided by natural reason but by the artificial reason and judgment of Law, which . . . requires long study and experience, before that a man can attain to the cognizance of it.[41]

Although the judiciary is appointed by the King to his nominal courts, its authority is nevertheless substantially self-legitimising, derived from a professional method that excluded the uninitiated – King and commoner alike.[42] 'James talked often of the *arcana imperii*, the secrets of state, that were reserved to the king alone', Richard Helgerson observes; '[a]s Coke presents (and represents) it, the common law has its own *arcana*'.[43]

James's fury at Coke's claims is legendary, and the Chief Justice hardly succeeded in redirecting the King's legal energies. In a speech from 21 March 1610, James declared that kings, like Gods, are 'Judges over all their subjects and in all causes'.[44] He went on to reassure parliament of his active concern:

> Yee have heard (I am sure) of the pains I took both in the causes of the Admiralty, and of the Prohibitions [i.e. in cases like Fuller's]: If any man therefore will bring me any just complaints upon any matters of so high a nature as this is, yee may assure your selves that I will not spare my labour in hearing it. In faith you never had a more painful King, or that will be readier in his person to determine causes that are fit for his hearing.[45]

Printed three times in 1610 – the year before Leontes was first represented onstage wresting power from the oracle and abusing legal procedure – this speech magnified James's interest in direct monarchal intervention at law, the effects of which would challenge the powers of the judiciary and parliament.[46]

In the Sicilian trial, the results of King Leontes's heavy-handed intervention propel him down a path of religious repentance and produce a highly mediated rule of state. In the wake of Mamillius's death, he confesses his own crimes and injustices against his best friend (Polixenes), his best counsellor (Camillo) and his 'sweet'st companion' (5.1.11) (Hermione), and commissions Paulina to supervise his punishment: a lifetime of rites at the single grave of his wife and son (3.2.231–40). To a radical degree, he goes on to delegate his will to Paulina, who, along with Camillo, is most clearly associated with the oracle.[47] At the end of the trial scene, in fact, she appears to adopt the 'priest-like' function Camillo once held. And, as with Camillo, this function is as legal as it is personal: Paulina's first object as Leontes' 'spiritual guide' is to usher the King out of the courtroom, removing him from the sphere of judicial decision-making where he proves dangerously incompetent. At the end of the trial scene, then, the play presents the relocation of legal authority squarely within oracular or judicial, rather than royal, hands, while the otherwise undisciplined mental-emotional life of the King's natural body is harnessed to daily acts of piety.

In an effective accommodation of common-law and royal ideologies, Leontes' abrupt shift in focus to religious practices both ejects the King from the judge's seat and redeems his character in accord with James I's own political theology. As Constance Jordan reminds us in her discussion of *The True Law of Free Monarchies*, according to James's schema, '[p]roper rule was guaranteed by [the King's] piety'.[48] With no legitimate recourse against tyrants, subjects could rest assured that the King's rule was in the service of god's by witnessing his religious self-fashioning.[49] James repeatedly asserted that only God could judge a King; nevertheless, a good King will submit himself to the law as an example to his people.[50] Here in Shakespeare's romance, Leontes is judged and punished by Apollo, in the form of his son's death, after which he makes a show of submitting himself to Paulina's direction, first to her supervision of his spiritual rites and then, in Act 5, to her legal-political counsel. The result is a face-saving balance of power that common-law authorities like Edward Coke would likely have approved, in which the king is removed from the judicial bench and relegated to the political role of ethical/religious exemplar. The promise of this new arrangement is put into practice in the last scene of Act 5. In the final moments of the play, I will argue, Leontes performs the kind of formal authorising or legitimating function that the sovereign assumed in parliament, while Paulina exhibits the more active judicial power associated with statute interpretation.

Lawful Art

To read Shakespeare's oracle as a figure for the early modern English judiciary is to relocate the immediate source of its authority in a professionally safeguarded method of self-fashioning, formally sanctioned by but independent of a higher, prior source of power, such as a King or divinity. Indeed, Howard Felperin observes that part of the uniqueness of Shakespeare's oracle is produced by its separation from its divine source: the contents of Apollo's judgement are reported during the trial but Apollo himself is never represented. This is an alteration of Greene's romance in which Apollo's voice is heard, and it is in contradistinction to the representation of divine authorities in Shakespeare's preceding romances, *Pericles* and *Cymbeline*.[51] The result, Felperin argues, is the destabilisation of the truth that the oracle is intended to represent:

> Since [the oracle] is supposed to be itself a validation, there is nothing left to fall back on when its validity is questioned [by Leontes], other than Cleomenes' reported awe. Once cut off from the presence of their divine speaker, with his univocality of meaning and intent, Apollo's words enter the realm of ... the interpretable, where they can be contradicted or dismissed, for all we know, with impunity.[52]

Felperin is right to underscore the human and linguistic mediation of Apollo's judgement: it is received at the temple, sealed in a document, carried by Cleomenes and Dion to Sicily, and read in court by a third lord. Instead of opening a chasm of interpretative uncertainty, however, the procedure instills in the visitors to Apollo's temple a sense that 'something rare … will rush to knowledge' (3.1.20–1) once the contents of the oracle are learned. According to Cleomenes and Dion, understanding or revelation is imminent rather than an impossibility in this process. 'I shall report', explains Dion, 'the celestial habits – / Me thinks I so should term them – and the reverence / Of the grave wearers. O, the sacrifice! / How ceremonious, solemn, and unearthly / It was i'th' offering!' (3.1.4–8). The unearthliness of the event, its supernatural quality, is here depicted as an aesthetic achievement, the artful and strategic result of the priests' practices. With no direct access to Apollo's deliberative method, nor his sealed words, the visitors construct an understanding of the authority – and from there, of the validity – of the oracle based on the ritual at the temple, on the ceremonial construction of the reception and transmission of its judgement. Like the early modern oracles of the law, Apollo's oracle establishes the legitimacy of its judgement through the integrity of a performance or procedure that strategically conceals and reveals. Most importantly, the report of the Delphic oracular process depicts a form of legitimate and conscientiously executed proceedings (quasi-legal in that they culminate in a just verdict or judgement) in contradistinction to the trial scene in Sicily that immediately follows.

The theatrics that surround the written oracle's transmission ensure that its validity (its authority as truth) is never really in doubt, though its ability to generate justice (its success as a speech act) is obstructed in the course of Hermione's trial. In her article on 'The Rhetoric of Animation in *The Winter's Tale*', Lynn Enterline identifies the failure of performative language in the trial, in which Leontes equates the law and the truth with his own 'linguistic prerogative', as the culmination of a play-wide pattern in which language exceeds or falls short of speakers' intentions. To see language and action or language and intention realigned, she maintains, we must wait until the final scene, in which Hermione transforms from a statue to a living body in imitation of Ovid's story of Pygmalion. Through the 'consciously and artistically controlled theatrical effects [of] Paulina's staging of Pygmalion's statue … language appears to perform the act it intends: "Music! awake her! … descend; be stone no more".' I argue that the misfiring speech acts that Enterline observes in the Sicilian courtroom are caused by the disingenuousness and illegitimacy of Leontes' 'open' proceedings. While the failure of performative language in the trial signals the failure of Sicilian justice, the subsequent success of performative language in the Pygmalion-like scene orchestrated by Paulina signals its final restoration. With the penitent Leontes' approbation, Paulina's resonance with both the mystic and legal aspects of Apollo's oracle solidifies over the course of Act 5, so that her theatrics and 'magically effective voice', her actions and her speech, successfully combine in the final scene as an expression of legitimate legal authority and practice.[53]

In 5.1, we discover Paulina upholding the oracle's judgement and appropriating its conditional, paradoxical, riddling style for herself. Clearly the most influential advisor at court, she counters the other voices that urge Leontes to remarry in order to obtain an heir despite the oracular ruling that 'the King shall live without an heir if that which is lost be not found'. She succeeds in obtaining Leontes' promise not to seek a new wife. In so doing, Paulina upholds the force of Apollo's oracle at the same time that she produces her own prophetic judgement: the King shall not have a wife 'Unless another / As like Hermione as is her picture / Affront his eye' (5.1.72–4). And 'That / Shall be when your first queen's again in breath. / Never till then' (5.1.82–4). Hermione's final return thus substantiates not only the original oracle but also the oracular function that Paulina self-consciously adopts. Her self-fulfilling prophecy simultaneously originates and demonstrates Paulina's legitimate judicial authority in the Sicilian court. Her association with the mystical and legal oracles is developed further in 5.2, a scene turned over to report, much like the earlier one between Cleomenes and Dion. An account is given here of her divided response to the news of Perdita's survival and Antigonus' demise. In the course of this exchange between nameless gentlemen, a portrait of her joy and grief is verbally painted that could not have been physically staged: 'oh, the noble combat that twixt joy and sorrow was fought in Paulina: she had one eye declined for the loss of her husband, another elevated that the oracle was fulfilled' (5.2.68–71). Our second last impression of Paulina, before she returns to the stage to bring Hermione back to life, consists of an image that suggests the trance-like state of an ancient oracle in action, evoking the ceremony of Apollo's temple that the play presents as emblematic of just legal proceedings.

In the *Metamorphoses*, Enterline observes, Pygmalion's statue is brought to life through a speech act: the sculptor's prayer to Venus initiates the extraordinary action that follows. It is a story motivated by a pun: '[d]rawing on the contemporary word for rhetorical power – the power, that is, to "move" (*movere*) – the narrator tells us that in his statue, Pygmalion believes he has an audience who "*wants* to be moved".' The statue's metamorphosis thus presents 'an erotic version of a rhetorician's dream'. In *The Winter's Tale*, the statue scene is the culmination of 'a rhetorically self-conscious play in which Shakespeare continues to test language's power as a mode of action rather than mere vehicle of representation, to search for a kind of voice that can effect the changes of which it speaks'.[54] Instead of a god, it is Paulina's imperatives that trigger Hermione's apparent metamorphosis that underscores the basic theatrical illusion of dramatic language. This is not, however, the only way word and action are aligned in this scene. Paulina's oracular verbal force ensures that the illusion of Hermione's transformation is accompanied by the performative power of a legal judgement.

Nowhere is the performative force of language more overt and more consequential than in the legal sphere. Thomas Wilson's *A Christian Dictionary* defines 'a lively oracle' as 'Making alive, or giving life. Such the words of the law are, in their own nature.'[55] A lively oracle is an oration, sentence or judgement that mobilises techniques of rhetorical mimesis such as energia in the pursuit of 'moving' an audience. The qualification added to the legal example suggests, however, that the law has a linguistic life that distinguishes it from traditional methods of mimesis. In fact, it surpasses the eloquent illusion of 'liveliness' achieved by rhetorical animation and the theatrical enactment of dramatic dialogue: embodied in documents such as statutes, legal language is authorised to alter or create not only the legal but also the social and political status of subjects and property. Within legal-political rhetoric, moreover, the gatekeepers of this performative power were represented as *bringing statutes to life*, the sovereign through his or her passive legitimising function and the oracular judiciary through its active interpretive function.

In *De Republica Anglorum*, Smith explains that the authority of Parliament ensured that laws were passed 'in peace & consultation where the Prince is to give life, and the last and highest commaundement' to legislative acts.[56] He goes on to elaborate on the typical sentiments expressed in the Lord Chancellor's closing speech to parliament, in which the country's highest-ranking legal official declares 'in the Princes name . . . that the doings [the Acts] might have perfect life & accomplishment by his princelie authoritie'.[57] In a much more remarkable amplification of this commonplace that 'princelie authoritie' gives 'perfect life' to the law, Christopher Yelverton, Speaker of the House in 1597–8, compares the Queen's function in parliament to the god's within the story of Pygmalion:

> The picture of Pigmalion, though by art it were never so curious and exquisite, and that in all the liniaments (almost) it had overcome nature and enticed the artisan himself, through the finenes of the faitures, to be fondly enamored with his owne creature, yet had it not the delight of life untill Jupiter, assuming some pittie of his wofull state and travell, inspired breath into it.

So these our petitions, howe fitt soever they be framed, and howe commodious soever they be imagined for your kingdome, yet be they but emptie and senceless shaddowes untill your Majestie takeing compassion on the common wealth, and entring into the examination of them by your princely wisdome, shall instill your most high and roiall assent, to geve full life and essence unto them.[58]

In the parliamentarian's speech, the mystification of aesthetic skill and effect subtends the mystification of political power. Ovid's story of mimetic skill that is inspired by a divine breath or voice provides a surprisingly apt analogy for the sovereign's authorisation of legal language and instruments. Motivating the comparison is a pun on statue and statute: just as Jupiter gives life to the statue, so Elizabeth breathes life into the parliamentary statutes. In the final scene of *The Winter's Tale*, Shakespeare adapts this pun to register and reconcile the jurisdictional tensions between James and his judiciary – tensions that were exacerbated by a King who identified his authority over the law with god's creative and destructive powers over life: 'God hath power to create, or destroy, make, or unmake at his pleasure, to give life, or send death, to judge all . . . And the like power have Kings.'[59]

If the sovereign gave statutes legal life by authorising parliamentary acts, it was the judiciary who made them walk and talk, put them into effect, through interpretive practices and the determination of cases. As we have seen, these oracles of the law established and defended their performative authority through a narrative that claimed what was in the process of coming to life had actually always already existed. Accordingly, judicial activity that appeared creative was dressed as a return to, or restoration of, the law's proper course or spirit that had been altered through erroneous interventions. In the Preface to the third volume of his *Reports*, Coke writes:

albeit some time by actes of Parliament, and sometime by invention and wit of men, some points of the auncient Common Law have been altered or diverted from his due course; yet in revolution of time, the same . . . have bin with great applause, for the avoyding of many inconveniencies, restored againe.[60]

The speciousness of this reasoning and the reality of judicial inventiveness were not lost on James. In his notes from a meeting between the King and the judiciary (13 November 1608), Julius Caesar reports an outburst by James in which he protests that '[t]he Judges are like the papists. They allege scriptures and will interpret the same. The Judges allege statutes and reserve the exposition thereof to themselves.'[61] The King's suspicions about judicial misrepresentation were not the byproduct of a tyrannical paranoia – far from it. The court was often forced to take it on faith that statutes and reports not only supported a legal authority's argument or interpretation, but that they even existed in the first place. There are instances of Coke, for example, alleging or 'vouching' in court for the existence of statutes and manuscript reports that, at times, could only be found in his own private collection.[62] In a later Elizabethan treatise attributed to Christopher Hatton, Lorna Hutson uncovers the concern that the judicial interpretation of statutes 'constituted a new form of political agency which no one as yet had seen fit to check': 'For the Sages of the Law, whose wits are exercised in such matters, have the interpretation in their hands, and their Authority no man taketh in hand to control: wherefore their Power is very great, and high, and we seek these Interpretations as Oracles from their mouthes.'[63] In the conclusion to *The Winter's Tale*, the Pygmalion intertext advances and resolves the question of the oracular Paulina's lawful or unlawful inventiveness and of Leontes' fitness or unfitness to intervene in Sicilian law.

The increasing political stability of Shakespeare's Sicily is writ large by the decorous exchange of courtesies between King and counsellor that opens the last scene set in Paulina's gallery (5.3.1–10), replacing the breaches on both sides that characterised the Leontes–Paulina relationship in the first half of the play. Nevertheless, as Paulina assumes the oracular function of bringing the statu(t)e to life, the scene insinuates the potential for her strategies to misfire and for Leontes to interfere once again with disastrous consequences. Her method of concealing and gradually revealing Hermione's continuing existence risks aggravating the royal humour that ignited the tragic plot in the first place. Indeed, the visible transformation of the King is registered in the concern expressed by Camillo, Polixenes, and Paulina (5.3.49–59). At the same time that she ostensibly attempts to comfort or calm the King, Paulina intentionally plants suggestions for his overactive imagination. 'I'll draw the curtain', she offers, since 'My lord's almost so far transported that / He'll think anon it lives' (5.3.68–70). 'No longer shall you gaze on't,' she proclaims, 'lest your fancy / May think anon it moves' (5.3.60–1). 'I am sorry, sir, I have thus far stirred you; but / I could afflict you farther' (5.3.74–5), she simultaneously apologises, promises, and threatens. These suggestions gradually prepare the way for Leontes's acceptance of a new reality at the same time that they expose to the gathered court his ongoing psychological susceptibility. Her stage-management keeps the King conscious of his mental-emotional instability and of his gross errors in judgement: the statue has his 'evils conjured to remembrance' (5.3.40). In effect, Paulina subverts Leontes' self-possession and exploits his reformed self-awareness and self-doubt in order to contain his tyrannical desire to intervene in oracular business. His two persistent character traits, his psychological excitability and his legal-political overreaching, are simultaneously demonstrated by his desire to kiss the statue (5.3.79–80). He is prevented from doing so by Paulina, who bars him from participating in the final oracular drama in a principal role. The King instead is forced to revert to his rightful authorising function, sanctioning both Paulina's stage show and the politically important marriage unions that conclude the play.[64] He orders Paulina to 'Proceed' (5.3.97–8) with her lawful art: 'What you can make [Hermione's statue] do, / I am content to look on; what to speak, / I am content to hear' (5.3.97, 91–3). And, along with Polixenes, he 'justifi[es]' Paulina's 'worth and honesty' to her future husband, Camillo (5.3.144–6).

We are repeatedly assured that the unique authority Paulina exercises in the last scene – that her 'business' (5.3.96), 'spell' (5.3.105) or 'art' (5.3.110) – is 'lawful' (5.3.105, 111). That is, she is not violating natural or positive law through the use of witchcraft to bring Hermione back to life. She is not fully exonerated of the suspicion of unnatural and unlawful creativity, however, until the on- and offstage audience appreciate that the Queen's revivification is the achievement of human agency and calculation rather than magic. Hermione has been in hiding for sixteen years, awaiting the return of her daughter. The Queen's absence was thus a sublimated presence, and her return represents the principle of continuity or temporal coherence that is as important to historical jurisprudence and artificial reasoning as it is to the personal virtue of constancy. Paulina has engineered an ideal version of the oracular method in which her restoration of Hermione puts Leontes' past judicial errors under erasure: the Queen's death was the beginning of an elaborate illusion. As J. H. Baker observes, 'the idea of law as prophecy . . . embraces a hope that the error [of a legal decision] will one day be rectified, or perhaps a prediction that its consequences will be minimized [and] will produce that right result when the time is ripe.'[65] The division of legal and political responsibilities inaugurated at the end of Hermione's trial ultimately leads to the restoration of the royal family and a stable political future for Sicily and Bohemia alike in the final scene. While offstage the relationship between James and Coke continued to sour until Coke was removed from the bench in 1616, the onstage accommodation of royal and common-law ideologies suggests that Leontes will continue his submission to the oracular direction of Paulina: 'Good Paulina, / Lead us from hence . . . Hastily lead away' (5.3.151–5).

Notes

1. Howard Felperin, '"Tongue-tied our queen?": The Deconstruction of Presence in *The Winter's Tale*', in Patricia Parker and Geoffrey Hartman (eds), *Shakespeare and the Question of Theory* (New York: Methuen, 1985), pp. 5–6.
2. Stephen Orgel, '*The Winter's Tale*: A Modern Perspective', in William Shakespeare, *The Winter's Tale*, ed. Barbara A. Mowat and Paul Werstine (New York: Washington Square Press, 1998), p. 262. For Orgel's more extensive treatments of the play, see 'The Poetics of Incomprehensibility', *Shakespeare Quarterly* 42 (1991), pp. 431–7, and his introduction to William Shakespeare, *The Winter's Tale*, ed. Stephen Orgel (Oxford: Oxford University Press, 1996).
3. Thomas Blount, *Nomo-lexikon, a Law-Dictionary Interpreting Such Difficult and Obscure Words and Terms as Are Found either in Our Common or Statute, Ancient or Modern Lawes* (London, 1670), sig. A2^r.
4. Lorna Hutson finds a similar overlap between the forensic rhetorical methods of justices of the peace (JPs) and popular literature. By the end of the sixteenth century, the JP's methods 'have already become indistinguishable from the "wit" and "judgement" exercised in more informal contexts by the variety of fictional social types (ne'er-do-wells, rogues, gallants, gentlemen, gentlewomen, clowns, maids) coming to prominence in satirical representations of urban fashionable life and low life both in print and on the stage' (*The Invention of Suspicion: Law and Mimesis in Shakespeare and Renaissance Drama* (Oxford: Oxford University Press, 2007), p. 304).
5. David M. Bergeron, 'The Apollo Mission in *The Winter's Tale*', in Maurice Hunt (ed.), *The Winter's Tale: Critical Essays* (New York: Garland, 1995), p. 376.
6. Lynn Enterline, '"You Speak a Language that I Understand Not": The Rhetoric of Animation in *The Winter's Tale*', *Shakespeare Quarterly* 48 (1997), p. 19. See also Lynn Enterline, *The Rhetoric of the Body from Ovid to Shakespeare* (Cambridge: Cambridge University Press, 2000).
7. Stuart M. Kurland, '"We Need No More of Your Advice": Political Realism in *The Winter's Tale*', *Studies in English Literature, 1500–1900* 31.2 (1991), pp. 365–86.
8. David Schalkwyk, *Shakespeare, Love and Service* (Cambridge: Cambridge University Press, 2008), p. 263.
9. See Harold J. Berman, 'The Origins of Historical Jurisprudence: Coke, Selden, Hale', *Yale Law Journal* 103.7 (1994), pp. 1651–738; Glenn Burgess, *The Politics of the Ancient Constitution* (University Park: Pennsylvania State University Press, 1993); J. G. A. Pocock, *The Ancient Constitution and the Feudal Law: A Study of English Historical Thought in the Seventeenth Century* (Cambridge: Cambridge University Press, 1987); and J. W. Tubbs, *The Common Law Mind: Medieval and Early Modern Conceptions* (Baltimore: Johns Hopkins University Press, 2000). On Edward Coke's contribution to historical jurisprudence and his reputation as an oracle of the law, see Richard Helgerson, *Forms of Nationhood: The Elizabethan Writing of England* (Chicago: University of Chicago Press, 1992), pp. 78–88.

10. Edward Coke, *The Selected Writings of Sir Edward Coke*, ed. Steve Sheppard, vol. 1 (Indianapolis: Liberty Fund, 2003), p. 479. Hereafter this edition is cited parenthetically as *Coke*, followed by volume and page numbers.
11. *Coke* 1: 59.
12. *Coke* 3: 1337.
13. J. H. Baker, *The Law's Two Bodies: Some Evidential Problems in English Legal History* (Oxford: Oxford University Press, 2001), p. 16. See also John P. Dawson, *The Oracles of the Law* (Westport, CT: Greenwood Press, 1978), pp. 50–65.
14. *Coke* 1: 60.
15. Robert Greene, *Pandosto. The Triumph of Time* (1588), in Geoffrey Bullough (ed.), *Narrative and Dramatic Sources of Shakespeare*, vol. 8 (New York: Columbia University Press, 1975), p. 169.
16. William Shakespeare, *The Winter's Tale*, in William Shakespeare, *The Norton Shakespeare*, ed. Stephen Greenblatt, Walter Cohen, Suzanne Gossett, Jean E. Howard, Katherine Eisaman Maus and Gordon McMullan, 3rd edn (New York: W. W. Norton, 2016), 3.2.130–3. All future Shakespeare quotations are from this edition, unless otherwise noted, and hereafter cited parenthetically by act, scene and line number.
17. Donald Beecher, 'Introduction', in Thomas Overbury, *Characters: Together with Poems, News, Edicts, and Paradoxes Based on the Eleventh Edition of A wife Now the Widow of Sir Thomas Overbury*, ed. Donald Beecher (Ottawa: Dovehouse Editions, 2003), p. 34. On charactery and Shakespeare, see Christy Desmet's *Reading Shakespeare's Characters: Rhetoric, Ethics, and Identity* (Amherst: University of Massachusetts Press, 1992).
18. Joseph Hall, *Characters of Vertues and Vices: In Two Bookes* (London, 1608), pp. 8–11.
19. Hall, *Characters of Vertues and Vices*, pp. 7–8.
20. Nicholas Breton, *The Good and The Badde: or, Descriptions of the Worthies, and Unworthies of This Age. Where the Best May See Their Graces, and the Worst Discerne Their Baseness* (London, 1616), p. 5.
21. John Earle, *Micro-cosmographie. Or, A Peece of the World Discovered, in Essayes and Characters* (London, 1628), sig. I8ᵛ.
22. Ernst H. Kantorowicz explains that 'jurists [were] styled by Roman Law so suggestively [as] "Priests of Justice"', and that this tradition made its way into works important to the development of the English common-law tradition, such as Bracton's and Fortescue's (*The King's Two Bodies* (Princeton: Princeton University Press, 1997), p. 16).
23. Barnabe Barnes, *Foure Bookes of Offices: Enabling Privat Persons for the Speciall Service of All Good Princes and Policies* (London, 1606), p. 142.
24. 'bench, v.', *OED Online* (Oxford University Press, September 2016).
25. Jonathan Goldberg, *James I and the Politics of Literature: Jonson, Shakespeare, Donne and Their Contemporaries* (Baltimore: Johns Hopkins University Press, 1983), p. 23. Kurland's conclusion that Camillo's moral character is tainted by his calculation of self-interest is, I would argue, misguided, since it is self-preservation that is really at stake. Where the counsellor may show moral weakness is in his abandonment of Hermione, as

A. E. B. Coldiron observes in "'Tis rigor and not law": Trials of Women as Trials of Patriarchy in *The Winter's Tale*', *Renaissance Papers* (2004), p. 45.

26. Overbury, *Characters*, p. 293.
27. Kurland writes 'the result [of the trial] is, as Hermione recognizes, foreordained' ('"We Need No More of Your Advice"', p. 375).
28. Coldiron, "'Tis rigor and not law"', p. 45; Bergeron, 'The Apollo Mission in *The Winter's Tale*', pp. 376–7; and Daniel Kornstein, *Kill All the Lawyers? Shakespeare's Legal Appeal* (Princeton: Princeton University Press, 1994), p. 83.
29. Kornstein is similarly sensitive to the self-reflexivity in these lines, but his attention to procedure is much more general. In reference to 3.2.4–7, he writes:

> Given such high-minded goals, the exact trial procedures to be used take on great importance. Who will be the judge? Will there be a jury? What kind of proof will be offered? What quantum of proof will suffice? A trial will prove nothing, neither Hermione's guilt nor Leontes's lack of tyranny, if the trial is merely a sham, a show trial. (*Kill All the Lawyers?*, p. 177)

Leontes' injustice and the sham nature of the trial, however, have been established for the audience long before 3.2 begins, foreclosing several of the questions that Kornstein raises. Kornstein further reads 'Hermione's request for trial by Apollo' as the queen's surrender of 'whatever procedural rights she has', while I argue here that her appeal to the oracle is revealed as an established feature of the Sicilian justice system (*Kill All the Lawyers?*, p. 179).

30. Bergeron, 'The Apollo Mission in *The Winter's Tale*', p. 372.
31. Felperin deconstructs the causal relationship that Leontes and generations of critics, audiences and readers have perceived between divine vengeance and the boy's death ('"Tongue-tied our queen?"', pp. 6–7).
32. Enterline, '"You Speak a Language that I Understand Not"', p. 28.
33. Thomas Smith, *De Republica Anglorum*, ed. Mary Dewar (Cambridge: Cambridge University Press, 1982), p. 60.
34. Smith, *De Republica Anglorum*, p. 60.
35. *Coke* 1: 479.
36. John Fortescue, *A Learned Commendation of the Politique Lawes of Englande*, trans. Richard Mulcaster (London, 1567), sig. E1^r.
37. James VI and I, *Political Writings*, ed. J. P. Sommerville (Cambridge: Cambridge University Press, 1994), pp. 184, 296.
38. Goldberg, *James I and the Politics of Literature*, p. 6.
39. Holger Schott, *The Trials of Orality in Early Modern England, 1550–1625* (Dissertation, Harvard University, 2004), p. 6. See also Holger Schott Syme, *Theatre and Testimony in Shakespeare's England: A Culture of Mediation* (Cambridge: Cambridge University Press, 2012).
40. *Coke* 1: 479.
41. *Coke* 1: 481.
42. See Allen D. Boyer, 'Sir Edward Coke, Ciceronianus: Classical Rhetoric and the Common Law Tradition', in Allen D. Boyer (ed.), *Law, Liberty, and Parliament: Selected Essays on the Writings of Sir Edward Coke* (Indianapolis: Liberty Fund, 2004), pp. 224–53.

43. Helgerson, *Forms of Nationhood*, p. 100.

44. James VI and I, *Political Writings*, p. 181.

45. James VI and I, *Political Writings*, pp. 191–2.

46. James VI and I, *Political Writings*, p. 295.

47. In the final scene of the play Leontes again cedes control to Paulina: 'Faced with the fantastic offer of a living Hermione, Leontes leaves his former control and acquiesces to the will of another: "What you can make her do, / I am content to look on; what to speak, / I am content to hear" (5.2.91–93)' (James A. Knapp, 'Visual and Ethical Truth in *The Winter's Tale*', *Shakespeare Quarterly* 55.3 (2004), p. 276).

48. Constance Jordan, *Shakespeare's Monarchies: Ruler and Subject in The Romances* (Ithaca: Cornell University Press, 1997), p. 16.

49. James I, *The True Law of Free Monarchies and Basilikon Doron*, ed. Daniel Fischlin and Mark Fortier (Toronto: Centre for Reformation and Renaissance Studies, 1996), pp. 57–68.

50. See, for example, James I, *The True Law of Free Monarchies*, pp. 66 and 72, and *Political Writings*, p. 184, quoted above.

51. Felperin, '"Tongue-tied our queen?"', p. 8.

52. Felperin, '"Tongue-tied our queen?"', p. 8. See also Bergeron's comparison of the mediated process of the oracle's transmission in Shakespeare's play with Greene's prose romance: the 'ceremony attached to Apollo's messengers and the formal reading of the oracle enhance the "presence" of the god, making him more real than in Greene's cursory treatment of the event' ('The Apollo Mission in *The Winter's Tale*', pp. 371–2).

53. Enterline, '"You Speak a Language that I Understand Not"', pp. 27, 40, 41.

54. Enterline, '"You Speak a Language that I Understand Not"', pp. 22, 31.

55. Thomas Wilson, *A Christian Dictionary* (London, 1612), p. 345.

56. Smith, *De Republica Anglorum*, p. 78.

57. Smith, *De republica Anglorum*, p. 84.

58. T. E. Hartley (ed.), *Proceedings in the Parliaments of Elizabeth I*, vol. 3 (Wilmington, DE: M. Glazier, 1981–95), pp. 198–9. On Shakespeare's knowledge of parliament, see Oliver Arnold, *The Third Citizen: Shakespeare's Theater and the Early Modern House of Commons* (Baltimore: Johns Hopkins University Press, 2007), pp. 20–4.

59. James VI and I, *Political Writings*, p. 181.

60. *Coke* 1: 73. See also Charles Gray, 'Reason, Authority, and Imagination: the Jurisprudence of Sir Edward Coke', in Perez Zagorin (ed.), *Culture and Politics from Puritanism to the Enlightenment* (Berkeley: University of California Press, 1980), pp. 41–2.

61. Roland G. Usher, 'James I and Sir Edward Coke', *English Historical Review* 18 (1903), p. 669.

62. For an instance of Coke 'vouching' for a record, see J. P. Kenyon (ed.), *The Stuart Constitution, 1603–1688: Documents and Commentary* (Cambridge: Cambridge University Press, 1966), p. 97. On Coke's manuscripts of reports, see Helgerson, *Forms of Nationhood*, p. 80. On manuscript reports generally, see L. W. Abbott, *Law Reporting in England, 1485–1585* (London: Athlone Press, 1973).

63. Lorna Hutson, 'Not the King's Two Bodies: Reading the "Body Politic" in Shakespeare's *Henry IV*, Parts 1 and 2', in Victoria Kahn and Lorna Hutson

(eds), *Rhetoric and Law in Early Modern Europe* (New Haven: Yale University Press, 2001), p. 176. Christopher Hatton, *A Treatise Concerning Statutes, or Acts of Parliament: and The Exposition Thereof* (London: 1677), p. 30.

64. On Elizabeth and James's royal 'regulation of marriage', see Leonard Tennenhouse, 'Representing Power: *Measure for Measure* in Its Time', in Stephen Greenblatt (ed.), *The Power of Forms in the English Renaissance* (Norman, OK: Pilgrim Books, 1982), pp. 151–3.

65. Baker, *The Law's Two Bodies*, p. 5.

Bibliography

Primary Sources

Aristotle, *The Nicomachean Ethics*, trans. David Ross, J. L. Ackrill and J. O. Urmson (Oxford: Oxford University Press, 1998).

Aristotle, *The Rhetoric and the Poetics of Aristotle*, intro. and trans. Edward P. J. Corbett (New York: Modern Library, 1984).

Bacon, Francis, *The Elements of the Common Lawes of England* (London, 1630).

Bacon, Francis, *The Essaies of Sr Francis Bacon Knight, the Kings Solliciter Generall* (London, 1612).

Bacon, Francis, *The Essayes or Counsels, Civill and Morall*, ed. Michael Kiernan (Oxford: Oxford University Press, 1985).

Bacon, Francis, *Francis Bacon: A Critical Edition of the Major Works*, ed. Brian Vickers (Oxford: Oxford University Press, 1996).

Bacon, Francis, 'A Letter of Advice, Written by Sir Francis Bacon to the Duke of Buckingham, when He Became Favourite to King James', in *The Works of Francis Bacon*, ed. James Spedding, Robert Leslie Ellis and Douglas Denon Heath, vol. 13 (London, 1872), pp. 13–26.

Bacon, Francis, *The Letters and Life of Francis Bacon*, ed. James Spedding, vol. 3 (London, 1868).

Bacon, Francis, 'An Offer to King James of a Digest to be Made of the Laws of England', in *The Works of Francis Bacon*, vol. 4 (London, 1826), pp. 375–82.

Bacon, Francis, *Of the Advancement and Proficience of Learning or the Partitions of Sciences*, trans. Gilbert Wats (Oxford, 1640).

Bacon, Francis, 'A Proposition to His Majesty by Sir Francis Bacon . . . Touching the Compiling and Amendment of the Laws of England', in *The Works of Francis Bacon*, ed. James Spedding, Robert Leslie Ellis and Douglas Denon Heath, vol. 13 (London, 1872), pp. 61–70.

Bacon, Francis, *Reading on the Statute of Uses*, in *The Works of Francis Bacon*, ed. James Spedding, Robert Leslie Ellis and Douglas Denon Heath, vol. 7 (London, 1879), pp. 389–450.

Bacon, Francis, 'The Speech which was used by the Lord Keeper of the Great Seal, in the Star-Chamber, before the Summer Circuits, the King being then in Scotland, 1617', in *The Works of Francis Bacon*, vol. 4 (London, 1826), pp. 497–500.

Bacon, Francis, 'Speeches of the Six Councillors', in *The Works of Francis Bacon*, ed. James Spedding, Robert Leslie Ellis, and Douglas Denon Heath, vol. 8 (London, 1862), pp. 332–43.

Baildon, William Paley (ed.), *Les Reportes del Cases in Camera Stellata, 1593 to 1609, from the Original MS. of John Hawarde* (London, 1894).

Barnes, Barnabe, *Foure Bookes of Offices: Enabling Privat Persons for the Speciall Service of All Good Princes and Policies* (London, 1606).

Beacon, Richard, *Solon His Follie, or A Politique Discourse Touching the Reformation of common-weales conquered, declined or corrupted*, ed. Clare Carroll and Vincent Carey (Binghamton, NY: Medieval & Renaissance Texts & Studies, 1996).

Blount, Thomas, *Glossographia: or A Dictionary, Interpreting all such Hard Words, Whether Hebrew, Greek, Latin, Italian, Spanish, French, Teutonick, Belgick, British or Saxon . . .* (London, 1656).

Blount, Thomas, *Nomo-lexikon, a Law-Dictionary Interpreting Such Difficult and Obscure Words and Terms as Are Found either in Our Common or Statute, Ancient or Modern Lawes* (London, 1670).

Breton, Nicholas, *The Good and The Badde: or, Descriptions of the Worthies, and Unworthies of This Age. Where the Best May See Their Graces, and the Worst Discerne Their Baseness* (London, 1616).

Buck, George, *The Third Universitie of England* (London, 1615).

Bullokar, John, *An English Expositor: Teaching the Interpretation of the hardest words used in our Language* (London, 1616).

Cawdrey, Robert, *A Table Alphabeticall, conteyning and teaching the true writing, and understanding of hard usuall English wordes, borrowed from the Hebrew, Greeke, Latine, or French* (London, 1604).

Cockburn, J. S. (ed.), *Western Circuit Assize Orders, 1629–1648: A Calendar* (London: Royal Historical Society, 1976).

Coke, Edward, *The Lord Coke His Speech and Charge. With a Discoverie of the Abuses and Corruption of Officers* (London, 1607).

Coke, Edward, *The Selected Writings of Sir Edward Coke*, ed. Steve Sheppard, 3 vols (Indianapolis: Liberty Fund, 2003).

A Complete Collection of State Trials and Proceedings for High Treason and Other Crimes and Misdemeanors from the Earliest Period to the Year 1783, with Notes and Other Illustrations, vol. 1 (London, 1816).

D'Ewes, Simonds, *A Compleat Journal of the Votes, Speeches and Debates, Both of the House of Lords and House of Commons Throughout the Whole Reign of Queen Elizabeth, of Glorious Memory* (London, 1693).

Dalton, Michael, *The Country Justice, Conteyning the Practise of the Justices of the Peace out of Their Sessions, Gathered for the Better Helpe of Such Justices of Peace as Have Not Beene Much Conversant in the Studie of the Lawes of This Realme* (London, 1618).

Daniel, Samuel, 'To Sir Thomas Egerton', in Samuel Daniel, *Poems and 'A Defence of Ryme'*, ed. Arthur C. Sprague (Cambridge, MA: Harvard University Press, 1930), p. 105.

Davies, John, *Hymes of Astraea, in Acrosticke Verse* (London, 1599).

Davies, John, *Le Primer Report des Cases & Matters en Ley Resolves & Adjudges en les Courts del Roy en Ireland* (Dublin, 1615).

Day, Angel, *The English Secretary, or Methode of Writing of Epistles and*

Letters: With a Declaration of Such Tropes, Figures, and Schemes, as either Usually or for Ornament Sake Are Therin Required (London, 1599).

Dickens, Charles, *Bleak House*, ed. Stephen Gill (Oxford: Oxford University Press, 1998).

Doddridge, John, *The English Lawyer* (London, 1631).

Donne, John, *The Complete Poems of John Donne*, ed. Robin Robbins (Harlow: Longman, 2008).

Donne, John, *Poems*, ed. Herbert J. C. Grierson, vol. 2 (Oxford: Oxford University Press, 1912).

Donne, John, *The Satires, Epigrams, and Verse Letters*, ed. W. Milgate (Oxford: Clarendon Press, 1967).

Donne, John, *Selected Letters*, ed. P. M. Oliver (New York: Routledge, 2002).

Dugdale, William, *Origines Juridiciales; or, Historical Memorials of the English Laws, Courts of Justice, Forms of Tryal, Punishment in Cases Criminal, Law-Writers, Law-Books, Grants and Settlements of Estate, Degree of Serjeant, Inns of Court and Chancery*, 3rd edn (London, 1680).

Earle, John, *Micro-cosmographie. Or, A Peece of the World Discovered, in Essayes and Characters* (London, 1628).

Egerton, Thomas, *A Discourse upon the Exposicion [and] Understandinge of Statutes; with Sir Thomas Egerton's Additions*, ed. Samuel E. Thorne (San Marino: Huntington Library, 1942).

Ellesmere, Thomas, *Certain Observations Concerning the Office of the Lord Chancellor* (London, 1651).

Elyot, Thomas, *The Book Named the Governor*, ed. S. E. Lehmberg (London: Everyman's Library, 1962).

Erasmus, Desiderius, *The Education of a Christian Prince*, trans. and ed. Lisa Jardine (Cambridge: Cambridge University Press, 1997).

Florio, John, *A World of Words* (London, 1598).

Floyd, Thomas, *The Picture of a Perfit Common Wealth* (London, 1600).

Fortescue, John, *A Learned Commendation of the Politique Lawes of Englande*, trans. Richard Mulcaster (London, 1567).

Gesta Grayorum: or, The History of the High and Mighty Prince, Henry Prince of Purpoole. . . Who Reigned and Died, A.D. 1594 (London, 1688).

Greene, Robert, *Pandosto. The Triumph of Time*, in Geoffrey Bullough (ed.), *Narrative and Dramatic Sources of Shakespeare*, vol. 8 (New York: Columbia University Press, 1975), pp. 156–99.

Greene, Robert, *Pandosto. The Triumph of Time. Wherein is Discovered by a Pleasant Historie, That although by the Meanes of Sinister Fortune Truth May Be Concealed, Yet by Time in Spight of Fortune It Is Most Manifestly Revealed* (London, 1588).

Greville, Fulke, *The Remains of Sir Fulk Grevill, Lord Brooke: Being Poems of Monarchy and Religion* (London, 1670).

Hall, Joseph, *Characters of Vertues and Vices: In Two Bookes* (London, 1608).

Hartley, T. E. (ed.), *Proceedings in the Parliaments of Elizabeth I*, 3 vols (Wilmington, DE: M. Glazier, 1981–95).

Hatton, Christopher, *A Treatise Concerning Statutes, or Acts of Parliament: and The Exposition Thereof* (London, 1677).

Hinckley, John, *Two Sermons Preached Before the Judges of Assize* (Oxford: 1657).

Holland, Philemon (trans.), *The Romane Historie Written by T. Livius of Padua. Also, The Breviaries of L. Florus: With a Chronologie to the Whole Historie: And The Topographie of Rome in Old Time* (London, 1600).

Hooker, John, *The Order and Usage of the Keeping of a Parlement in England, and The Description of Tholde and Ancient Cittie of Fxcester* [*sic*] (London, 1575).

James I, *The True Law of Free Monarchies and Basilikon Doron*, ed. Daniel Fischlin and Mark Fortier (Toronto: Centre for Reformation and Renaissance Studies, 1996).

James VI and I, *Political Writings*, ed. Johann P. Sommerville (Cambridge: Cambridge University Press, 1994).

Johnson, Samuel, *Lives of the English Poets*, vol. 1 (Oxford: Oxford University Press, 1906).

Jonson, Ben, *The Complete Poems*, ed. George Parfitt (London: Penguin Books, 1996).

Juvenal, *Juvenal and Persius*, ed. and trans. Susanna Morton Braund, Loeb Classical Library 91 (Cambridge, MA: Harvard University Press, 2004).

Lambarde, William, *Archeion, or, A Discourse Upon the High Courts of Justice in England* (London, 1635).

Lambarde, William, *Eirenarcha; or, Of The Office of the Justices of Peace, in two Bookes* (London, 1582).

Legh, Gerard, *The Accedens of Armory* (London, 1562).

Luders, Alexander et al. (eds), *Statutes of the Realm*, vol. 4 (London, 1810–28).

McCutcheon, Elizabeth, *Sir Nicholas Bacon's Great House Sententiae* (Amherst: English Literary Renaissance Supplements, III, 1977).

The Office of the Clerk of Assize: Containing the Form and Method of the Proceedings at the Assizes, and General Gaol-Delivery, as Also on the Crown and Nisi Prius Side. Together with The Office of the Clerk of the Peace. Shewing the True Manner and Form of the Proceedings at the Court of General Quarter-Sessions of the Peace (London, 1682).

Overbury, Thomas, *Characters: Together with Poems, News, Edicts, and Paradoxes Based on the Eleventh Edition of A wife Now the Widow of Sir Thomas Overbury*, ed. Donald Beecher (Ottawa: Dovehouse Editions, 2003).

Quintilian, *The Orator's Education, Volume V: Books 11–12*, ed. and trans. Donald A. Russell, Loeb Classical Library 494 (Cambridge, MA: Harvard University Press, 2002).

Peacham, Henry, *Minerva Britanna; or, A Garden of Heroical Devises, Furnished, and Adorned with Emblemes and Impresa's of Sundry Natures* (London, 1612).

Plato, *Timaeus*, Donald J. Zeyl (trans.), in *Plato: Complete Works*, ed. John M. Cooper (Indianapolis: Hackett, 1997).

Puttenham, George, *The Arte of English Poesy*, ed. Frank Whigham and Wayne A. Rebhorn (Ithaca: Cornell University Press, 2007).

Rastell, John, *Le livre des assises et pleas del' corone, moves* [*et*] *dependants devant les justices sibien en jour circuits come aylours, en temps du Roy Edward le Tiers* (London, 1679).

Saint German, Christopher, *Here after foloweth a Dialoge in Englisshe, bytwyxte a Doctour of Dyvynitie and a Student in the Lawes of Englande* (London: 1531).

Sclater, William, *Civil Magistracy by Divine Authority* (London, 1653).

Shakespeare, William, *The Comedy of Errors*, ed. Charles Whitworth (Oxford: Oxford University Press, 2002).

Shakespeare, William. *The Norton Shakespeare*, ed. Stephen Greenblatt, Walter Cohen, Suzanne Gossett, Jean E. Howard, Katherine Eisaman Maus, and Gordon McMullan, 3rd edn (New York: W. W. Norton, 2016).

Shakespeare, William, *The Winter's Tale*, ed. Stephen Orgel (Oxford: Oxford University Press, 1996).

Sidney, Henry, *A Viceroy's Vindication? Sir Henry Sidney's Memoir of Service in Ireland, 1556–1578*, ed. Ciaran Brady (Cork: Cork University Press, 2002).

Smith, Thomas, *De Republica Anglorum*, ed. Mary Dewar (Cambridge: Cambridge University Press, 1982).

Southwell, Robert, *An Humble Supplication to Her Majestie* (London, 1595).

Southwell, Robert, *An Humble Supplication to Her Majestie*, ed. R. C. Bald (Cambridge: Cambridge University Press, 1953).

Spenser, Edmund, *The Faerie Queene*, ed. A. C. Hamilton, revised 2nd edn (London: Routledge, 2013).

Spenser, Edmund, *A View of the State of Ireland*, ed. Andrew Hadfield and Willy Maley (Oxford: Blackwell, 1997).

The Third Part of Reports of Cases, Taken and Adjudged in the Court of Chancery, in the Reigns of King Charles II, King William, and Queen Anne, vol. 3 (London, 1716).

Thomas, Thomas, *Dictionarium linguae Latinae et Anglicanae* (London, 1587).

Townshend, Heywood, *Historical Collections: or, An Exact Account of the Proceedings of the Four Last Parliaments of Q. Elizabeth of Famous Memory. Wherein is Contained the Compleat Journals Both of the Lords [and] Commons, Taken from the Original Records of Their Houses* (London, 1680).

Virgil, *Eclogues, Georgics, Aeneid: Books 1–6*, trans. H. R. Fairclough, Loeb Classical Library 63 (Cambridge, MA: Harvard University Press, 1916).

Walshe, Edward, 'Edward Walshe's "Conjectures" Concerning the State of Ireland [1552]', ed. D. B. Quinn, *Irish Historical Studies* 5 (1946–7), pp. 303–22.

Walton, Izaak, *The Lives of Dr. John Donne, Sir Henry Wotton, Richard Hooker, George Herbert, and Dr. Robert Sanderson* (Boston, 1860).

Westerman, William, *Two Sermons of Assise: The One Intituled; A Prohibition of Revenge: The other, A Sword of Maintenance* (London, 1600).

Wilson, Thomas. *The Arte of Rhetorique, for the Vse of All Soche as Are Studious of Eloquence, Sette Forth in English, by Thomas Wilson* (London, 1553).

Wilson, Thomas, *A Christian Dictionary* (London, 1612).

Wilson, Thomas, *The Rule of Reason, Conteinyng the Arte of Logike* (London, 1563).

Secondary Sources

Abbott, L. W., *Law Reporting in England, 1485–1585* (London: Athlone Press, 1973).

Adlington, Hugh, 'Restoration, Religion, and Law: Assize Sermons, 1660–1685', in Hugh Adlington, Peter McCullough and Emma Rhatigan (eds), *The Oxford Handbook of the Early Modern Sermon* (Oxford: Oxford University Press, 2011), pp. 423–41.

Anderson, Judith H., '"Nor Man It Is": The Knight of Justice in Book V of Spenser's *Faerie Queene*', *PMLA* 85.1 (1970), pp. 65–77.

Anderson, Judith H., *Reading the Allegorical Intertext: Chaucer, Spenser, Shakespeare, Milton* (New York: Fordham University Press, 2008).

Anderson, Judith H., 'Spenser's *Faerie Queene*, Book V: Poetry, Politics and Justice', in Michael Hattaway (ed.), *A Companion to English Renaissance Literature and Culture* (Malden, MA: Blackwell, 2000), pp. 195–205.

Arnold, Oliver, *The Third Citizen: Shakespeare's Theater and The Early Modern House of Commons* (Baltimore: Johns Hopkins University Press, 2007).

Axton, Marie, *The Queen's Two Bodies: Drama and the Elizabethan Succession* (London: Royal Historical Society, 1977).

Baker, J. H., 'The Common Lawyers and the Chancery: 1616', in Allen D. Boyer (ed.), *Law, Liberty, and Parliament: Selected Essays on the Writings of Sir Edward Coke* (Indianapolis: Liberty Fund, 2004), pp. 254–81.

Baker, J. H., *An Introduction to English Legal History*, 2nd edn (London, Butterworths, 1979).

Baker, J. H., *An Introduction to English Legal History*, 4th edn (Oxford: Oxford University Press, 2007).

Baker, J. H., *The Law's Two Bodies: Some Evidential Problems in English Legal History* (Oxford: Oxford University Press, 2001).

Baker, J. H., *The Legal Profession and the Common Law: Historical Essays* (London: Hambledon Press, 1986).

Baker, J. H., *The Oxford History of the Laws of England: Volume VI, 1483–1558* (Oxford: Oxford University Press, 2003).

Baker, J. H., *Readers and Readings in the Inns of Court and Chancery* (London: Seldon Society, 2000).

Baker, J. H., *The Third University of England: The Inns of Court and the Common Law Tradition* (London: Selden Society, 1990).

Bald, R. C., *John Donne: A Life* (Oxford: Clarendon Press, 1970).

Barbour, Richmond, '"There is our commission": Writing and Authority in *Measure for Measure* and the London East Indian Company', *Journal of English and Germanic Philology* 99.2 (2000), pp. 193–214.

Barkan, Leonard, *Nature's Work of Art: The Human Body as Image of the World* (New Haven: Yale University Press, 1975).

Baumlin, James S., 'Donne's Christian Diatribes: Persius and the Rhetorical Persona of "Satyre III" and "Satyre V"', in Peter Amadeus Fiore (ed.), *Just So Much Honor: Essays Commemorating the Four-Hundredth Anniversary of the Birth of John Donne* (University Park: Pennsylvania State University Press, 1972), pp. 92–105.

Bergeron, David M., 'The Apollo Mission in *The Winter's Tale*', in Maurice Hunt (ed.), The Winter's Tale: *Critical Essays* (New York: Garland, 1995), pp. 361–79.

Berman, Harold J., 'The Origins of Historical Jurisprudence: Coke, Selden, Hale', *Yale Law Journal* 103.7 (1994), pp. 1651–738.

Bernthal, Craig A., 'Staging Justice: James I and the Trial Scenes of *Measure for Measure'*, *Studies in English Literature, 1500–1900* 32.2 (1992), pp. 247–69.

Bevington, David, 'The Comedy of Errors in the Context of the Late 1580s and Early 1590s', in Robert S. Miola (ed.), *The Comedy of Errors: Critical Essays* (New York: Garland, 1997), pp. 335–53.

Boyer, Allen D., *Sir Edward Coke and the Elizabethan Age* (Stanford: Stanford University Press, 2003).

Boyer, Allen D., 'Sir Edward Coke, Ciceronianus: Classical Rhetoric and the Common Law Tradition', in Allen D. Boyer (ed.), *Law, Liberty, and Parliament: Selected Essays on the Writings of Sir Edward Coke* (Indianapolis: Liberty Fund, 2004), pp. 224–53.

Braddick, Michael J., 'Administrative Performance: The Representation of Political Authority in Early Modern England', in Michael J. Braddick and John Walter (eds), *Negotiating Power in Early Modern Society: Order, Hierarchy and Subordination in Britain and Ireland* (Cambridge: Cambridge University Press, 2001), pp. 166–87.

Braddick, Michael J., *State Formation in Early Modern England, c.1550–1700* (Cambridge: Cambridge University Press, 2000).

Brady, Ciaran, 'Court, Castle, and Country: The Framework of Government in Tudor Ireland', in Ciaran Brady and Raymond Gillespie (eds), *Natives and Newcomers: Essays on The Making of Irish Colonial Society, 1534–1641* (Dublin: Irish Academic Press, 1986), pp. 22–49.

Brady, Ciaran, 'Spenser's Irish Crisis: Humanism and Experience in the 1590s', *Past and Present* 111 (1986), pp. 17–49.

Brewer, John and Styles, John (eds), *An Ungovernable People: The English and Their Law in the Seventeenth and Eighteenth Centuries* (London: Hutchinson, 1980).

Brown, Piers, '"Hac ex consilio meo via progredieris": Courtly Reading and Secretarial Mediation in Donne's The Courtier's Library', *Renaissance Quarterly* 61 (2008), pp. 833–66.

Brooks, Christopher W., *Law, Politics and Society in Early Modern England* (Cambridge: Cambridge University Press, 2008).

Briggs, Julia, 'Shakespeare's Bed-Tricks', *Essays in Criticism* 44.4 (1994), pp. 293–314.

Bullough, Geoffrey, 'Donne, The Man of Law', in Peter Amadeus Fiore (ed.), *Just So Much Honor: Essays Commemorating the Four-Hundredth Anniversary of the Birth of John Donne* (University Park: Pennsylvania State University Press, 1972), pp. 57–94.

Burgess, Glenn, *The Politics of the Ancient Constitution: An Introduction to English Political Thought, 1603–1642* (University Park: Pennsylvania State University Press, 1993).

Burrow, Colin, 'Reading Tudor Writing Politically: The Case of 2 Henry IV', *The Yearbook of English Studies* 38 (2008), pp. 234–50.

Cain, Tom, 'Donne and the Prince D'Amour', *John Donne Journal* 14 (1995), pp. 83–111.

Campbell, John, *The Lives of the Lord Chancellors and Keepers of the Great Seal of England*, vol. 2 (London, 1846).

Chapman, Alison A., 'Milton and Legal Reform', *Renaissance Quarterly* 69 (2016), pp. 529–65.

Clare, Janet, *Shakespeare's Stage Traffic: Imitation, Borrowing and Competition in Renaissance Theatre* (Cambridge: Cambridge University Press, 2014).

Clark, Ira, '*Measure for Measure*: Chiasmus, Justice, and Mercy', *Style* 35.4 (2001), pp. 659–80.

Cockburn, J. S., *Calendar of Assize Records: Home Circuit Indictments, Elizabeth I and James I: Introduction* (London: Her Majesty's Stationery Office, 1985).

Cockburn, J. S., *A History of English Assizes, 1558–1714* (Cambridge: Cambridge University Press, 1972).

Cohen, Stephen, 'From Mistress to Master: Political Transition and Formal Conflict in *Measure for Measure*', *Criticism* 41.4 (1999), pp. 431–64.

Coldiron, A. E. B. '"'Tis rigor and not law": Trials of Women as Trials of Patriarchy in *The Winter's Tale*', *Renaissance Papers* (2004), pp. 29–69.

Collinson, Patrick, 'Sir Nicholas Bacon and the Elizabethan *Via Media*', *Historical Journal* 23 (1980), pp. 255–73.

Condren, Conal, *Argument and Authority in Early Modern England: The Presupposition of Oaths and Offices* (Cambridge: Cambridge University Press, 2006).

Condren, Conal, 'Unfolding "the Properties of Government": The Case of *Measure for Measure* and the History of Political Thought', in David Armitage, Conal Condren and Andrew Fitzmaurice (eds), *Shakespeare and Early Modern Political Thought* (Cambridge: Cambridge University Press, 2009), pp. 157–75.

Coquillette, Daniel R., *Francis Bacon* (Stanford: Stanford University Press, 1992).

Cormack, Bradin, 'Locating *The Comedy of Errors*: Revels Jurisdiction at the Inns of Court', in Jayne Elisabeth Archer, Elizabeth Goldring, and Sarah Knight (eds), *The Intellectual and Cultural World of the Early Modern Inns of Court* (Manchester: Manchester University Press, 2011), pp. 264–85.

Cormack, Bradin, *A Power to Do Justice: Jurisdiction, English Literature, and The Rise of Common Law, 1509–1625* (Chicago: University of Chicago Press, 2007).

Corthell, Ronald J., '"Coscus onely breed my just offence": A Note on Donne's "Satire II" and the Inns of Court', *John Donne Journal* 6.1 (1987), pp. 25–31.

Corthell, Ronald J., *Ideology and Desire in Renaissance Poetry: The Subject of Donne* (Detroit: Wayne State University Press, 1997).

Cotterell, Mary, 'Interregnum Law Reform: The Hale Commission of 1652', *English Historical Review* 83.329 (1968), pp. 689–704.

Crane, Mary Thomas, *Framing Authority: Sayings, Self, and Society in Sixteenth-Century England* (Princeton: Princeton University Press, 1993).

Cromartie, Alan, *The Constitutionalist Revolution: An Essay on the History of England, 1450–1642* (Cambridge: Cambridge University Press, 2006).

Cromartie, Alan, '*Epieikeia* and Conscience', in Lorna Hutson (ed.), *The Oxford Handbook of English Law and Literature, 1500–1700* (Oxford: Oxford University Press, 2017), pp. 321–36.

Cunningham, Karen, *Imaginary Betrayals: Subjectivity and the Discourses of Treason in Early Modern England* (Philadelphia: University of Pennsylvania Press, 2002).

Cunningham, Karen, 'Opening Doubts Upon the Law: *Measure for Measure*', in Richard Dutton and Jean E. Howard (eds), *A Companion to Shakespeare's*

Works, Volume IV: The Poems, Problem Comedies, Late Plays (Malden, MA: Wiley-Blackwell, 2003), pp. 316–32.

Davis, Natalie Zemon, 'The Reasons of Misrule: Youth Groups and Charivaris in Sixteenth-Century France', *Past and Present* 50 (1971), pp. 41–75.

Dawson, John P., *The Oracles of the Law* (Westport, CT: Greenwood Press, 1978).

Dean, David, *Law-making and Society in Late Elizabethan England: The Parliament of England, 1584–1601* (Cambridge: Cambridge University Press, 1996).

Dean, D. M. and Jones, N. L. (eds), *The Parliaments of Elizabethan England* (Oxford: Basil Blackwell, 1990).

Desmet, Christy, *Reading Shakespeare's Characters: Rhetoric, Ethics, and Identity* (Amherst: University of Massachusetts Press, 1992).

Dollimore, Jonathan, 'Introduction: Shakespeare, Cultural Materialism and the New Historicism', in Jonathan Dollimore and Alan Sinfield (eds), *Political Shakespeare: New Essays in Cultural Materialism* (Manchester: Manchester University Press, 1985), pp. 2–17.

Dollimore, Jonathan, 'Transgression and Surveillance in *Measure for Measure*', in Jonathan Dollimore and Alan Sinfield (eds), *Political Shakespeare: New Essays in Cultural Materialism* (Manchester: Manchester University Press, 1985), pp. 72–87.

Dolven, Jeff, *Scenes of Instruction in Renaissance Romance* (Chicago: University of Chicago Press, 2007).

Dolven, Jeff, 'Spenser's Sense of Poetic Justice', *Raritan* 21.1 (2001), pp. 127–40.

Dubrow, Heather, '"No man is an island": Donne's Satires and Satiric Traditions', *Studies in English Literature* 19 (1979), pp. 71–83.

Dunne, Derek, *Shakespeare, Revenge Tragedy and Early Modern Law: Vindictive Justice* (Basingstoke: Palgrave Macmillan, 2016).

Eden, Kathy, *Poetic and Legal Fiction in the Aristotelian Tradition* (Princeton: Princeton University Press, 1986).

Eggert, Katherine, *Showing Like A Queen: Female Authority and Literary Experiment in Spenser, Shakespeare, and Milton* (Philadelphia: University of Philadelphia Press, 2000).

Elsky, Stephanie, '"Wonne with Custome": Conquest and Etymology in the Spenser–Harvey *Letters* and *A View of the Present State of Ireland*', *Spenser Studies* 28 (2013), pp. 165–92.

Elton, G. R., *English Law in the Sixteenth Century: Reform in an Age of Change* (London: Selden Society, 1979).

Elton, G. R., *Reform and Reformation: England, 1509–1558* (Cambridge, MA: Harvard University Press, 1977).

Elton, G. R., *Reform and Renewal: Thomas Cromwell and The Common Weal* (Cambridge: Cambridge University Press, 1973).

Elton, G. R., *Reform by Statute: Thomas Starkey's Dialogue and Thomas Cromwell's Policy* (London: Oxford University Press, 1968).

Elton, G. R., *The Tudor Revolution in Government: Administrative Changes in the Reign of Henry VIII* (Cambridge: Cambridge University Press, 1953).

Engle, Lars, '*Measure for Measure* and Modernity: The Problem of the Sceptic's Authority', in Hugh Grady (ed.), *Shakespeare and Modernity: Early Modern to Millennium* (London: Routledge, 2000), pp. 85–104.

Enterline, Lynn, *The Rhetoric of the Body from Ovid to Shakespeare* (Cambridge: Cambridge University Press, 2000).

Enterline, Lynn, '"You Speak a Language that I Understand Not": The Rhetoric of Animation in *The Winter's Tale*', *Shakespeare Quarterly* 48.1 (1997), pp. 17–44.

Felperin, Howard, '"Tongue-Tied our Queen?": The Deconstruction of Presence in *The Winter's Tale*', in Patricia Parker and Geoffrey Hartman (eds), *Shakespeare and the Question of Theory* (New York: Methuen, 1985), pp. 3–18.

Finkelpearl, Philip J., *John Marston of the Middle Temple: An Elizabethan Dramatist in His Social Setting* (Cambridge, MA: Harvard University Press, 1969).

Fletcher, Anthony, 'Honour, Reputation and Local Officeholding in Elizabethan and Stuart England', in Anthony Fletcher and John Stevenson (eds), *Order and Disorder in Early Modern England* (Cambridge: Cambridge University Press, 1985), pp. 92–115.

Fletcher, Anthony, *Reform in the Provinces: The Government of Stuart England* (New Haven: Yale University Press, 1986).

Fletcher, Anthony and Stevenson, John, 'Introduction', in Anthony Fletcher and John Stevenson (eds), *Order and Disorder in Early Modern England* (Cambridge: Cambridge University Press, 1985), pp. 1–40.

Flynn, Dennis, 'Donne's Most Daring *Satyre*: "richly For services paid, authoriz'd"', *John Donne Journal* 20 (2001), pp. 107–20.

Flynn, Dennis, 'John Donne in the Ellesmere Manuscripts', *Huntington Library Quarterly* 46.4 (1983), pp. 333–6.

Fortier, Mark, *The Culture of Equity in Early Modern England* (London: Routledge, 2005).

Fortier, Mark, 'Equity and Ideas: Coke, Ellesmere, and James I', *Renaissance Quarterly* 51.4 (1998), pp. 1255–81.

Fowler, Elizabeth, 'The Failure of Moral Philosophy in the Work of Edmund Spenser', *Representations* 51 (1995), pp. 47–76.

Garver, Eugene, *Aristotle's Rhetoric: An Art of Character* (Chicago: University of Chicago Press, 1994).

Gibbons, Brian, '"Bid Them Bring the Trumpets to the Gate": Staging Questions for *Measure for Measure*', *Huntington Library Quarterly* 54 (1991), pp. 31–42.

Gillespie, Vincent, 'Monasticism', in Brian Cummings and James Simpson (eds), *Cultural Reformations: Medieval and Renaissance in Literary History* (Oxford: Oxford University Press, 2010), pp. 480–501.

Goldberg, Jonathan, *James I and the Politics of Literature: Jonson, Shakespeare, Donne, and Their Contemporaries* (Baltimore: Johns Hopkins University Press, 1983).

Gras, Henk, '*Twelfth Night*, *Every Man out of His Humour*, and the Middle Temple Revels of 1597–98', *Modern Language Review* 84.3 (1989), pp. 545–64.

Gray, Charles, 'Further Reflections on "Artificial Reason"', in Allen D. Boyer (ed.), *Law, Liberty, and Parliament: Selected Essays on the Writings of Sir Edward Coke* (Indianapolis: Liberty Fund, 2004), pp. 121–6.

Gray, Charles, 'Reason, Authority, and Imagination: The Jurisprudence of Sir Edward Coke', in Perez Zagorin (ed.), *Culture and Politics from Puritanism to the Enlightenment* (Berkeley: University of California Press, 1980), pp. 25–66.

Green, A. Wigfall, *The Inns of Court and Early English Drama* (New York: Benjamin Blom, 1965).

Greenblatt, Stephen, *Hamlet in Purgatory* (Princeton: Princeton University Press, 2001).

Greenblatt, Stephen, *Shakespearean Negotiations: The Circulation of Social Energy in Renaissance England* (Oxford: Clarendon Press, 1988).

Greenberg, Janelle, *The Radical Face of the Ancient Constitution: St Edward's 'Laws' in Early Modern Political Thought* (Cambridge: Cambridge University Press, 2001).

Gregory, Tobias, 'Shadowing Intervention: On the Politics of *The Faerie Queene* Book 5 Canto 12', *English Literary History* 67. 2 (2000), pp. 365–97.

Griffiths, Paul, 'Secrecy and Authority in Late Sixteenth- and Seventeenth-Century London', *Historical Journal* 40.4 (1997): 925–51.

Guibbory, Achsah, '"Oh, let me not serve so": The Politics of Love in Donne's *Elegies*', *English Literary History* 57 (1990), pp. 811–33.

Hadfield, Andrew, 'Introduction', in Edmund Spenser, *The Faerie Queene: Book Six and the Mutabilie Cantos*, ed. Andrew Hadfield and Abraham Stoll (Indianapolis: Hackett, 2007), pp. vii–xxii.

Hadfield, Andrew, *Edmund Spenser's Irish Experience: Wilde Fruit and Salvage Soyl* (Oxford: Clarendon Press, 1997).

Hale, David George, *The Body Politic: A Political Metaphor in Renaissance English Literature* (The Hague: Mouton, 1971).

Hall, G. D. G., 'An Assize Book of the Seventeenth Century', *American Journal of Legal History* 7 (1963), pp. 228–45.

Halper, Louise, '*Measure for Measure*: Law, Prerogative, Subversion', *Cardozo Studies in Law and Literature* 13.2 (2001), pp. 221–64.

Hartley, T. E., *Elizabeth's Parliaments: Queen, Lords, and Commons, 1559–1601* (Manchester: St. Martin's Press, 1992).

Hawkins, Harriet, '"The Devil's Party": Virtues and Vices in *Measure for Measure*', in Harold Bloom (ed.), *Measure for Measure* (New York: Chelsea House, 1987), pp. 81–94.

Hayne, Victoria, 'Performing Social Practice: The Example of *Measure for Measure*', *Shakespeare Quarterly* 44.1 (1993), pp. 1–29.

Helgerson, Richard, *Forms of Nationhood: The Elizabethan Writing of England* (Chicago: University of Chicago Press, 1992).

Herrup, Cynthia, *The Common Peace: Participation and the Criminal Law in Seventeenth-Century England* (Cambridge: Cambridge University Press, 1987).

Hester, M. Thomas, *Kinde Pitty and Brave Scorn: John Donne's Satyres* (Durham, NC: Duke University Press, 1982).

Hindle, Steve, *The State and Social Change in Early Modern England, c.1550–1640* (Basingstoke: Palgrave Macmillan, 2000).

Hunt, Arnold, *The Art of Hearing: English Preachers and Their Audiences, 1590–1640* (Cambridge: Cambridge University Press, 2014).

Hurley, Ann, 'Interruption: The Transformation of a Critical Feature of Ritual from Revel to Lyric in John Donne's Inns of Court Poetry of the 1590s', in Douglas F. Rutledge (ed.), *Ceremony and Text in the Renaissance* (Cranbury, NJ: Associated University Presses, 1996), pp. 103–21.

Hutson, Lorna, 'The Evidential Plot: Shakespeare and Gascoigne at Gray's Inn', in Jayne Archer, Elizabeth Goldring and Sarah Knight (eds), *The Intellectual and Cultural World of the Early Modern Inns of Court* (Manchester: Manchester University Press, 2013), pp. 245–63.

Hutson, Lorna, 'Imagining Justice: Kantorowicz and Shakespeare', *Representations* 106.1 (2009), pp. 118–42.

Hutson, Lorna, *The Invention of Suspicion: Law and Mimesis in Shakespeare and Renaissance Drama* (Oxford: Oxford University Press, 2007).

Hutson, Lorna, 'Rethinking the "Spectacle of the Scaffold": Juridical Epistemologies and English Revenge Tragedy', *Representations* 89.1 (2005), pp. 30–58.

Hutson, Lorna, 'Not the King's Two Bodies: Reading the "Body Politic" in Shakespeare's *Henry IV*, Parts 1 and 2', in Victoria Kahn and Lorna Hutson (eds), *Rhetoric and Law in Early Modern Europe* (New Haven: Yale University Press, 2001), pp. 166–98.

Ingram, Martin, 'Reformation of Manners in Early Modern England', in Paul Griffiths, Adam Fox and Steve Hindle (eds), *The Experience of Authority in Early Modern England* (New York: St. Martin's Press, 1996), pp. 47–88.

Ingram, Martin, *Church Courts, Sex, and Marriage in England, 1570–1640* (Cambridge: Cambridge University Press, 1988).

Jardine, Lisa, *Francis Bacon: Discovery and the Art of Discourse* (Cambridge: Cambridge University Press, 1974).

Jensen, Pamela K., 'Vienna Vice: Invisible Leadership and Deep Politics in Shakespeare's *Measure for Measure*', in John A. Murley and Sean D. Sutton (eds), *Perspectives on Politics in Shakespeare* (Lanham, MD: Lexington Books, 2006), pp. 105–54.

Jones, W. J., 'The Crown and the Courts in England, 1603–1625', in Allen D. Boyer (ed.), *Law, Liberty, and Parliament: Selected Essays on the Writings of Sir Edward Coke* (Indianapolis: Liberty Fund, 2004), pp. 282–301.

Jones, W. J., *The Elizabethan Court of Chancery* (Oxford: Clarendon Press, 1967).

Jones, W. J., 'Ellesmere and Politics, 1603–1617', in Howard S. Reinmuth Jr, *Early Stuart Studies: Essays in Honor of David Harris Willson* (Minneapolis, MN: University of Minnesota Press, 1970), pp. 11–63.

Jones, William R., 'The Bishops' Ban of 1599 and the Ideology of English Satire', *Literature Compass* 7.5 (2010), pp. 332–46.

Jordan, Constance, *Shakespeare's Monarchies: Ruler and Subject in The Romances* (Ithaca: Cornell University Press, 1997).

Joseph, Miriam, *Shakespeare's Use of the Arts of Language* (Philadelphia: Paul Dry Books, 2005).

Kamps, Ivo, 'Ruling Fantasies and the Fantasies of Rule: *The Phoenix* and *Measure for Measure*', *Studies in Philology* 92.2 (1995), pp. 248–73.

Kantorowicz, Ernst H., *The King's Two Bodies: A Study in Mediaeval Political Theology* (Princeton: Princeton University Press, 1997).

Kenyon, J. P. (ed.), *The Stuart Constitution 1603–1688: Documents and Commentary* (Cambridge: Cambridge University Press, 1966).

Kesselring, K. J., *Mercy and Authority in the Tudor State* (Cambridge: Cambridge University Press, 2003).

Kiralfy, A. K. R., 'Law Reform by Legal Fictions, Equity and Legislation in

English Legal History', *American Journal of Legal History* 10 (1966), pp. 3–14.

Knafla, Louis A. (ed.), *Law and Politics in Jacobean England: The Tracts of Lord Chancellor Ellesmere* (Cambridge: Cambridge University Press, 1977).

Knafla, Louis A., 'Mr. Secretary Donne: The Years with Sir Thomas Egerton', in David Colclough (ed.), *John Donne's Professional Lives* (Cambridge: D. S. Brewer, 2003), pp. 37–73.

Knafla, Louis A., 'The Law Studies of an Elizabethan Student', *Huntington Library Quarterly* 32.3 (1969), pp. 221–40.

Knapp, James A., 'Visual and Ethical Truth in *The Winter's Tale*', *Shakespeare Quarterly* 55.3 (2004), pp. 253–78.

Knapp, Margaret and Kobialka, Michal, 'Shakespeare and the Prince of Purpoole: The 1594 Production of *The Comedy of Errors* at Gray's Inn Hall', *Theatre History Studies* 4 (1984), pp. 71–81.

Kneidel, Gregory, 'Coscus, Queen Elizabeth, and Law in John Donne's "Satyre II"', *Renaissance Quarterly* 61 (2008), pp. 92–121.

Kneidel, Gregory, 'Donne's *Satyre* I and the Closure of the Law', *Renaissance and Reformation/Renaissance et Réforme* 28.4 (2004), pp. 83–103.

Kneidel, Gregory, *John Donne and Early Modern Legal Culture: The End of Equity in the Satyres* (Pittsburgh: Duquesne University Press, 2016).

Kocher, Paul H., 'Francis Bacon on the Science of Jurisprudence', Brian Vickers (ed.), *Essential Articles for the Study of Francis Bacon* (Hamden, CT: Archon Books, 1968), pp. 167–94.

Kornstein, Daniel J., *Kill All the Lawyers? Shakespeare's Legal Appeal* (Princeton: Princeton University Press, 1994).

Kreps, Barbara, 'Playing the Law for Lawyers: Witnessing, Evidence and the Law of Contract in *The Comedy of Errors*', *Shakespeare Survey* 63 (2010), pp. 262–71.

Kurland, Stuart M., '"We Need No More of Your Advice": Political Realism in *The Winter's Tale*', *Studies of English Literature, 1500–1900* 31.2 (1991), pp. 365–86.

Laffitte, Susan Cameron Miller, *The Literary Connections of Sir Thomas Egerton: A Story of the Influence of Thomas Egerton Upon Major Writers of Renaissance Literature* (Dissertation, Florida State University, 1971).

Lake, Peter, 'Ministers, Magistrates and the Production of "Order" in *Measure for Measure*', *Shakespeare Survey* 54 (2001), pp. 165–81.

Lanier, Douglas, '"Stigmatical in Making": The Material Character of *The Comedy of Errors*, *English Literary Renaissance* 23 (1991), pp. 81–112.

Lauritsen, John R., 'Donne's Satyres: The Drama of Self-Discovery', *Studies in English Literature, 1500–1900* 16.1 (1976), pp. 117–30.

Leggatt, Alexander, 'Substitution in *Measure for Measure*', *Shakespeare Quarterly* 39.3 (1988), pp. 342–59.

Leinwand, Theodore B., 'Negotiation and New Historicism', *PMLA* 105.3 (1990), pp. 477–90.

Leishman, J. B., *The Monarch of Wit: An Analytical and Comparative Study of the Poetry of John Donne* (London: Hutchinson, 1965).

Leonard, Nancy S., 'Substitution in Shakespeare's Problem Comedies', *English Literary Renaissance* 9 (1979), pp. 281–301.

Lerer, Seth, 'An Art of the Emetic: Thomas Wilson and the Rhetoric of Parliament', *Studies in Philology* 98.2 (2001), pp. 158–83.

Lewis, C. S., *The Allegory of Love: A Study in Medieval Tradition* (New York: Oxford University Press, 1958).

Lewis, John Underwood, 'Sir Edward Coke (1552–1634): His Theory of "Artificial Reason" as a Context for Modern Basic Legal Theory', in Allen D. Boyer (ed.), *Law, Liberty, and Parliament: Selected Essays on the Writings of Sir Edward Coke* (Indianapolis: Liberty Fund, 2004), pp. 107–20.

Lim, Walter S. H., 'Knowledge and Belief in *The Winter's Tale*', *Studies in English Literature, 1500–1900* 41.2 (2001), pp. 317–34.

Lockey, Brian C., '"Equitie to measure": The Perils of Imperial Imitation in Edmund Spenser's *The Faerie Queene*', *Journal for Early Modern Cultural Studies* 10.1 (2010), pp. 52–70.

Lockey, Brian C., *Law and Empire in English Renaissance Literature* (New York: Cambridge University Press, 2006).

Lupton, Julia Reinhard, *Citizen-Saints: Shakespeare and Political Theology* (Chicago: University of Chicago Press, 2005).

Lyon, Hastings and Block, Herman, *Edward Coke: Oracle of the Law* (Littleton, CO: Fred B. Rothman, 1992).

McCabe, Richard A., *Spenser's Monstrous Regiment* (Oxford: Oxford University Press, 2002).

MacCaffrey, Wallace T., 'Sidney, Sir Henry (1529–1586)', *Oxford Dictionary of National Biography* (Oxford University Press, 2004; online edn, January 2008).

McCune, Pat, 'Order and Justice in Early Tudor Drama', in Frances E. Dolan (ed.), *Renaissance Drama and the Law* (Evanston, IL: Northwestern University Press and the Newberry Library Center for Renaissance Studies, 1996), pp. 171–96.

Mack, Peter, *Elizabethan Rhetoric: Theory and Practice* (Cambridge: Cambridge University Press, 2002).

McLane, Bernard William, 'Juror Attitudes Toward Local Disorder: The Evidence of the 1328 Trailbaston Proceedings', in J. S. Cockburn and Thomas S. Green (eds), *Twelve Good Men and True: The Criminal Trial Jury in England, 1200–1800* (Princeton: Princeton University Press, 1988), pp. 36–64.

Magnusson, Lynne, 'Danger and Discourse', in Jeanne Shami, Dennis Flynn, and M. Thomas Hester (eds), *The Oxford Handbook of John Donne* (Oxford: Oxford University Press, 2011), pp. 743–55.

Magnusson, Lynne, '"Power to Hurt": Language and Service in Sidney Household Letters and Shakespeare's *Sonnets*', *English Literary History* 65.4 (1998), pp. 799–824.

Magnusson, Lynne, 'Scoff Power in *Love's Labour's Lost* and the Inns of Court: Language in Context', *Shakespeare Survey* 57 (2004), pp. 196–208.

Majeske, Andrew, 'Equity's Absence: The Extremity of Claudio's Prosecution and Barnardine's Pardon in Shakespeare's *Measure for Measure*', *Law and Literature* 21.2 (2009), pp. 169–84.

Majeske, Andrew, *Equity in Renaissance Literature* (London, Routledge, 2006).

Marcus, Leah S., *Puzzling Shakespeare: Local Reading and Its Discontents* (Berkeley: University of California Press, 1988).

Marotti, Arthur F., 'John Donne and the Rewards of Patronage', in Guy Fitch Lytle and Stephen Orgel (eds), *Patronage in the Renaissance* (Princeton: Princeton University Press, 1981), pp. 207–34.

Marotti, Arthur F., *John Donne, Coterie Poet* (Madison: University of Wisconsin Press, 1986).

Martin, Julian, *Francis Bacon, the State, and the Reform of Natural Philosophy* (Cambridge: Cambridge University Press, 1992).

Matthews, Nancy L., *William Sheppard, Cromwell's Law Reformer* (Cambridge: Cambridge University Press, 1984).

Maule, Jeremy, 'Donne and the Words of the Law', in David Colclough (ed.), *John Donne's Professional Lives* (Cambridge: D. S. Brewer, 2003), pp. 19–36.

May, Steven W., 'Donne and Egerton: The Court and Courtship', in Jeanne Shami, Dennis Flynn and M. Thomas Hester (eds), *The Oxford Handbook of John Donne* (Oxford: Oxford University Press, 2011), pp. 447–59.

Mukherji, Subha, *Law and Representation in Early Modern Drama* (Cambridge: Cambridge University Press, 2006).

Musolf, Gil Richard, 'Role-Taking and Restorative Justice: Social Practices of Solidarity and Community in Shakespeare's *Measure for Measure*', *Contemporary Justice Review* 5.3 (2002), pp. 211–30.

Nardo, Anna K., 'John Donne at Play in Between', in Claude Summers and Ted Larry Pebworth (eds), *The Eagle and the Dove: Reassessing John Donne* (Columbia: University of Missouri Press, 1986), pp. 157–65.

Neale, J. E., *Elizabeth I and Her Parliaments, 1584–1601*, 2 vols (London: Cape, 1953–7).

O'Callaghan, Michelle, *The English Wits: Literature and Sociability in Early Modern England* (Cambridge: Cambridge University Press, 2007).

O'Connell, Michael, '*The Faerie Queene*, Book V', in A. C. Hamilton (ed.), *The Spenser Encyclopedia* (Toronto: University of Toronto Press, 1997), pp. 280–3.

O'Day, Rosemary, *The Professions in Early Modern England, 1450–1800: Servants of the Commonweal* (Harlow: Longman, 2000).

Orgel, Stephen, 'The Poetics of Incomprehensibility', *Shakespeare Quarterly* 42.4 (1991), pp. 431–7.

Orgel, Stephen, '*The Winter's Tale*: A Modern Perspective', in William Shakespeare, *The Winter's Tale*, ed. Barbara A. Mowat and Paul Werstine (New York: Washington Square Press, 1998), pp. 257–72.

Owens, Judith, 'Warding off Injustice in Book Five of *The Faerie Queene*', in Donald Beecher, Travis DeCook, Andrew Wallace and Grant Williams (eds), *Taking Exception to the Law: Materializing Injustice in Early Modern English Literature* (Toronto: University of Toronto Press, 2015), pp. 204–24.

Patterson, Annabel, 'All Donne', in Elizabeth D. Harvey and Katharine Eisaman Maus (eds), *Soliciting Interpretation: Literary Theory and Seventeenth-Century Poetry* (Chicago: University of Chicago Press, 1990), pp. 37–67.

Patterson, Annabel, 'John Donne, Kingsman?', in Linda Levy Peck (ed.), *The Mental World of the Jacobean Court* (Cambridge: Cambridge University Press, 1991), pp. 251–72.

Patterson, Annabel, 'Satirical Writing: Donne in Shadows', in Achsah Guibbory (ed.), *The Cambridge Companion to John Donne* (Cambridge: Cambridge University Press, 2006), pp. 117–31.

Peltonen, Markku, 'Bacon's Political Philosophy', in Markku Peltonen (ed.), *The Cambridge Companion to Bacon* (Cambridge: Cambridge University Press, 1996), pp. 283–310.

Peltonen, Markku, 'Politics and Science: Francis Bacon and the True Greatness of States', *Historical Journal* 35.2 (1992), pp. 279–305.

Pocock, J. G. A., *The Ancient Constitution and the Feudal Law: A Study of English History Thought in the Seventeenth Century* (Cambridge: Cambridge University Press, 1987).

Pocock, J. G. A., Schochet, Gordon, and Schwoerer, Lois G., 'Introduction', in David Armitage (ed.), *British Political Thought in History, Literature and Theory, 1500–1800* (Cambridge: Cambridge University Press, 2006).

Prest, Wilfrid R., *The Inns of Court under Elizabeth I and the Early Stuarts, 1590–1640* (London: Longman, 1972).

Prest, Wilfrid R., 'Judicial Corruption in Early Modern England', *Past and Present* 133 (1991), pp. 67–95.

Prest, Wilfrid R., 'Legal Education of the Gentry at the Inns of Court, 1560–1640', *Past and Present* 38 (1967), pp. 20–39.

Prest, Wilfrid R., 'William Lambarde, Elizabethan Law Reform, and Early Stuart Politics', *Journal of British Studies* 34.4 (1995), pp. 464–80.

Quarmby, Kevin A., *The Disguised Ruler in Shakespeare and His Contemporaries* (New York: Routledge, 2016).

Rabb, Theodore K., 'Francis Bacon and the Reform of Society', in Theodore K. Rabb and Jerrold E. Seigel (eds), *Action and Conviction in Early Modern Europe: Essays in Memory of E. H. Harbison* (Princeton: Princeton University Press, 1969), pp. 169–93.

Rackley, Erika, 'Judging Isabella: Justice, Care and Relationships in *Measure for Measure*', in Paul Raffield and Gary Watt (eds), *Shakespeare and the Law* (Oxford: Hart, 2008), pp. 65–80.

Raffield, Paul, 'The Ancient Constitution, Common Law and the Idyll of Albion: Law and Lawyers in *Henry IV, Parts 1 and 2*', *Law and Literature* 22.1 (2010), pp. 18–47.

Raffield, Paul, *Images and Cultures of Law in Early Modern England: Justice and Political Power, 1558–1660* (Cambridge: Cambridge University Press, 2004).

Raffield, Paul, *Shakespeare's Imaginary Constitution: Late Elizabethan Politics and the Theatre of Law* (Oxford: Hart, 2010).

Raffield, Paul, '"Terras Astraea reliquit": *Titus Andronicus* and the Loss of Justice', in Paul Raffield and Gary Watt, *Shakespeare and the Law* (Oxford: Hart, 2008), pp. 203–20.

Rivlin, Elizabeth, 'Theatrical Literacy in *The Comedy of Errors* and the *Gesta Grayorum*', *Critical Survey* 14.1 (2002), pp. 64–78.

Schalkwyk, David, *Shakespeare, Love and Service* (Cambridge: Cambridge University Press, 2008).

Schoek, R. J., 'Rhetoric and Law in Sixteenth-Century England', *Studies in Philology* 1 (1957), pp. 110–27.

Schott, Holger, *The Trials of Orality in Early Modern England, 1550–1625* (Dissertation, Harvard University, 2004).

Scodel, Joshua, *Excess and the Mean in Early Modern English Literature* (Princeton: Princeton University Press, 2002).

Shagan, Ethan H., *The Rule of Moderation: Violence, Religion and the Politics of Restraint in Early Modern England* (Cambridge: Cambridge University Press, 2011).

Shapiro, Barbara, 'Classical Rhetoric and the English Law of Evidence', in Victoria Kahn and Lorna Hutson (eds), *Rhetoric and Law in Early Modern Europe* (New Haven: Yale University Press, 2001), pp. 54–72.

Shapiro, Barbara, 'Codification of the Laws in Seventeenth Century England', *Wisconsin Law Review* 2 (1974), pp. 428–65.

Shapiro, Barbara, 'Law Reform in Seventeenth Century England', *American Journal of Legal History* 19.4 (1975), pp. 280–312.

Shapiro, Barbara, 'Political Theology and the Courts: A Survey of Assize Sermons *c*.1600–1688', *Law and Humanities* 2.1 (2008), pp. 1–28.

Shapiro, Barbara, *Probability and Certainty in Seventeenth-Century England: A Study of the Relationships between Natural Science, Religion, History, Law, and Literature* (Princeton: Princeton University Press, 1983).

Shapiro, Barbara, 'Sir Francis Bacon and the Mid-Seventeenth Century Movement for Law Reform', *The American Journal of Legal History* 24.4 (1980), pp. 331–62.

Shapiro, I. A., 'John Donne and Parliament', *TLS* (10 March 1932), p. 172.

Sharpe, J. A., *Crime in Early Modern England, 1550–1750* (London: Longman, 1984).

Sharpe, Kevin, *Remapping Early Modern England: The Culture of Seventeenth-Century Politics* (Cambridge: Cambridge University Press, 2000).

Shawcross, John T., 'All Attest His Writs Canonical: The Texts, Meaning and Evaluation of Donne's Satires', in Peter Amadeus Fiore (ed.), *Just So Much Honor: Essays Commemorating the Four-Hundredth Anniversary of the Birth of John Donne* (University Park: Pennsylvania State University Press, 1972), pp. 245–72.

Shuger, Debora Kuller, *Political Theologies in Shakespeare's England: The Sacred and the State in* Measure for Measure (Basingstoke: Palgrave, 2001).

Smith, David Chan, *Sir Edward Coke and the Reformation of the Laws: Religion, Politics and Jurisprudence, 1578–1616* (Cambridge: Cambridge University Press, 2014).

Staines, John D., 'Pity and the Authority of Feminine Passions in Books V and VI of *The Faerie Queene*', *Spenser Studies: A Renaissance Poetry Annual* 25 (2010), pp. 129–61.

Strain, Virginia Lee, 'Preventive Justice and *Measure for Measure*', in Kevin Curran (ed.), *Shakespeare and Judgment* (Edinburgh: Edinburgh University Press, 2017), pp. 21–44.

Strain, Virginia Lee, 'The "Snared Subject" and the General Pardon Statute in Late Elizabethan Coterie Literature', in Donald Beecher, Travis DeCook, Andrew Wallace and Grant Williams (eds), *Taking Exception to the Law: Materializing Injustice in Early Modern English Literature* (Toronto: University of Toronto Press, 2015), pp. 100–19.

Strain, Virginia Lee, 'The Winter's Tale and the Oracle of the Law', *English Literary History* 78.3 (2011), pp. 557–84.

Stretton, Timothy, *Women Waging Law in Elizabethan England* (Cambridge: Cambridge University Press, 1998).

Syme, Holger Schott, *Theatre and Testimony in Shakespeare's England: A Culture of Mediation* (Cambridge: Cambridge University Press, 2012).

Syme, Holger Schott, *The Trials of Orality in Early Modern England, 1550–1625* (Dissertation, Harvard University, 2004).

Tennenhouse, Leonard, 'Representing Power: *Measure for Measure* in its Time', in Stephen Greenblatt (ed.), *The Power of Forms in the English Renaissance* (Norman, OK: Pilgrim Books, 1982), pp. 139–56.

Tittler, Robert, 'Education and the Gentleman in Tudor England: The Case of Sir Nicholas Bacon', *History of Education* 5.1 (1976), pp. 3–10.

Tittler, Robert, *Nicholas Bacon: The Making of a Tudor Statesman* (London: Cape, 1976).

Tubbs, J. W. *The Common Law Mind: Medieval and Early Modern Conceptions* (Baltimore: Johns Hopkins University Press, 2000).

Tubbs, J. W., 'Custom, Time and Reason: Early Seventeenth-Century Conceptions of the Common Law', *History of Political Thought* 19.3 (1998), pp. 363–406.

Usher, Roland G., 'James I and Sir Edward Coke', *English Historical Review* 18 (1903), pp. 664–75.

Veall, Donald, *The Popular Movement for Law Reform, 1640–1660* (Oxford: Clarendon Press, 1970).

Vickers, Brian, 'Bacon and Rhetoric', in Markku Peltonen (ed.), *The Cambridge Companion to Bacon* (Cambridge: Cambridge University Press, 1996), pp. 200–31.

Vickers, Brian, *Francis Bacon and Renaissance Prose* (Cambridge: Cambridge University Press, 1968).

Visconsi, Elliott, *Lines of Equity: Literature and the Origins of Law in Later Stuart England* (Ithaca: Cornell University Press, 2007).

Wall, Alison, '"The Greatest Disgrace': The Making and Unmaking of JPs in Elizabethan and Jacobean England', *EHR* 481 (2004), pp. 312–32.

Wallace, Karl R., 'Discussion in Parliament and Francis Bacon', in Brian Vickers (ed.), *Essential Articles for the Study of Francis Bacon* (Hamden, CT: Archon Books, 1968), pp. 195–205.

Wallace, Karl R., *Francis Bacon on Communication and Rhetoric, Or: The Art of Applying Reason to Imagination for the Better Moving of the Will* (Chapel Hill, NC: University of North Carolina Press, 1943).

Ward, Ian, *Shakespeare and the Legal Imagination* (London: Butterworths, 1999).

Warren, Christopher N., *Literature and the Law of Nations: 1580–1680* (Cambridge: Cambridge University Press, 2015).

Watt, Gary, 'Earl of Oxford's Case (1615)', in Peter Cane and Joanne Conaghan (eds), *The New Oxford Companion to Law*, online edn (Oxford University Press, 2009).

Wasson, John, '*Measure for Measure*: A Text for Court Performance?', *Shakespeare Quarterly* 21.1 (1970), pp. 17–24.

West, William N., '"But this will be a mere confusion": Real and Represented Confusions on the Elizabethan Stage', *Theatre Journal* 60 (2008), pp. 217–33.

White, R. S., *Natural Law in English Renaissance Literature* (Cambridge: Cambridge University Press, 1996).

Williams, I. S., 'Early-modern judges and the practice of precedent', in P. Brand and J. Getzler (eds), *Judges and Judging in the History of the Common Law and Civil Law* (Cambridge: Cambridge University Press, 2012), pp. 51–66.

Williams, I. S., 'The Tudor Genesis of Edward Coke's Immemorial Common Law', *Sixteenth Century Journal* 43.1 (2012), pp. 103–23.

Wilson, Luke, *Theaters of Intention: Drama and Law in Early Modern England* (Stanford: Stanford University Press, 2000).

Winston, Jessica. *Lawyers at Play: Literature, Law, and Politics at the Early Modern Inns of Court, 1558–1581* (Oxford: Oxford University Press, 2016).

Wolfe, Jessica, *Humanism, Machinery, and Renaissance Literature* (Cambridge: Cambridge University Press, 2004).

Wrightson, Keith, 'Two Concepts of Order: Justices, Constables and Jurymen in Seventeenth-Century England', in John Brewer and John Styles (eds), *An Ungovernable People: The English and Their Law in the Seventeenth and Eighteenth Centuries* (London: Hutchinson, 1980), pp. 21–46.

Yates, Francis A., *Astraea: The Imperial Theme in the Sixteenth Century* (London: Routledge & Kegan Paul, 1975).

Zurcher, Amelia A., *Seventeenth-Century English Romance: Allegory, Ethics, and Politics* (New York: Palgrave Macmillan, 2007).

Zurcher, Andrew, 'Consideration, Contract and the End of *The Comedy of Errors*', in Paul Raffield and Gary Watt (eds), *Shakespeare and the Law* (Oxford: Hart, 2008), pp. 19–37.

Zurcher, Andrew, *Shakespeare and Law* (London: Methuen Drama, 2010).

Zurcher, Andrew, *Spenser's Legal Language: Law and Poetry in Early Modern England* (Cambridge: D. S. Brewer, 2007).

Index

Initials in brackets after names indicate the works in which they appear, e.g. (FQ) *Faerie Queene, The.*